NAKED IN EDEN

My Adventure and Awakening
in the Australian Rainforest

NAKED *in* EDEN

Robin Easton

Library of Congress Cataloging-in-Publication Data

Easton, Robin.
  Naked in Eden : my adventure and awakening in the Australian rainforest / by Robin Easton.
  p. cm.
Includes poems by Russell Hume.

ISBN – 978-1-7344281-0-0
1. Daintree (Qld. : Region)—Description and travel. 2. Easton, Robin—Travel—Australia—Daintree (Qld. : Region) 3. Rain forests—Australia—Daintree (Qld. : Region) 4. Outdoor life—Australia—Daintree (Qld. : Region) 5. Natural history Australia—Daintree (Qld. : Region) 6. Travelers—Australia—Daintree (Qld. : Region)—Biography. 7. Adventure and adventurers—Australia—Daintree (Qld. : Region)—Biography. 8. Nature, Healing power of—Case studies. 9. Philosophy of nature—Case studies.
I. Hume, Russell. II. Title.
DU280.D14E185 2010
919.43'6—dc22

2010012645

Copyright ©2010 Robin Easton

All rights reserved. Printed in the United States of America. No part of this publication may be reproduced, stored in a retrieval system, or transmitted in any form or by any means, electronic, mechanical, photocopying, recording, or otherwise, without the written permission of the publisher.

2019 Publisher: Robin Easton Productions, LLC.
robineaston2@gmail.com
www.robineaston.com

First Edition printed by: Health Communications, Inc., 2010

Cover and all interior art: Robin Easton www.robineaston.com
Interior design, layout and formatting by Pi Luna Press, www.pilunapress.com

*To the valiant souls who strive to protect earth's wildness.
I am deeply grateful for your efforts.*

*To the Daintree Rainforest and my wild friends.
You gave me life when I was dying.*

*To my father who lives on in my heart.
You are with me ... always.*

Contents

Foreword by Michael J. Roads — vii

Acknowledgments — vii

Author's Note — vii

Introduction: Snake in My Face — vii

1. The Journey Begins — vii
2. Weirdos and Washouts — vii
3. The Old Man by the Sea — vii
4. Goin' Troppo — vii
5. Things Eating Things — vii
6. The Way of the Earth — vii

7. **There is No Separation**	vii
8. **Crocodiles, Feral Pigs, and Pitch Black**	vii
9. **Do Not Intervene**	vii
10. **I Am an Animal**	313
Notes	vii
Robin's Glossary of Strine	vii
Contributing Writer	vii
About the Author	vii

FORWARD by Michael J. Roads

EVERY NOW AND THEN A BOOK COMES ALONG that, by its very authenticity, makes you sit up and take notice. *Naked in Eden: My Adventure and Awakening* is just such a book. As the author shares her experience of being eyeball to eyeball with a deadly snake, I felt an instant rapport. I, too, have been in this situation.

This is a moment when not only the wrong move, but also the wrong thought, can prove to be fatal. Thought sends messages to a snake faster and more subtly than the blink of an eyelid, with the snake's reaction even faster.

Reading an account of a very courageous woman healing herself in Nature, learning—and sharing through her book—many of her profound insights, can not only heal, but can also affect the very reality of your life.

We are conscious Beings, and Robin's great lesson was to access this consciousness on an aware and elevated level, thus powerfully and positively affecting every cell of her body.

We can communicate on a two-way level with Nature, but we generally need to be jolted out of our complacent and apathetic relationship with life before this can happen. Robin's illness and the harsh tropical rainforest combined to provide that necessary jolt.

I enjoyed the author's writing. I enjoyed her exploratory ramblings both in the forest of Nature and the forest of her thoughts. This book is fresh; it moves, it is uplifting, and it contains a positive contribution toward the life of anyone who reads and digests it.

Michael J. Roads is the author of Talking with Nature/Journey into Nature; The Magic Formula; More Than Money, True Prosperity; *and the 1998 award-winning visionary novel* Getting There. *Visit Michael's website at: www.michaelroads.com. Michael is well known in the United States, Australia, Holland, Sweden, Norway, Germany, Switzerland, Japan, and other countries as you will see from the "events" list on his website.*

∾

I was born in the Australian rainforest
at the age of twenty-five. Anything before
was only an illusion. My soul drifted into the forest,
a fading shadow cast from wounded spirit and aching heart.

—ROBIN EASTON

ACKNOWLEDGMENTS

Barbara Neighbors Deal/Literary Associates—my literary agent and dear friend: You inspire courage, compassion, and integrity. You are dynamic and sensitive, a rare combination. In your generous support of this book, you ventured beyond agent and into the realm of humanitarian. That's the way of your life and spirit. I could not have entered the literary arena with a finer human being.

Joseph Dispenza: My guardian angel. When I was ready to fly, you were there to guide me, every time. You knew, you saw, and you cared. What a gift. Thank you for the beautiful title for this book.

Stephen: You fostered my writer's voice so I wouldn't remain trapped inside myself, full of a hundred lifetimes lived in one. You helped me unravel almost two-thousand pages that I wrote when I came out of the rainforest, pages written to save my sanity while I readjusted to human-society. I thank you for your belief in me and all that you so generously gave. I deeply treasure the memory of our late-night editing, laughing, dreaming and sharing creativity. You are a gifted editor and, more importantly, a beautiful and highly gifted soul.

Mom: You understood my desperate desire to really live the life I've been given. You encouraged me to follow my dreams. In the end, you knew me. I knew you. Without words. Without explanation. You are always with me.

Pi Luna: It is pure joy to work with you. I could not have done this second edition without your highly skilled help. You are not only extremely professional, but you are kind, patient and delightful to work with. You instill confidence and trust, which I deeply value. Pi Luna can be found at www.pilunapress.com

Dr. Hugh Spencer: Your input on this book was invaluable. I'm familiar with the conditions you've worked under; they're hot, humid and full of torrential rain, mold, and insects. You've kept going despite insufficient funds and made do with primitive living conditions, all of which make your support of this book additionally precious.

Allison Janse: I am honored that you saw something in my story worth sharing with the world. Right from the start you reflected to me someone who lives from her heart. In doing so you confirmed a way of being that I hold dear.

Emily Easton, Sara Hume and Robin Clarke: Thank you from my heart for your research or editing. I could not have done it without you. Your counsel, encouragement, and love made all the difference.

Kuku Yalanji rainforest people: I give you my heartfelt gratitude for the privilege of being in your rainforest. Its great love healed my soul and spirit. To those of you who befriended me, I carry you in my heart.

Australian people: You are earnest, hardworking, and loving. You're a high-spirited, happy-go-lucky bunch of wonderful people. I loved my years spent in your country.

My dear family of friends (both online and off-line): You helped me in one way or another to edit, to keep going, to relax, to cry, to laugh, to grow, to heal, to take charge, to let go, to live . . . to love. I am a better person because of you. Without your help I might not have come this far.

Thank you to the following individuals and organizations for verifying facts and sharing information: Environment Australia; Tim Bamster; Mary Barber; Dr. Adam Britton, crocodile specialist; Brian Bush; Elizabeth Cameron, Australian Museum; Hartley's Creek; Don Herbison-Evans; John Fowler; Ken Parker, Friends of Hitchenbrook Society, Inc.; Cairns Frog Hospital; Peter Hitchcock; Nicky Hungerford; Doon McColl, Wet Tropics Management Authority; Geof Monteith; Chris Motz; Queensland Museum–Brisbane; Lyall Naylor; Sheryl Sackman; Australian Butterfly Sanctuary.

Author's Note

EVERY ATTEMPT HAS BEEN MADE TO respect the privacy of the people in this story. All names and identifying details of the characters, some exact locations, dates, and time sequences have been changed or compressed. Although a dose of Queensland storytelling has been added, the story is drawn from and faithful to my adventures in the Daintree Rainforest of Queensland, Australia, and is written from the perspective of the twenty-five-year-old woman who went into the rainforest.

Introduction

Snake in My Face

THE GENTLE BREEZE THAT usually filled our valley had abandoned us. I knew the day would soon be intolerably hot. If I wanted to go for a morning hike I had to leave immediately. I slugged down almost a liter of water, grabbed a handful of dried fruit from the tent, and wandered up the hill that rose behind our camp. I was eager to reach the crest and see what lay beyond. Was there a grand vista or perhaps an undiscovered creek full of ancient palms? But the top of the hill never came, beyond each rise was yet another hill. I kept climbing and climbing and was annoyed when the pain in my bladder begged me to stop and let go of the water I'd drunk earlier.

I pulled my frayed denim shorts down around my thighs and squatted barefoot to pee. Oh man, the simple pleasures people miss; warm urine pooled around my toes, and warm air caressed my bare arms and legs. Suddenly, out of the corner of my eye I saw something move. A six-foot, red-bellied black snake raced toward my feet and the urine streaming from between my legs. I gasped, pulled back. Startled, the snake rose to strike position, twelve inches from my face. With head and neck flattened, he lashed out three times in a false strike within two inches of my nose. I froze. Oh God, I'm still alive. His fangs didn't snag my face. *Robin, stay calm. Don't move a muscle. If he bites, you could be paralyzed.*

Head to head, eye to eye, I didn't dare breathe; my moist breath might provoke a serious strike. Inches from my face, my neck, it would be the worst place for venom to enter my body, immediate envenomization. I could see each individual scale on his head. His rapidly throbbing throat stretched so tautly it appeared distorted. Two glasslike black eyes bulged with fear and stared straight into mine. His tongue flicked between black scaly lips to taste the air. *Can he taste my fear? I have to let him know I'm no threat. How do I communicate that to the snake's tongue? His eyes are almost popping out of his head. Boy, I know how he feels. Wait a minute; he's more terrified than me.*

When I realized this, I knew that the way to reassure him was to act and feel as if his presence were almost irrelevant to me, as if I were a tree or a rock. Surprisingly, that was not as hard as you might think. I knew he'd either bite or he wouldn't, but if I flailed about or even moved he'd most likely strike. Since we were already nose to nose I decided the best course was to calm myself in earnest by pretending I faced only an earthworm and had nothing to fear. Something shifted in me and let go. I actually began to relax. Time slipped into slow motion. Time within time, face-to-face, I started to comprehend this maligned creature. I began to think and not merely react. Gradually, compassion calmed my racing heart, and within that calm I heard the snake's thoughts.

"I don't know who you are. I'm terrified. Confused. I don't want to harm you. You just happened to be on the path of my flight—though I will protect myself, fight for my life if I have to. You don't seem ready to attack. You're too big to eat. You're much bigger than I am and could easily crush me. Aaah, so you hadn't thought of that. You don't realize your own strength, do you? Not that I fear that strength. So, you're afraid too. What'll you do with your fear? Strike out? Kill me? I'd like to pass unharmed. Will you let me do that? I don't dare take my eyes from your face. You might hurt me. I must remain in strike readiness to protect myself. If you look away and allow me to escape I won't harm you. Can I trust you? Can you trust me? We've reached an impasse."

While the snake directed his thoughts into my consciousness, I heard a lizard dart among the leaves, a fly zip past my right ear. A kookaburra in a distant tree gave a brief laugh; the midday sun sweltered too hot for anything more raucous.

The snake flicked his tongue.

I blinked.

Swallowed.

Waited.

All of a sudden, I felt more awareness than I'd ever experienced. I was taken aback that I could feel such crisp clarity. More surprising, I immediately had a memory I didn't know I could recall, a memory of being connected to all other life forms, a time when all beings communicated with each other, awareness-to-awareness.

The snake waited, motionless.

Thoughts drifted from my mind. With the ease of a child, I talked with Red-belly, thought-to-thought.

"Okay, Red-belly, I hear you. One of us has gotta be vulnerable. I'll take the risk. I need to test my courage. And you're right; I'm heaps larger than you. I must appear huge. Since I've intruded into your space, I'll retreat first. You can trust me. Please let me trust you. I don't wanna become paralyzed from your bite. I'll slowly turn my head away so you won't see my eyes, and my eyes won't see where you're going. I've no interest in following you. You're safe. Just don't bite me. Okay? Sloooowly, I'm turning my head and eyes away from your space. See? I'm completely at your mercy. Don't harm me. You're free to leave. I won't hurt you."

With my head turned side on, the snake took one huge black lunge and whipped half of his six-foot length up and over the rest of his body and vanished into the rainforest faster than my peripheral vision could follow.

I collapsed, grinning to the urine-soaked ground. I felt elated. In the face of potential death, I discovered a courage I didn't know I possessed.

Tested and passed, I began my initiation into the mysteries of the Australian rainforest. There were many more tests. Each one I embraced with loving spirit and open arms. Daily the whisper of this ancient rainforest beckoned me to enter and discover life's most intimate secrets. In time I shed all of my clothes along with my fear, and walked naked into the jungle.

one

THE JOURNEY BEGINS

"Aaaahhh! There's a leech on my leg. Ian, hurry up."

"Youse got your bloody dacks on. You'll be right."

"No, Ian. He's *in* my pants. Oh noooooooo! He's moving up my leg. Toward my . . ."

My fingers pressed the side of my knee to stop the black, bloodsucking glob's progress toward my crotch. Beneath the fabric of my jeans I felt a fat squishy lump writhe under my touch. I frantically unzipped my pants to get at the leech. When I lowered my jeans it abruptly dropped off. Instead of falling into the mud he fell to the bottom of my pant leg, trapped inside the sock I'd pulled up over the cuff of my jeans.

"Yuck. He's still in my pants. He's climbing up again."

"Okay, mate. Pass me the hammer. Quick smart. Before I lose this bloody nail in the stinking mud."

In the slimy water around my legs, two more leeches moved toward me. Flat and ribbonlike they squirmed their way to food. Forgetting the leech trapped under my pant leg, I struggled to pull up my jeans and tuck my T-shirt into the waistband.

"Ian, this is sick. I can't take it. Oh God! How can you go naked? You're probably covered with 'em."

"Freaking strewth! Dropped me bloody nail in the mud. Damned mozzies." Ian slapped a mosquito that drilled his left temple. The insect's squished abdomen sprayed blood across his eyelid. His face was a painted collage of mud, blood, and dead mosquitoes.

"Righty-o, mate. Pass me another nail. Here, hold the bloody hammer while I put the pin in place. Okay. Quick, give me back the hammer. Strewth. Wipe the mud off it so's I don't drop her. Almost done, mate. Just a tick longer. Crikeys! The bloody mozzies. Keep them away from me eyes. I can't see what I'm doing."

Standing in a foot and half of slimy brown mud, I tried to pass tools to Ian while I swished leeches away and swatted the cloud of mosquitoes that swarmed around our heads. I'd never seen such hungry mosquitoes. They were everywhere at once, in my nose, mouth, and ears. *Oh maaaan, how the hell did I end up here? Not that long ago I was living a young woman's dream when Dad gave me a dozen red roses on my wedding day.*

When we stopped to check the depth of the mudhole before crossing I cringed at the sight of writhing leeches and wiggling mosquito larvae. The leeches were only about two inches long. As a child growing up on Lake Pennesseewassee in Maine, I'd seen them four inches long. But leeches are leeches, black, rubbery, squirmy things that attach to your skin to drink blood. I tried desperately not to think about them as I passed Ian the hammer.

"Deadset, Rob-o. If we hadn't hit this submerged log, we'd have driven right through this bloody bog hole. No worries."

The winch's last cotter pin had snapped when we attempted to winch the truck over the log. We'd run out of spare pins earlier in the day, so Ian had pulled some old nails out of a fence a few miles back, "just in case." We were about to test them as cotter pins.

∽

It was 1979; Ian was twenty-four and I was twenty-five. We had been on the road for weeks, driving at a lazy pace along the coast from Melbourne. Late March marked the start of the Australian autumn, but the days rolled by warmer than a Maine summer. We drove through coastal regions where I swam in aqua blue seas and renewed my spirit on hot sandy beaches. Fruit stands along the road begged us to stop and devour twenty-five-cent watermelons and sticky-sweet pineapples.

Every time we stopped at a rest area, magpies chortled in the gum trees and hopped and flapped about the truck, expecting, maybe demanding, a free lunch. I'd heard tales of people being attacked by magpies during the nesting season, so I never fed them. But I loved to listen to their rich undulating melodies. Australian magpies are huge black-and-white ravenlike birds with white beaks tipped with black. They're cheeky and bold. I marveled every time they landed on the highway in front of us to peck at roadkill. As our Toyota sped toward them they continued to eat. They waited until the last second. Often I squirmed in my seat, gasped, and covered my eyes with my hands, unable to watch our tires grind them to magpie pâté. I needn't have worried. Unruffled with the truck barreling down on them, they casually hopped to the road's edge in a dignified manner. Their heads thrown back and beaks in the air, they sauntered just far enough out of reach so that our tires didn't paste them to the tarmac. Once we passed, they returned to their roadkill, business as usual.

We sweated our way through a searing-hot inland route, from Rockhampton to Sarina, just south of Mackay. The only water in existence floated miles ahead on the road, a silvery mirage. "The outback" was an area so long without rain, grass grew sparse as hair on an ancient mummy.

Cattle wandered aimlessly, nearly sucked dry of all moisture as they waited for death. The already-dead lay on their sides or propped against a barbed wire fence, as if staying upright might prolong life. Dehydrated carcasses lay on their backs and sides and sprouted legs so stiff they stuck straight out. These horrifying apparitions no longer resembled cows. They were tanned hides wrapped taut over grotesque skeletons.

Have you ever heard heat? One noon we stopped to stretch our legs and eat lunch. Hot air blasted me like a giant oven and sucked the breath from my lungs. Apart from the constant chainsaw buzz of cicadas, the air hung hushed and lethargic, too hot for birds to sing. Dry fallen leaves curled and crackled before my eyes. Shimmering heat hummed as it rose off black asphalt and metal truck. Lizards scurried across sizzling rock and fallen bark. I once read that when the Australian explorers Wills and Burke trekked from Melbourne to the Gulf of Carpentaria they faced temperatures of 140 degrees. Hell, that's halfway to baking cookies. Or maybe just halfway to hell.

Ian sat in the front of the truck with the map while I dropped the tailgate to search for food and water. The spot we pulled into claimed to be a rest stop for travelers. Without toilet or table, its only amenities were the shade of a gigantic old gum tree and a trash can that hung between a set of two-by-fours. I rummaged for lunch and went to join Ian at the front of the truck when out of the corner of my eye I noticed the trash can begin to sway. Faster and faster, the bin swung back and forth. Creak. Reek. Creak. Reek.

"Ian. I think there's something in the garbage out here."

Two deadly looking claws hooked over the lip of the trash can. What the hell is in there?

My tentative steps to investigate ended abruptly when an enormous gray scaly head with a long forked tongue appeared over the edge of the bin. I yelped when a six-foot lizard leapt from the trash onto the ground with a thump. He raised his upper body on his front legs like an athlete doing push-ups, turned in my direction, and snapped out a long "tssssssss." In a blink, he decided to flee instead of fight. Ian stuck his head out the window and laughed.

"Hey, a bloody big old goanna, mate. Strewth. He won't hurt youse unless he thinks youse a bloody tree and runs up your leg. Then his claws will rip your bloody guts open. Glad I'm in the truck."

Holy mackerel, no goanna is gonna mistake me for a tree.

Chased by Ian's laughter, I raced for the hood of the Toyota with visions of my intestines trailing behind me. I hardly noticed the truck's scorching metal as I watched the goanna run at a high-speed waddle for the nearest gum tree. His long, razor-sharp claws sunk easily into the bark as he clambered up the side of the tree trunk and disappeared into the greenery. *What kind of weird place is this?*

On one of those hot and dry stretches, I saw my first kangaroo. The day's relentless heat wore itself out and gentle air wafted through the truck window with a promise of evening's cool. Slanting rays of late afternoon sun shone through dry savanna and spun an aura of golden light over everything they touched. When I first spotted the kangaroo he appeared to change his very form, golden grass transformed into boundless energy. Time slowed as he hung suspended between each jump, fur haloed by sunlight.

Grayish-colored kangaroos often bounded across the road in twos or threes. I didn't know what kind they were, but figured they must be a type of wallaby because they weren't very tall. Their carcasses sometimes lay on the roadsides where they'd probably been hit by huge trucks carrying goods north. Most trucks, even small ones, sported bullbars across the front and wrapped around the sides to protect the vehicle against 'roo damage. At the sight of my first dead kangaroo I stopped our vehicle and got out to take a closer look. It hurt to see such magnificence dead and covered with flies, lying bloated on hot tarmac.

From Sarina we drove to Proserpine and took a boat to the Whitsunday Islands. Most of our fellow passengers were retired American and Australian tourists, with a few young newlyweds thrown in. About ten minutes before we reached the islands, a little white-haired woman shouted, "Oh, look at the dolphins. I can almost touch them."

Her traveling companions rushed to the low railing like a flock of dainty sandpipers. When I arrived at the boat's edge their hands strained to touch a dolphin's dorsal fin. Over the top of one white-haired, neatly permed head, I caught a glimpse of something in the water beside the boat, about two feet below deck level. I learned a lot about dolphins that day. Everyone on board sounded like an expert.

"Look. There's two of them. They're very intelligent, you know."

"I wonder if they can read our thoughts."

"I've heard they communicate with aliens on other planets."

"Did you know they strap explosives to their backs and send them out to blow up enemy ships?"

"Which enemies? The Russians?"

"Don't be silly, luv. The Russians are too bloody poor to have boats."

"Oh, that's nonsense. You'd be surprised what the Russians have."

"Strewth. It's not the bloody Russians youse gotta worry 'bout, mate. It's those billions of little Chinamen. They's the ones we gotta keep a bloody eye on, eh?"

"Aw come on, mate. Forget the bloody little Chinks. Just blow up a few Pommies."

"What's a Pommy?"

"You can always tell a dolphin by its fin, and those are dolphins, not porpoises."

I stood a head taller than most of the gathering so I had a good look at the broad-backed forms in the water. I chuckled and said, "You might wanna move back a bit. Those are sharks you're trying to pet."

I thought it might be fun to discuss the difference between horizontal and vertical tail fins, gills, and lungs, mammals and fish, but after the captain shouted, "Sharks off the bow," the area by the railing rapidly emptied. Similar to a school of tiny fish, the sightseers turned in unison to escape the sharks. All dignity lost, the tourists shoved and jostled to the safety of center deck like sandpipers dodging ocean waves. The mysticism of dolphin intelligence and alien communication vaporized like sea spray, quickly forgotten as they released their nervous fear of sharks.

"I read somewhere that sharks can smell blood."

"Boy, you wouldn't wanna swim with a cut."

"Or when you're having your . . . uhhh, never mind."

"Actually, they don't know much about them. I've read they're extremely intelligent, but unpredictable."

"Fair dinkum, mate. Those things will bloody well eat you no matter what you do. Forget the bloody ships. They oughta attach bloody bombs to the bleeding sharks and blow them up, eh?"

"Forget the bloody sharks, mate. Just blow up a few Pommies."

"Whaaat's a Pommy?"

Ian and I stood at the railing and watched the sharks. I didn't know what kind they were, but I related to the others' apprehension. The sharks swam with primordial power, an almost insular confidence that made shivers skitter up my spine. I felt tremendous awe and respect for such mighty creatures, although I wouldn't have jumped in the water right then.

Back on the mainland that evening we hit the road again and headed north for Bowen, Ayr, and Townsville. The dark night pulsated with strange life. Snakes that stretched longer than any I'd ever seen lay on the road absorbing the last degrees of the day's heat. Our headlights searched the darkness for eyes of different shapes and colors, and found them. I was glad I rode safely in the truck. Cool, pungent air blew on my face. In a few hours we'd be able to stop and sleep in the back of the Toyota.

Before we'd left Melbourne—once we knew we were "going bush"—we got an old red PMG Toyota truck (PMG: Postmaster-General's Department), formerly used as a mail truck. It had a cab in the front and a long tray bed on the back, long enough to sleep in. We put a cap over the tray of the truck and rigged out the inside with a mattress and sleeping bags, jerry cans of water, dried fruit and beans, nuts and whole grains, sprout seeds, and a few clothes. We placed a bullbar on the Toyota in case we accidentally hit any kangaroos on the road or, as Ian said, had to "thrash" our way through brush. I also helped Ian mount a large winch at the front of the truck. It was a contraption that ran off the truck's engine —"PTO," Ian called it, "power take-off." It consisted of a horizontal drum on which was wound a long steel cable with a hook at the end, kind of like a fishing reel. Ian explained how it worked.

"It's like this, Roby. We's can unwind the bloody cable and hook her to a tree, rock, or some other stable object, and pull ourselves out of trouble if we's to get stuck somewhere."

The gleam of anticipation in Ian's eyes when he said, "out of trouble," worried me. He looked just a little too happy at the thought of trouble for me to perceive the winch as security.

Last of all, we added a second gas tank and painted the used Toyota in swirls of camo' green. When I asked Ian, "Why bother?" he told me, "Privacy, mate. Don't want no one seeing us in the jungle. We can stay as long as we bloody well like, and this way no one will ever know we's there."

Momentarily forgetting the truck, I asked Ian, "Why do you always say 'ain't' and 'don't want no one?' Didn't your folks send you to one of the best schools in the world? I thought you said princes and kings went there? So why talk like that? You're not dumb."

Ian's grin turned devilish when he said, "Eh, it's me old man, bloody hates it when I talk that way. Always correcting me. Sent me to a fair dinkum fancy school, and I talk like a bloody old outbacker."

"But why, Ian? It only aggravates him?"

"There you go, mate. Precisely me point. Bloody strewth. Got to hang onto meself somehow."

Ian laughed and told me the more his father corrected him the more he said "ain't." I made a mental note to remember that dynamic since I'd also corrected Ian on occasion and found him proudly stubborn. Years later, I realized that many young people feel a need to rebel, at least until they have a strong sense of self. In some cases it may be a natural part of pushing our parents away so we can find out who we are—independent of them.

As disappointing as it may sound, we originally had no profound spiritual motives or courageously brave intentions of living in the rainforest. At first we planned to live in Melbourne near Ian's folks, get jobs, and be one big happy family. When I first met Ian in Salt Lake City, he had painted a picture of a middle-class, close-knit, absolutely perfect family. I later discovered how much he'd embellished the portrait and realized his family was like most other families, including my own. I once saw the TV show *The Waltons* at a friend's house. That's the kind of family I had always wanted and the kind of family I hoped awaited my arrival in Melbourne. I thought I'd find a warm kitchen filled with the soft aroma of freshly baked oatmeal cookies, gentle and wise parents, and loving siblings. Even through hardships, we'd all be safe and loved, and every drama would have a happy ending. After my bubble burst and I realized his family was just like my own, I couldn't decide if *The Waltons* provided a good example or an impossible and unrealistic role model.

I'd grown up in middle-class America. In my family of six kids, we frequently wore hand-me-down clothing and the furniture showed many signs of good-natured roughhousing. I was unprepared for the house I walked into when we arrived at Ian's parents. Chrome, leather, glass, Persian rugs, swimming pool with cabana, Mercedes, speed boat, yacht, private schools, expensive clothes, jewelry, and money were the norm.

At the time I was too young to realize that it didn't really matter whether someone was rich, poor, or anywhere in between. Underneath all the trappings, most families are basically the same. We may have varied hues of skin and hair, have more money or less money, but basically we are the same the world over. We worry about our health, our children, our safety, our freedom or lack of it, our right to love and be loved, and on it goes—life.

Ian's family fascinated me because discussions often revolved around "the business." In his early twenties, Ian left for America because he couldn't handle the pressure of being the oldest son prepped to take over the family enterprise. I felt just the opposite and often wished I had been prepped for *something*. I didn't yet see the unique gifts that I *had* been given.

Ian once said, "Crikey, Rob, don't even know who I am, and already me whole life is mapped out." When he told me that, I thought how I wished mine had been more mapped out. As much alike as we were, in other ways we were very different.

I didn't fully understand Ian's need to escape, but I did know I wanted to be with him. That was all that mattered to me. He was wild and wacky and brilliantly bright. Nothing seemed to stop him. All things were possible with Ian.

When I left America, my family and friends knew only that I was going to Melbourne, Australia. Once Ian and I left Melbourne, no one knew our whereabouts for months, eventually years. We'd only been in Melbourne a few weeks when Hal, a friend of Ian's, told us about a place he'd camped on the northeast coast of Queensland called Cape Tribulation, located in the Daintree Rainforest.

After I commented on the peculiar name, he told me, "Aw, she's a stunning place. The only reason it's named Tribulation is because bloody good ol' Captain Cook named it when his ship, the *Endeavour*, ran aground on the Great Barrier Reef just off the coast. It's easy to get to. Go all the way up the coast to Queensland. Keep right on going, mate, until the bloody road runs out, eh? North of Mossman you take the dirt road out to the ferry, and catch the punt across the Daintree River. If the track isn't washed out or the creek's too high, slog through the rainforest and down to the beach. You can camp there forever. It's virgin rainforest, bloody beaut place."

That was that. Ian jumped at "the great escape." He never did anything in half measures. One day we planned to live in Melbourne, the next day we were on the road to Far North Queensland.

The evening we left the Whitsunday Islands and the "dolphin experts," Ian drove into the night while I dozed. Around midnight he parked the Toyota on the edge of a rocky beach, and we crawled into the back of the truck to sleep. When we woke, the air was so heavy and humid I remembered dreaming that I had a dry cleaner's plastic bag over my head. Since our return to the edge of the Coral Sea, I craved to loll about in the warm water, but gladly avoided it. I'd heard tales that north of Rockhampton and the Tropic of Capricorn you could die from the sting of the box jellyfish.

While we sat on the beach and ate breakfast, we chatted with a musclebound lifeguard with spiky blond hair and zinc oxide smeared across his nose. He knew a fair bit about "the Box."

"Eh, it's best to stay out the water. The bloody stingers are here from about October to May. Tend to swim in bunches, they do. Come in to breed in the warm shallow water. They's got four sets of tentacles, about sixty tentacles in all. At least ten to fifteen feet long, sometimes longer. There's nasty little nematocyts all over the tentacles, yer see? They's venomous barbs that puncture your bloody skin, inject poison, and kill you. Sometimes in five minutes or less. Usually stops yer bloody breathing. Deadset, the pain from it is hell on fire, mate."

"Have you ever seen anybody get stung?" I asked.

"Sure, I's seen it. A bloke got a tentacle wrapped around his leg. Bloody ugly sight. Poor bastard actually made it to shore, thrashed around on the sand, screaming his bloody gob off. Red welts all over one of his legs. Strewth. One of those buggers alone could kill a few dozen people, eh?"

"But we saw guys surfing north of the Tropic of Capricorn. How come they don't get stung?" I asked.

"They's the smart ones. Wear bloody ladies' pantyhose in the surf. You know, nylon stockings. Stops the bloody tentacles from stinging you. Just pull an extra large pair of pantyhose up over yer cozzie or board shorts, right up over yer chest to yer bloody armpits. Cut a hole in the crotch of another pair. Put yer head through the hole, yer arms and hands into the bloody legs, pull the waist down over the other pair, and youse right as rain.[1] Done it meself. Could use a full-body wet suit or dry suit if you can afford it. Just keep yer bloody fool head out of the water or else smear it with some kind of thick grease."

"Is that all we gotta watch out for in the water?" I asked.

"Bloody oath, no! Further north youse gonna have to watch out for big ol' 'salties.' Crocodiles, mate. They swim in the sea. Sometimes come right up onto the beaches. Let's see, then there's yer bloody sea snakes, stingrays, cone shells, stonefish, sharks, and blue-ringed octopus. They's all potentially deadly."

Oh geeeez, why'd I have to ask? I don't wanna know this. Not yet. Maybe eventually . . . maybe NEVER.

Thinking about deadly stuff brought back stories Ian's dad, John Barkworth, told us before we left Melbourne. Sometimes I felt intimidated around John, but at the same time I couldn't help but love and respect him. He was dynamic and larger than life, an extremely proud self-made man. He had created his prosperity with his own hands, with hard work and sweat, from the ground up. A part of me empathized with his desire to give all he'd achieved to his oldest son. Although Ian was independent like his father, he wanted to live his own dreams and cared little for financial success. I think it was hard for John when Ian and I left for the jungle thousands of miles away. He stood in the drive and silently watched us ready the truck. A black cloud hung over his head as we hung sunny-yellow curtains in the cap's windows and burlap water bags off the bullbar.

"Strewth, mate. Youse must be mad to live in the bloody jungle. What'll youse do there?"

"We's going to bloody live there," Ian calmly said, as if living in the jungle were the most natural thing in the world. That frustrated his father even more. A part of me wanted to hug John because I knew he was hurting. He hoped Ian would change his mind and stay in Melbourne to help run the business. I knew it would never happen. If he stayed, pressures would mount and conflicts arise. They were too much alike—stubborn, independent, and strong.

A few days before we left Melbourne, Ian and I dined with his family. One of the humorous aspects of John's character was that he sometimes did all kinds of finagling to get what he wanted. Maybe he thought if he could frighten me I wouldn't want to go to the jungle, and Ian would stay home. Between mouthfuls of Chinese fried rice, he turned mischievous with stories of the taipan, "the world's deadliest snake."

"Over three bloody meters long," he laughed, arms fully extended. "It's got the longest bloody fangs of any Australian snake. A bloody multiple striker, he is." He held up his first and middle fingers and hooked them to imitate the two front fangs of a snake, and then continued. "Strikes faster than the human eye can follow." His arm lashed out. "Strewth. Youse gonna have to watch out for that bloody bastard, Rob. There's the common brown snake too, yeah know? He's so bloody aggressive and mean, I wouldn't piss on him if he caught fire."

"Rob, did I ever tell youse," he asked as if he'd known me for years instead of weeks, "years ago I got bit by one of them bloody tiger snakes? Got a huge black sac on the back of me leg where he bit me. They rushed me off to hospital just in time. Don't reckon they's got hospitals in the bloody jungle, eh?"

I laughed off John's attempts to terrify me. After all, he didn't know I'd hung out with four brothers and handled water snakes at the lake in Maine. Terrified or not, it didn't matter. Either way I loved Ian breathlessly and would have ridden with him to the moon on a meteor, no matter how frightened. It would take more than a little ol' snake to scare me. Obviously my brain wasn't ready to compare a two-foot harmless water snake with a ten-foot taipan—one of the world's deadliest snakes.

How ironic then, the closer we got to the jungle, the more gingerly I stepped from the truck. In an attempt to be sensible and learn about my new world I told Ian, "I wanna visit a reptile park. I gotta know something about all these deadly creatures I'm gonna live with."

Instead of setting my mind at ease, my trepidation only increased. When we left the park that day I checked the truck floor and seat before I climbed in. My head reeled with creepy-crawly images, similar to a child awakened by a nightmare. As we drove out of the parking lot, I watched all the happy laughing tourists with a jaundiced eye. *Oh sure, it's all right for you,* I thought. *Go ahead and laugh. You aren't gonna live with 'em.*

Reality hit hard. In one day at the park I saw the poisonous redback spider with her bulbous black body and needle-fine legs. A hundred dot-sized babies clustered in a corner. Thank heavens they were in a glass case. I couldn't even touch the glass, just like the kid whose fingers can't touch the insect-infested pages of the *National Geographic* issue on spiders or ants, creatures photographed so close you see venom drip from their fangs as they leap off the page to attack your face.

All the snakes I saw that day slithered around in my mind like a dark horror movie that wouldn't let go. The taipan, the tiger, the death adder, and the common brown, some of the world's deadliest snakes, sat coiled behind a piece of glass that wouldn't be there when I went to the jungle.

A huge saltwater crocodile lay in six inches of water behind a wire fence. Even from twenty feet, I thought he still looked way too big and definitely had an evil reptilian skulk about him.

There were other creatures I shut out and couldn't even remember. After all, I could only take in so much potential death in a day. The connection between my childhood water snakes and these eight- and ten-foot monsters-of-death finally formed . . . ooooh yeah. I was glad John Barkworth wasn't there to witness my fear. The thought made me chuckle and feel a bit happier.

After the day at the park, I cringed every time I stepped out of the truck, afraid I'd tread on a deadly snake or spider. In my imagination they lurked everywhere, behind every rock and log, draped in the trees and hanging from every branch. A forest of slithering spaghetti. For my own peace of mind I stopped asking Ian or anyone else, "Are there deadly snakes where we're going? Do those kinds of spiders live there? Are the ticks poisonous there?"

Of course they were poisonous. Yes. Yes. YES, to ALL of it. I'd have been better off asking, "What isn't poisonous?" I decided I didn't want to know. I wanted to enjoy the remains of my tattered ignorance and pretend that I was just another smiling tourist. Do you know the old adage "ignorance is bliss"? Well, at that point in my life I strongly agreed. If the road north had gone all the way around Australia I would have written a book titled, *I Drove Around Australia: Three Hundred Times.*

Unfortunately, the coastal route didn't go all the way around the continent. It stopped in Daintree, Queensland, a tiny black dot on the map. Each day I hauled out the map and watched the line shrink between Daintree and us. The shorter the line, the greater my misgivings. I truly believed that we'd live in the rainforest forever. Every turn of the Toyota's wheels drew me closer to the forest and nearer the dark jungles of my own fear. Time and space began to distort. Flashbacks from my youth wove their way in and out of my thoughts.

I'd lived in Salt Lake City for three years before I met Ian. Most days I walked in a dark shadow of vague fear, lost and detached from all that most people hold dear: friends, family, and a sense of home and belonging.

On the surface I appeared too normal to warrant notice. I worked various jobs and tried to go back to school to study wild, edible, and medicinal plants, despite the fact that death rapidly consumed both my body and spirit. My kidneys were failing, and my body ached from infection. Daily, the doctor pumped my bladder full of liquid antibiotics that did nothing except turn my pee red. I finally sought out another doctor who gently told me I had a precancerous vaginal cyst. Some of the cells in my body grew at a rapid rate, out of control. I was more terrified than I'd ever been in my life, and I never told anyone what I'd found out. Even when I later met and fell in love with Ian, I couldn't tell him. It wasn't that I didn't trust him; I could be completely honest with him. It was my own terror that stopped me telling him or anyone else. I just couldn't let the word *cancer* pass through my lips for fear that death might become too real and I would drown in it, never to rise again.

The second doctor finally referred me to a holistic practitioner in hopes that a diet change might help. He told me he couldn't do anymore unless I wanted to undergo surgery. I didn't stick around long enough to ask what that involved. The mere mention of surgery flashed a bright red warning in my brain.

My new diet agreed with me, but at times I worried it wouldn't be enough. If I didn't somehow awaken to life, I'd die. I didn't really know what "awakening" meant or how to go about it. Some days I doubt I cared. Then there were those days when I hungered for something drastically different from the world I lived in, but I saw no way of attaining it. Maybe I was *too* awake and had no way of deadening myself to survive. I often felt that way as a child. My wraith of a spirit had no defense against the demoralizing experience of school. I felt trapped and angry as social conditioning pressed in around me, determined to leave me no quarter of privacy, no thoughts of my own. Somewhere between A+ and D−, 8:00 AM and 3:00 PM, 1 to 100 and A to Z, I began to lose my connection to the earth and her love.

Fortunately, growing up in beautiful western Maine I sometimes could retreat into the woods during my free time. It helped ease some of my loneliness. I'd sit under a tree and dream of love and adventure and faraway places. For a few golden hours, I had time to simply feel. Time stood still. Late afternoon sun glowed warm on my innocent skin. The sky was so blue I thought I'd die from such luscious beauty. Birds didn't *just* sing. They sang for *me*. During those intimate hours alone in the woods, I didn't need to look in a mirror to see if I was beautiful, I just *knew* I was beautiful. The contrast between my days in the woods and my "real life" at school was so inconceivable I thought I'd go insane.

Someday someone will ask me, "What do you do for a living?" and I will say, "I feel."

Once during a grade school "show-and-tell" the teacher scolded me when I couldn't stop telling the class about all the things I'd seen in the woods. She said, "One cannot live in the woods forever. After all, there is the *real* world, Robin."

I fell through the cracks of life while the world moved on without me. I was unbearably bored in school. Book learning was dry and tiresome, and I seemed to have very selective retention ability, extremes of good and bad memory, depending on the topic. In class, the teachers' voices, no matter how softly spoken, sounded so loud they made me want to run screaming from the room. If a teacher lectured too fast, I was unable to register the individual meaning of words, and heard only noise. When given instructions for an exam or homework assignment, I often felt confused and overwhelmed. Yet, as I looked around the classroom, my fellow students appeared perfectly at ease and seemed to understand what was expected of them. I was horrified that I didn't. My heart raced, I broke out in a sweat, felt faint, and desperately fought back tears. The whole situation drove me to a state of panic, but I didn't know why or what to do about it. Sometimes I put one hand over my mouth and clutched my stomach with the other as I threw down my pencil and mumbled something about "feeling sick," while I raced for the girls' room. My mother was called, told that I was ill and advised to come and pick me up. Safe for one more day.

By the time I reached high school, I'd learned to hide my strange behavior from the world, but in the process of doing this, part of me shut down. I lost a vital connection to my truest self. However, the blessed side was that the ostracism and isolation I'd previously experienced in school ended, and I was inexplicably well liked and very popular. I was invited to all the usual school parties and dances, chosen for the

American Legion Auxiliary Girls State program, voted homecoming and winter carnival queen and class secretary, and earned letters for my sweater in several sports, but it all had little or no meaning to me. I had tons of friends and yet didn't feel *really* close to anyone. It never occurred to me that I could reciprocate an invitation. It didn't exist in my reality. While on the outside I appeared to laugh and joke, inside I was scared. I felt removed and wandered through these functions in a daze. They swirled around me, and I didn't even know why I was part of them. They just happened; and although my life appeared normal, I desperately hungered for something more. I knew something was very wrong. When my senior year of high school came to an end, I had no idea what do with my life and no comprehension of how to build a future. The thought of college made me want to kill myself. To go to college would be the end of all my hopes, dreams, and sense of adventure. Silently, I despaired like an inmate given a taste of freedom and then told to live four more years in prison.

The sound of Ian humming Cat Stevens's song "Wild World" momentarily ended my wandering thoughts and brought me back to the drive. He was lost in his own thoughts and absentmindedly drummed his fingers on the truck's big black steering wheel while he sang. The thick heat made me drowsy. I didn't know how Ian managed to stay awake. He looked so strong and confident. Although he was a year younger than me, I depended on him completely. As I devoured the strong lines of his handsome face, my thoughts lazily drifted and again returned to my past, but to a time long before high school.

As an adolescent there were many things I didn't understand about myself. I desperately wanted to be held, but could hardly stand being held by *anyone*, even my mother. Light touch particularly irritated me. At times the slightest noise painfully ripped through my body. I found it hard to say people's names. Eye contact was very challenging. Often when I entered a room and one of my siblings or parents would look at me, I'd yell at them, "Don't look at me!" I wanted to be left alone and not be talked to or forced to interact. But at the same time I wanted my family nearby because my biggest fear was of being alone. I was easily overwhelmed, and peace and rest came only with solitude and motion. I'd rocked myself since infancy. Night after night, for years, I sat cross-legged on my bed, rocked my back against the wall, and made repetitive sing-song sounds until I fell asleep. By the time I was eight years old, I'd developed a large callus on my spine. I think my parents simply thought I was a challenging child and prayed I'd outgrow any worrisome behavior.

In my teen years the horrendous motion sickness I'd had all my life began to abate, and in its place I started to occasionally have convulsions when I was under stress. I never actually blacked out, but my arms and legs would convulse while I battled for consciousness. Dad would help me to a chair and lower my head between my legs until it passed. While we waited, he vigorously rubbed my arms and legs and encouraged me to take deep breaths. Thankfully, when puberty ended and I entered high school, the convulsions stopped. My body calmed down, and I never had convulsions again.

Once I left high school I passed my days as the shadow of a ghost. I didn't know how to clutch at someone's sleeve and say, "Please help me. Something's wrong. I'm dying." How could I ask for help when I had no sense of other? Feelings of isolation and fear dominated my days. Unless someone or something intervened, I lived apart from the rest of the world, just outside the jar of society, sometimes looking in, more often than not looking away.

Ian's singing again broke into my reminiscence, and I felt his warm hand on my leg, safe and reassuring, but my thoughts continued to pull me into the past. Six months before I met Ian, my grandmother passed away. Her death left me locked in my Salt Lake City apartment. I sat cross-legged on the living room floor. With my back against the wall and the curtains closed, I rocked myself for hours. Peace and rest came only with motion. My grandmother's death devastated me. I didn't know death was forever . . . I didn't even know it was real. *If death is real then life also must be real.*

Faced with the permanency of death, I slammed the door on a rush of pain, but not before I imagined my parents grown old and gone and my own life passed away, unlived.

I couldn't let that happen.

As my grief deepened, a sense of self began to form for the first time in my life. Something familiar called me. Another soul reached out over great distance; I'd felt him since I was four years old. Now I had to find him or die. I'd waited my entire life for destiny to arrive. Little did I know that within less than a year I'd travel more than halfway around the globe and live in one of the world's oldest tropical rainforests. My life would unravel in a way I couldn't imagine.

My destiny's name was Ian. When I met him in Salt Lake City I was involved with a personal-awareness group, one of many such groups that were happening all over the country during the sixties and seventies. We all explored thoughts, feelings, and insights. Ian had come to the States from Australia to become part of the group with some of his Aussie buddies who lived in Salt Lake. The first time I saw him I thought he looked about as handsome as a man could. He was just over six feet tall with a well-muscled lumberjack's build. Blond hair feathered wild and wispy around his face. Intense blue eyes and a strong square chin were enough to knock out any woman. And if that didn't do it, his captivating Australian accent did. Ian's most enchanting aspect was that he remained unaware of his charm.

Wild and spontaneous, he lived life at full throttle. He loved American "Yank tanks," freeways, and twenty-four-hour supermarkets. He didn't really care what people thought of him and seemed oblivious to the possibility that someone might think *anything* about him. He'd speak his mind in a situation where other people cowered under intimidation. This came naturally to Ian. He often said, "It's good shock value, mate."

With a genius-level IQ and a near-photographic memory, he was high stimulus.

On the other hand, I always tried to do the right thing. Be polite. Orderly. Don't rock the boat. Never contradict anyone or break the rules, and always "think before you act." Yet I quivered with anticipation when someone else stood up for himself or herself, broke a rule, spoke out of turn, or showed some sign of spontaneity.

I grew up in the woods of Maine and small-town, middle-class America. Ian grew up in the city with private schools and money. We appeared opposites, and yet at "our" core we were more alike and familiar to each other than anyone either of us had ever known.

The first day I met Ian, complete recognition washed over me. I felt I had *always* known him. I knew he was the person I'd waited for since I was four and a half years old. I had waited since the summer day my sister and I sat by our stone wall in Maine—little girls playing—and I told her someday a tall man who spoke funny would come from far away. And I would marry him. I accurately described Ian to her on that sunny day, and spent my time after that searching every pair of eyes and every voice for that one familiar soul, my other half. The one I couldn't forget. When I met Ian, my life finally became real. One of life's most profound mysteries is to look into another face and see our own soul looking back. Human souls extend far beyond fragile bodies of bone and flesh. Like two comets about to crash head on, Ian and I had a meeting with destiny that would change both our lives forever.

One of the things I loved most about him was that he instilled shining freedom in me. He had an ability to live beyond social conditioning and didn't become trapped in the pressure to be certain ways or do certain things. I eventually told him that I wanted to leave the personal-awareness group because I felt that the continual study of every thought and emotion was making me crazy. I was tired of being in my head, questioning every impulse until it vanished. That was unhealthy. It was time to let the river of my life run freely, let it find its own course. I wanted to walk away and take back my spontaneity and trust in myself. However, I knew that some people in the group thought I was wrong to leave. Ian said that even if everyone in the group thought I should stay, even if they all rejected me when I left, it didn't matter. What mattered was that I follow my impulses, whatever they were. He told me that I could let go and trust life. It would teach me what I needed to know. The only important thing was that I follow my heart. Shortly after that, Ian quit the group, but I still couldn't. I wanted to, but I hemmed and hawed and kept analyzing my impulse until it no longer felt real, and I was left feeling dead and despaired. It seemed I always tried to work everything out before I did anything, and I always tried to do the "right" thing, as opposed to doing what I was guided to do. Ian didn't judge me; he only encouraged.

That first year after I met Ian and he moved into my apartment, I started taking modeling classes. Each year, the agency I worked with chose a few girls to promote and send to Paris, London, and New York. I was one of the "chosen." But unlike the other girls I did not feel elated. I felt depressed about being chosen, as if I'd stepped off solid ground into quicksand. I'd only taken up modeling because I needed a job, and several people said I'd make a good model. But I soon felt like I was being sucked into a world of makeup, clothes, and hairspray.

Late one night, I came home from a class to find Ian happily making avocado and miso sandwiches for supper. When I walked in the door, he immediately asked what was wrong. I told him I hated the modeling and the layers of makeup and wearing four-inch heels that hurt my back. As we sat on the living room floor to eat our sandwiches, Ian asked what I *did* like doing. I told him that the thing I loved most was being in the mountains hiking and camping. He listened intently and openly while I talked. Ian had a curious and innocent quality, which I found refreshing. He never put on airs or acted with pretense; he was easy to talk to. There were no barriers, so I could be really honest with him. I cried as I told him about the pain of modeling. When I finished it was almost midnight, and yet Ian's eyes were sparkling. Grinning, he jumped up and said he'd be right back. The front door closed behind him before I could respond. I thought he'd gone to a twenty-four-hour grocer to buy a special dessert to cheer me up. A half hour later he burst in with a bag of groceries, two gallons of water, and a new green tarp. He told me to put on the warmest clothes I had, find a box of matches, and get both of our sleeping bags out of the closet. He grabbed our red cooler from under the kitchen table and threw in a loaf of bread, a handful of bananas, some apples, and a bag of marshmallows. On top of the marshmallows he threw in an iron skillet and bag of potatoes.

He glanced around and saw me still standing there and said, "Come on, go change and grab the other stuff, mate. We's going to the mountains."

Stunned, I reminded him that it was already past 1:00 AM. We didn't have a tent. Where would we sleep if it rained? It was freezing out. And where was the rest of the food? Ian stopped what he was doing and came over to me. He held me firmly by the shoulders and said, "Trust me, Rob, there is a reason you need to do this *right now*; you'll understand later. And besides, it's good to sometimes do things just for the hell of it. We'll sleep in the bloody car if it rains. So go grab our sleeping bags, and then help me load this gear into the trunk. Don't forget to lock the door behind you."

Ian's spontaneity was shattering my ordered world. I felt both elated and somewhat disoriented. I liked it. But still . . . in the middle of the night? In the mountains? In freezing autumn? I'd never done *that* before.

The car was warm as toast when I climbed in and sat next to Ian. He drove into the night and up into the mountains. At one point he pulled to the side of the road and said he was going to make sandwiches. He reached behind the seat into the cooler and pulled out the bread and some bananas and said, "Okay, mate, here's something I've never shown you before, the bloody sandwich du jour." He peeled a banana, put it between two pieces of bread, slapped the whole mess between his palms, and then squished. Instant banana sandwiches.

We put the food away and drove deeper into the mountains until we reached a bumpy dirt road that came to an end in a little valley. Within fifteen minutes I had a fire glowing inside a ring of rocks, and we were happily toasting marshmallows. I breathed the sweet smell of pine and relaxed to the babble of a nearby creek. Modeling felt a thousand miles away, as if it had never been a part of me. It hadn't. I began to understand why Ian had brought me to the mountains immediately. I knew what I needed to do when I returned to Salt Lake City. I would never be a model. Robin Easton loved the woods. Ian gave me that gift, not with words, but simply by taking me to the thing I loved most, right when I needed it. He didn't wait or try to talk me out of modeling. He simply connected me with my truest self. I loved him for it. The longer I knew Ian, the freer I felt.

That night we zipped the two sleeping bags together and slept cuddled on the ground near the fire, just like the cowboys under the stars. I never did get cold or hungry, and it never rained. I lay in the dark looking at millions of stars, and it was the first time in my life that I experienced true sovereignty. There beneath the galaxy, my impulse to leave the personal awareness group returned. I knew it was over; I'd never go back. I marveled at the power of following an impulse. Freedom and life were the outcome. Two days later on our return trip to the city, Ian asked me to marry him. I said yes and knew that being with him would be an astounding journey that would change my life.

Several months after our midnight mountain trip, we decided to live in Australia. We concluded our affairs in Salt Lake City and flew to Maine to see my parents one last time. We were married in a simple ceremony in my childhood home. It was a blue-jean wedding. I wore clogs and a lacey blouse, and Ian wore cowboy boots and a Western shirt. He was captivated by anything Western as he had seen that style of dress in the American movies he'd watched on Australian TV.

As with all young newlyweds, neither of us could believe we were husband and wife. Madly in love, we were forever. Unrealistic? Who knows? Everyone should feel "forever" at least once. Eternal love binds all life. In a parting of tears and hugs, I said good-bye to my parents and left for Australia and my new family.

My spirit rode on the wings of a plane in the night sky, transported through time to another reality. At long last, life began to stir. I sensed freedom was near. I'd waited for the right spark of life to arrive. Finally it was here. And on that very night, thousands of feet above earth, my weary spirit found respite.

Thin ties and familiarities vaporized in the jet stream. Ian became my family, my whole life. It never occurred to me to do anything but follow him. He was the destiny I'd waited for, and I knew it. I didn't know where this soul journey would take me; I only knew that I might never have this chance again. I had no plans or connections other than Ian. He brought movement into my life. When one is dying, movement often is life.

Ian's persistent voice returned my attention to the present and the drive north. "Hey, mate? Rob-o? Roby?"

"Oh sorry, Ian. I was just thinking about stuff."

"So, Rob, you reckon bloody Oz is a right beaut place, eh?"

"At least there aren't tigers and lions in Australia that could rip the back of my skull open and eat me."

Ian chuckled, and I continued.

"And thank God we won't be near the funnel-web spider. At the reptile park I read that its territory is mainly around Sydney. The guy at the desk said the funnel-web's pinchers could bite through a man's fingernail. That thing could kill you in five minutes. No time for writin' out a last-minute will."

Ian chuckled again and pulled me closer to his side of the truck.

While driving north we'd stayed with a friend of Ian's in Sydney, Graham Tucker. He warned me to watch out for funnel-web spiders that ended up in his swimming pool. "They fall into the pool and can be underwater, down in the corners. I've scooped 'em out with the pool net, and they's still bloody kicking. So youse going to have to check before you swim. Me neighbor was bitten by one."

I didn't know if Graham was just trying to scare me or if they really did get funnel-webs in the pool, but I carefully checked for itty-bitty black things every time I dove in.

"Ian, I know there are crocodiles up north, but they stay near the water, right? And I'll have to watch I don't step on a snake, and remember to check my sleeping bag every night and my clothes every morning for spiders. But we'll be all right . . . won't we?"

Ian acted brave enough. He hadn't reacted to all the deadly creatures at the reptile park the way I had. In fact, he'd sort of clammed up and hadn't spoken while we were there. At the time I didn't know why. All I knew was that I felt perfectly safe with him. I found his ability to fix anything and improvise to make do with what we didn't have very reassuring. We had a survival book and natural healing book in the back of the truck, and we were young and invincible. We knew it all, man.

After a few more days on the road I pushed the apprehension of the reptile park to the farthest corner of my mind. South of Innisfail we stopped to rest near the Tully River. Earlier that day we bought a couple of watermelon-sized papaya—or "pawpaws" as Ian called them—and I couldn't wait to try one.

With a clang of metal I lowered the tailgate and sat on it cross-legged. The pawpaw stretched from knee to knee, braced in my lap. I hacked open the sweet, orange flesh with my Buck knife, a wedding present from Mom. I loved to cut my fruit into bite-sized squares, stab a chunk, and pop it into my mouth.

Ian squatted on the ground at the end of the truck, engrossed in our now well-worn map.

"Not much farther, Rob. We can hit bloody Cairns tonight and find a place to camp, or we can nick off first thing in the morning and go all the way to bloody Mossman."

"It's pretty here. Why don't we set up camp now, while it's warm and sunny."

"Righty-o. We'll leave after brekkie tomorrow."

The next morning began bright and clear. As we hopped into the truck, Ian said, "Here we go again, mate." At the start of each day we went through the same ritual with me parroting Ian's words. "Yup, here we go again."

We stopped in Cairns to grab a bite of "normal food." We were both vegetarians, so we ordered two thick veggie and cheese sandwiches. Cheese didn't usually agree with me. I'd given it up months before, but it sure tasted good in a sandwich with pickled beetroot—as the Aussies called beets. Of course Ian had to have an ice cream cone. He ate more ice cream than anyone I knew. I once watched him eat three pints before he felt only slightly sick. I didn't have ice cream, but I'll never forget those sandwiches. They were such a treat compared to the food we ate on the road, raw fruit and veggies sold by the honor system.

I liked that honor system. Way out on an empty road in the middle of nowhere there'd be a produce stand and an old wooden table. On the table was an open tin can with the words CASH HERE written across it. Prices were hastily scrawled on a piece of scrap wood. I usually saw no farmhouse or other signs of life, not human anyway, yet the can overflowed with money. We sat on the roadside for an hour, ate our lunch, and didn't see one car pass by.

How often did the farmer collect the money? Did a few customers stop every couple of hours, or do the Aussies look at things kind of long term? Maybe the tin held a week's worth of sales, maybe more. I didn't know. I would have needed to sit on the road for days to find out. I could think of worse pastimes.

The road from Cairns to Mossman invigorated me with its spectacular beauty. Aqua-blue sea stretched to the horizon on my right, and steep rainforest hillsides rose up on my left where liquid-silver waterfalls tumbled from lush greenery. Sun warmed my arm as it rested on the truck's open window. In the presence of such beauty I thought our adventure might not be so bad after all. But as we approached Mossman, aqua-blue ocean gave way to a sea of tall, green sugar cane that extended for miles on either side of the road and right up to the base of the mountains. I didn't much like it.

"This is kinda depressing, Ian. I don't really wanna live in this. Do you?"

"Rob, we'll just keep looking until we find the right bloody place. Ain't real sure where this spot is that Hal mentioned. I can see it on the map. Cape Tribulation. Strewth! Wish we'd got better bloody directions. He said there's a dirt road a few miles past Mossman that will take us down to the Daintree River. Then we take a ferry across the river to get into the jungle. Tomorrow we'll drive a bit farther and have a stickybeak. If we don't find it, we'll go back to one of the other roads. Righty-o, mate?"

In Mossman we stopped for gas and supplies. The small town intrigued me so completely that I forgot to ask for directions to Cape Tribulation. I was surprised and delighted to see grown men wearing shorts with kneehigh socks and leather dress shoes. I told Ian that American men wouldn't be caught dead wearing knee-high socks with shorts. At least not a Mainer. I had to laugh since I associated knee-highs with junior-high-school girls. But apparently as dorky as *I* thought it looked, the men didn't seem to feel it threatened their masculinity at all, which I thought was very cool.

Pubs commandeered almost every street corner. By late afternoon, raucous laughter and bawdy songs spilled from their windows and bubbled like beer into the street. Women of all colors and shapes, in flowered dresses and white cotton shifts, stood outside pub doors rocking baby-filled strollers: Aboriginal women with blue-black skin and ebony eyes, mixed-descent women with mocha skin and blue eyes, Anglo women with white skin and red hair, and even one albino Aboriginal woman with white hair and red eyes. They all had one thing in common;

they waited for their men to finish their drink and come home to supper. I shared my amazement with Ian.

"How can they stand there in this heat waiting for their husbands? Why don't they just go home? Aren't women allowed in the pubs?"

"Don't bloody know, Rob."

When a brawl broke out in one of the pubs, I wasn't too anxious to stick around.

Most of the Aboriginals on the street were exceptionally warm. They happily returned my smiles as if they'd known me for years. While Ian ran to grab more ice cream, I stood by the truck with three young Aboriginal women. The remarkable thing was that I didn't even know them, but nonetheless they leaned with me against the truck, just smiling and being friendly. They all wore simple cotton dresses, sleeveless and straight, and two of them were barefoot. The other one wore old white canvas sneakers minus the laces.

All at once we noticed a small tan dog wander out of a nearby pub and walk slowly up to the Mossman Bank entrance. We giggled when he jerkily cocked his leg toward the bank door, but before the mutt could urinate, he suddenly toppled onto his side. One of the girls nudged me and said, "Pissed," which I knew meant drunk in Australian slang. Slowly, the dog scrambled to his feet and braced himself for another try. He was determined to mark his territory. That was *his* bank. While we held our breath, waiting and watching, he raised his leg, teetered for one second on three legs, then boom, over he went again. He whined in frustration as he got up, staggered to the door, cocked his wavering leg, and tried again. *Okay, almost there, you can do it.* Teeter. Teetering. Tipping. Ooops, down he goes yet again.

Worn out and unable to do his male thing, he drunkenly staggered off, leaving a trail of pee as he went. Someone in the pub had given him beer.

At Ian's approach one of the girls took my hand, pointed to herself and then toward Mossman Gorge, shrugged her shoulders, and said, "Come."

Then off the girls went smiling and waving. They walked a little ways, turned to smile and wave once more, and then vanished around a corner.

For the first time in my life I felt like I fit in. They didn't care who I was, what I'd done or not done, whether I had money or not, what kind of career I had, where I'd gone to school or even if I *had* gone to school. I could be myself, a nothing, and be accepted. They didn't even know or care where I'd come from. They only cared that I was kind to them. I liked their priorities. It made me happy all day, and I found myself loving them for it.

Ian and I continued with our errands. In the grocery store I returned to the 1950s as I wandered up and down the four isles.

"Ian, is this all the cereal brands you have in Australia?"

"Yeah, that's it, mate."

The cereal section contained five brands of cereal.

"Geez, Ian, this is refreshing. In America we have so much stuff in our stores. The choices are overwhelming. After awhile nothing seems special. I like this. It's simple and uncomplicated."

I remembered Ian's incredulity over a twenty-four-hour grocery store back in the States, where one whole aisle, on both sides, devoted itself to dozens of different cereals.

Here, frozen orange juice didn't exist. Ian hadn't even heard of it. Popsicles were called paddle pops, and everyone ate meat pies. Everyone ate meat. Lots of it.

This would be our last chance to purchase fresh food and fill up with water. Ian filled the dual gas tanks with petrol before we jumped into the truck and continued north to Daintree. We'd only traveled the length of Main Street when suddenly one of our burlap water bags came loose. Ian pulled over to the edge of the road to tighten the strap. As I got out of the truck to sit on the cool grass, I heard a shout and looked up to see a skeletal-thin Aboriginal man smile and wave at me. His wiry, gray hair ballooned thick and magnificent. Encouraged by my returned smile, he teetered forward on legs as thin as my arms wearing only tan, baggy shorts that almost lost their hold on his frail, naked body. He pointed to the camera around my neck and back to his people who sat at a picnic table under a huge rain tree. We shook hands, and he spoke in a language full of *oohs, uuus,* and *lllls,* which I didn't understand, but I knew from his gestures that he wanted me to follow. The group rose to meet me as I approached and gathered around, all smiles and giggles, while the elder spoke to them and indicated my camera.

After I took the photo, the old man pointed to me and began to converse with a youth in his early twenties. With a couple of gentle nudges from his elder, the young man shyly introduced me to each member of the group, and then said, "My grandfather says you took our picture so the world will not forget us."

Ian and I drove in silence. At sunset we pulled off the washboard road and parked beneath two old mango trees. Between the millions of midges that wriggled through the cap's screen windows and the memory of my new Aboriginal friends, it took some tossing and turning before sleep had its way.

Morning arrived with the winking of sun through mango leaves. After a breakfast of sweet, juicy pineapple, we hit the road in search of the turnoff to the Daintree River and the ferry. It lay somewhere between Mossman and the tiny town of Daintree. I regretted not having gotten directions when we had stopped in Mossman.

"Ian, there was a house back there. Why don't we stop and I'll see if they know where the road is?"

"Naaaahh. We'll be right. I'll bloody find it, eh."

I didn't know if it was all men or just Ian, but having to ask for directions was like stopping at a stranger's house and asking if you could use their toilet to take a dump. It just wasn't done. We'd driven away from society in a self-contained unit and had a date with a jungle that had been in existence long before we were born. A day or two more wouldn't alter the grand scheme of things.

Jackhammer vibrations rattled my teeth in their sockets and bounced the truck to the washed-out edge of the dirt road. A shift into four-wheel drive pulled us out of the ditch. I nervously hummed, "There's a place for us, somewhere a place for us . . ."

"You oughta slow down a bit, Ian. We'll miss the turnoff."

"Not sure where the bloody turnoff is, Rob-o, but I saw a sign back there. Said STATE FOREST. Maybe we could live there instead of Cape Tribulation. Let's pull over and suss it out, eh?"

Sure enough, a track veered up the hill and into the forest. A barbed wire fence ran along the side of the main road, and a white gate hung across the forestry track. The gate boasted a heavy-duty padlock.

"My oath, didn't know they'd lock up the freakin' jungle. Where's me bolt cutters, Roby? Thanks, mate. Aaahhh, they's not bloody strong enough. Crikeys. We should've bought the bigger ones. Whenever youse buying tools always buy the biggest and the best, or it's a waste of bloody money."

I'd known Ian only a bit over a year, but I knew how his mind worked. He went about things in a big way. Visions of the winch attached to the gate and the gate ripped from the ground flashed through my mind. Fortunately alternative visions came equally as fast.

"Hey, Ian. Why don't we undo the barbed wire fence along the road here? We can do the fence back up, go through this field, and cut over to the forestry road. If we hide well enough, no one'll ever know we got in."

Unfortunately, my ideas were almost as asinine as Ian's, but not as dramatic. They got us into as many crazy adventures, just at a slower pace.

Out with the wire cutters and pliers; we had enough tools and extra wire to build a whole new fence. Maybe it would have been easier to rip apart the gate, drive through, and then put it back together. Illegal? I'm sure, but living between realities made *everything* seem bizarre. I was rapidly losing my hold on any kind of normalcy, and I wagered it would only get worse.

"Right-o, everybody stand back. This bloody fence might recoil when I cut her." Snip. Ping. Snip. Ping. Snip. Ping. "She's a goer, Rob-o. You want to drive? No? Okay. I'll drive then. We's home and hosed now, mate."

After Ian added new wire and reattached the strands to the post, we drove 100 feet into the field going great guns. Then something weird happened. We hit these outlandishly large tussocks of grass, two feet high. Not the grass itself, but the tough mounds the grass created where it grew. They hid every three feet in front of us.

"Bloody strewth. Look at these things. They's like moguls on a fair dinkum ski slope."

Ian had skied moguls in Utah, on his backside, headfirst down the mountain.

"Should've sussed her out, Rob. Righty-o then. We'll use the winch. No worries, mate."

I scanned the hill for trees as Ian bent to unhook the cable and ready the winch. I didn't know whether to laugh or cry. Smack in the middle of the field grew one spindly naked palm. That was it.

"Uh, Ian? Hey, Ian! You might want to check this out first."

"What's that, mate?"

Clang.

Bang.

The winch cable came free. Ian still had his back to the lone tree and me.

"Hey, Ian? What size tree do we need? Can a winch rip trees out of the ground?"

Ian turned and looked at me, ready to say, "Can't you tell I'm on a mission here?" But he never had the chance. Slowly, his features rearranged as he spotted the lonely little palm and my words sunk in. I waited.

"Bloody strewth! Bloody bleeding strewth! If this don't suck blowies out of a dead 'roo's arse. Deadset. More drama. But we's not going back, mate. Already closed up the bloody wires. We'll wrap that piece of inner tube around the tree way down low, then put the bloody winch cable over it. She'll be right. But let's not fartarse around gasbagging. Let's get right on 'er, eh?"

Ian didn't say anything directly, but he looked really worried. I knew enough about plants to know that palm trees have shallow root systems and enough about winching to know that the grass moguls would be a challenge.

One thing we had going for us was time. When you drop out of society, it's not as if you have to get home or be at work at a certain time. If it rained or grew dark we could crawl into the back of the truck and play cards, read, play the guitar, sing, make love, sleep, make love, sleep. If we got lost we had months' and even years' worth of food. In four days we could grow and eat fresh sprouts from the vast assortment of seeds we'd stored in the truck.

Ian had a .22 caliber repeating rifle with his tools, and I had a medical kit that would have made a surgeon proud. My bright red tackle box contained straight and curved-edged scalpels, 100 yards of silk sutures and 36 inches of polyester sutures, taper-cut and circle-cut edged needles, suture grips and suture scissors, xylocaine, topical anesthesia, plus all the other supplies a normal first aid kit contains.

None of the stuff bothered me or felt foreign, not after years spent inside other people's mouths while Dad cut them open and sewed them back together. As a small-town dentist and oral surgeon, he taught all of his children how to dental assist in case we needed "something to fall back on." Dad enthusiastically shared what he knew with us kids. He prepped us so well that we performed repair surgery on ourselves and an assortment of cherished animals. "I wonder if I can stitch this finger-foot-leg-dog-cat-chicken back together?" Experimental surgery was a family pastime, a bit like TV for other families.

Ian's impatience made me quicken my stride as I trudged up the hill, wrapped the inner tube around the tree, and hooked the cable into place.

I flashed the thumbs-up sign, but mud already sprayed from behind the tires as the winch kicked into gear and the engine revved to move the Toyota forward. I gave directions twenty feet in front of the truck.

"Turn this way. Now that way. Let the winch do the work. Don't turn the wheel so hard and fast. Slow it down. SLOW DOWN!"

The slower I told Ian to turn the wheel, the faster he cranked. Stubborn determination drove him to get the Toyota through the field right now, not in a few minutes' time. He got out to investigate when he realized the winch had suddenly gone slack and no longer pulled the truck up the hill.

"Bugger me dead. We's snapped the bloody cotter pin in two. Luckily there's three more. Crikey. This reminds me why I hate working on bloody bleeding engines for a living."

I didn't know anything about cotter pins. Ian grew up with machines and worked on everything short of helicopters. I only knew the winch wouldn't work without a nail-sized pin in place, and it seemed to take forever to replace it. After hours in the grueling sun, two more tries up the hill, and two more broken pins, I felt crazed with frustration.

Holy Toledo! Why don't they make the damned things stronger?

Our next-to-last pin snapped. So did Ian. He leapt from the truck, dropped to his knees, and slammed his wrench over and over into the red earth, until he sobbed. I knew how he felt.

"Crikeys, Rob-o, I'll replace this one last bloody pin then I've got to ask you to drive, mate. Maybe you'll have better luck."

I'd never used a winch or driven a four-wheel drive vehicle up a slope like this. But could I do any worse than Ian? In his present condition he'd pop the tires clean off their rims in no time. They were already bent at an agonizing angle. One of us had to get a handle on the situation. We had one pin left. I just might be able to do it if I turned the wheel more gently and hit the moguls at an angle.

I sat in the driver's seat, barely able to see the rear tires with my side mirrors tipped down as far as they'd go. Slowly, I turned the wheel left and right as the winch pulled the truck at a precarious angle up the hill and over the moguls. All the way I chanted, "Come on baby, light my fire. You can do this. Just a little higher." At the top, I stopped the truck and painfully uncurled my claws from the black steering wheel. I got out on shaky legs and plopped to the ground. Ian's grin of amazement and pride made it all worthwhile. When I looked back down the torn up, mud-sprayed field, I thought, *Yeah right, no one will ever know we got in here.*

We cut across the top of the pasture onto the dirt forestry road. Ian ground the truck to a halt and hollered, "My oath, I've got a beaut idea. We'll nick some nails from the bloody gate back there. Let's grab the hammer. We'll walk down the hill and suss her out, mate. Might be the same size as the bloody useless cotter pins. They's about as useless as tits on a bull."

We celebrated as Ian pulled six nails out of the fence that were the exact size of the broken cotter pins. His ingenuity doubly impressed me when he thought to remove nails that didn't affect the structure of the gate. I also spied a couple of them on the ground that had been dropped when the gate was built. Although rusty, they were straight and strong.

Several miles into the forest, we stopped at the top of a mountain and ate a late lunch in cool fresh air. Silence swallowed the memory of our engine's roar when Ian turned off the Toyota. Bird songs filtered down through the canopy and hit the trunks of trees in soft-echoed tones.

"Maybe this is where we're supposed to live, Rob. She's a right beaut place, eh?"

"Yeah, but we'd have to go further into the forest so we're not so close to the road. We've gotta look for a nice place to camp with a creek."

We finished lunch and drove deeper into the bush. Several miles along, we approached a washout. Rain had rushed in a torrent down the steep mountainside and taken the road and three trees with it. Next to the washout was a fifteen-foot flat area covered with brown slimy mud. Ian jumped from the truck to take a closer look. After the last mogul disaster, I jumped out behind him.

"Mud's pretty shallow. Ground's solid enough. Look, Rob." Ian's stick sank a foot into the bog. "She's a goer. Put her in four-wheel drive and she'll go through, no bloody worries."

I felt a bit squeamish about the two-inch leeches that squirmed in the fetid water. They went all flat and wiggly when Ian stirred the muck with his stick. I walked away, grateful to be inside the truck while we drove through the mud.

With the Toyota in four-wheel drive we slowly pushed into the bog hole, steady and firm. Halfway across, the truck suddenly lurched forward as if the front wheels had fallen into a hole. Wham! Thud!

"What the bloody hell?"

Ian revved the engine and shifted gears. I figured we'd hit a rock. Disgusted, he kicked off his thong sandals and flung open the truck door. I almost gagged when he jumped barefoot into the mud, leeches and all.

"You want something on your feet? There's 'things' in the mud."

"Oh crikeys, mate. It's only leeches, not a bloody nest of taipans."

"I just thought . . . "

Ian waded to the front of the truck carrying the stick. I crawled out my window and onto the hood of the Toyota for a better look. I could only move so far before I hit a tangle of branches that overhung the front of the vehicle. Ian crouched by the winch in a foot and a half of mud. His stick made a solid thunk, thunk noise against a submerged log.

"How big is it, Ian? How high? How wide?"

"Strewth. Forgot me bloody tape measure."

When I gave an exasperated sigh, Ian laughed and said, "Just funning you, mate. There's a bloody big arse hole here, about a foot and a half deep with a big arse tree in it almost two feet across. Sticks up pretty high, too. Crikey, there's sharp little stubs on her where the branches broke off. Strewth! We's best make sure we miss those so's we don't puncture the bloody tires.

"Oh great."

"Aaaahh, she's a goer, Rob-o. We can winch over it. One good thing, they'll have to repair the road before they find us. It'll keep people out."

Keep people out? Oh yes, it'll keep people out. I'm sure. So what the hell are we doing here? It's okay, Robin. You and Ian are just insane. That's all. It'll keep out the rest of the world. The saner portions.

"Oh God, Ian, we can't do this again. The only cotter pin we have left is in the winch. What if it breaks and the nails don't work? What then? How the hell do we get out of here?"

"Oh, Rob, it won't break."

"Of course not. How silly of me. It's not like we've broken any cotter pins or anything lately."

Ian was grinning when we got into the truck. We started across the mudhole with the winch wrapped around a solid gum tree. Branches obscured the windshield and screeched against the glass as the front wheels rose up and over the log. The truck settled back to level. The pin snapped and the winch went slack. Of course.

Gritting my teeth, I avoided the childhood taunt of, "Na na, na, na, na, na. Told you so," and simply asked, "*Now* what'll we do, Ian?"

"Listen, Roby. There'll probably be water in the bloody mountains here, real soon."

I laughed and said, "I know, Ian, like your mother used to say, 'Just around the corner, luv.'"

Ian grinned sheepishly and replied, "We've come this far, might's well keep bloody going. Strewth. We can't back up now, even if we wanted to. We's straddling the bloody log. We have to go forward, Rob."

"Okay. But how will we change the cotter pin in the mud?"

"That's right, Rob, in the mud."

Before I registered what Ian meant, he stripped naked and laid his Tshirt and pants on the hood of the Toyota. He then walked back to the tailgate of the truck and stood calmly in the muck while he sorted through his toolbox.

"You better strip down, Rob. I'll need you to pass me tools."

"Are you serious? What about the leeches? You want me to remove my clothes and squat in the mud with you? Crikeys, Ian, they could crawl anywhere. Doesn't that bother you?"

"We've got to bloody well change this pin if we want to crawl anywhere. I still have to get the back wheels over the bloody tree. Just pray the nails work. By crikey, mate, the ratbag who sold me these cotter pins should have his bloody knackers nailed to the dunny door."

Ian rifled through his toolkit. Then he glanced up and saw the panicked expression on my face.

"Look, I'll pull the bloody leeches off you. Okay? They won't hurt you. They's only trying to suck your bloody blood. Why waste a pair of clean dacks?"

"Oh thanks for telling me that, Ian. It really makes a big difference. And by the way, what's this 'bloody blood' crap anyway? Next you'll be saying, 'your bloody bleeding blood.'"

"Damned mosquitoes, I hate 'em. Where's that bug dope, Ian? Maybe I can crawl under these branches, lay on the hood, and pass you tools."

"'Fraid not, Rob-o. Me fingers are like bleeding hamburger from changing the other ratbag pins. I'll need you to hold a few things down here. Me fingers are just too bloody chafed. You'll be right, mate. Come on. 'Ave a go."

Maybe Ian just needed me in the mud with him. Ten minutes later I'd stalled for as long as I could. Clothes still on, socks pulled up over my pants, I stood in brown slime up to my knees and held tools for Ian. With a branch full of leaves, I swatted at the thickest cloud of mosquitoes I'd ever seen. Maybe if I swatted really hard at the mosquitoes, it might keep the leeches away. I clenched my thighs together and tried not to think about crawly squirmy things. After what seemed hours, my legs ached and my neck and back throbbed from bending to avoid overhanging limbs covered with ants. I desperately wanted to sit. Oh what the hell, why not? The leeches won't kill me.

I sank gratefully to my knees in front of the truck. The mud rose to my hips.

Silence made me aware that Ian's tools had stopped their busyness. I twisted my head to look at him through the gloom of leaves and branches. He stared at me intently. Tears glistened in his deep blue eyes as he said, "Good onya, mate. Look at youse in the bloody mud with me, surrounded with leeches and mossies, with mud on your nose. Youse so beautiful right now. I love you, Robin."

With the nail finally in place, muddy clothes and leeches pulled off, I sat naked in the truck as we cruised over the submerged log to the other side.

"We's home an' hosed, mate. What'd I tell you?"

I couldn't remember what he'd told me. I didn't care. We were on solid ground. At a much slower pace, Ian wound the Toyota along the mountainside while I kept both eyes open for further washouts, fallen trees, or bog holes. Sure enough "just around the corner" the rain had left a hole in the road twenty feet across. Thirty feet in front of the truck, the road dropped one hundred and fifty feet into a gully of rubble and uprooted trees. Far below, draped across one of the dying branches, lay a long black snake. The snake didn't bother me, but the look on Ian's face did.

"No, Ian, there's no way. I won't ride in the truck across thin air. Do you hear me?"

Ian tried not to grin while I talked on.

"Oh, I get it now. You'll chop down ten two-foot-diameter trees with our panel saw, de-limb them with the campfire ax, lay them across the washout, and drive over it. Forget it. I'll swim through leeches if I have to before you take the truck across that."

"Strewth, Rob-o. There's about a foot and a half of bloody road left here. We could put one wheel up on the cutaway bank and the other on this little strip of . . ."

"Nope, absolutely not. And what? Drive across at a thirty-degree angle and fall into the gully to die?"

At that point Ian chuckled and said, "Righty-o, mate, you win."

"There never was any contest, Ian."

In tiny increments, we turned the Toyota around on the narrow road and drove down the mountain. On our way back through the leech-infested mudhole, the nail held and the winch pulled us up and over the log like greased lightning. I thanked God for good old nails. As unbelievable as it sounds, I was so relieved to be away from the mudhole that I forgot about the field full of moguls until we got to the bottom of the forestry road. So much had filled the intervening time that our earlier slog through the pasture felt like it had happened years before. But no, there in front of me sat the smirking field, taunting, daring me to try again. Dead ahead, on the solid dirt road, stood the locked gate. Luckily Ian stopped the truck to plan our next move. Despite his extremely distressing memories of broken cotter pins and hours of hot work, he still surprised me when he came up with a sane solution.

"Let's sleep here tonight. Tomorrow we'll lock the truck, leave it here, and walk to that farmhouse a few miles back. Maybe they got a key to the gate, and we won't need to go through the bloody paddock."

Early afternoon of the next day, after we walked forever in sweltering heat and the fattest rain I'd ever seen, we reached the old white farmhouse. A middle-aged farmer with a military haircut, waxed wiffle, and starched green coveralls answered our knock. He stood deadpan while we told him about the Toyota and asked if he might have a key for the gate. In a grunt of disgust, he waved us away and closed the door. Shocked and concerned, we plodded back down the road. I hoped we'd make it to the truck before dark. Lost in thought and worry, I almost didn't hear the rattle and pop of a very sick vehicle. The battered old Land Rover stopped with a clatter of gravel ten feet behind us. A young rakish head popped out of the window and yelled, "You and yer missus 'op in, mate.

Me name's Brett. I got the bloody key 'ere. Lemme take youse to the gate and unlock 'er, eh?"

We eagerly piled into the Land Rover's dusty passenger seat, and Brett sped off to the forestry gate. As we banged over the bumpy dirt road, he tried to apologize for his father's rudeness.

"Me dad's a bit of an ol' wanker, but he's not a bad sorta bloke."

I suspected Brett heard us come to the door and then waited awhile, long enough to make it look believable when he asked his father if he could use the truck to go to town.

Our blond-haired young friend exuded wild, hungry energy and ran on a tank full of testosterone. He'd grown up in the area and seemed eager for outside contact. He had the thickest Australian accent I'd heard so far. A year or two younger than Ian, he could have passed for his equally handsome brother.

Brett grinned and said, "They gave us the key so's we could open the gate when our bloody cows stray into the forest."

We apologized for any inconvenience, but Brett wasn't worried.

"Oh, she's right, mate. Good to see some bloody new faces 'round 'ere. Besides, it's a chance to get away from me oldies. Can't figure why you two 'ould wanna live in the bloody bush. I's jack of it 'ere. Me oldies are pushing me to run the bloody farm, cows and all. Strewth. Not me, mate. I've had enough of it. Ain't into shovelin' no more bloody cow crap. Can't ever get the stink off. Bloody bovines always bellowin' and slobberin'. I'll be 'eadin' for Sydney straight away. What's it cost to get to bloody 'merica? Exy, is it? Strewth, that's an even better idea, eh?"

Brett turned the key, flung the gate open, and I drove the Toyota safely to the other side. We waved good-bye as our new friend rattled down the track with two of our fresh pineapples bouncing around on his front seat.

We took to the road in search of a place to sleep the night. Back to the mango trees. Once again, in our relief to be away from leeches, mud, and moguls, we forgot to ask Brett how to get to the Daintree River and Cape

Tribulation. But that was okay; we'd return to Mossman in the morning for detailed directions.

∽

The shadow moon rose
Drawing me out, onto the unknown path
Through the stuttering uncertainty
Toward the knowing of the native soul

—RUSSELL HUME

two

Weirdos and Washouts

Late the next day, we entered the hardware store in Mossman. Ian bought bolt cutters strong enough to cut anchor chain, and I asked for detailed directions to the Daintree River and the ferry. The manager grabbed a piece of scrap paper and drew a mud map that showed the turnoff to the Daintree River Ferry.

"Ferry master will tell youse how to get to Cape Tribulation, luv."

"So tell me, mate, what's this bloody ferry like anyway?" Ian asked.

"It's a punt. A big flat thing. You drive your bloody car onto it, and huge cables haul you across the river. Fare's not too bloody exy, maybe a buck or two? Not sure if it runs after 6:00 PM though. Or on weekends. You might see a bloody croc if youse look along the river bank."

Back on the road headed north, we searched for the turnoff to the ferry. The dirt track appeared on the right, just like the storeowner had described. Since it was almost six o'clock, Ian drove like a man possessed. If we missed the last run of the ferry, we'd need to spend another night on this side of the river. The only way into the rainforest was by the Daintree River Ferry or boat. There was no other vehicle access to the rainforest of Cape Tribulation.

When the Toyota slid sideways through a tight bend, Ian slowed to a slightly safer pace. On both sides of the road, sugar cane grew more than six feet tall like blades of a giant's lawn. Around the last corner I saw the ferry master's house. It sat atop tall stilts like most of the coastal homes in Far North Queensland. A guy at the hardware store told Ian that during the wet a good heavy rain might raise the river fifteen feet. Between Cairns and Mossman I'd seen white posts along the roadside with black lines marked on them every foot or so. I asked Ian what they were for.

"They's to let people know if the bloody water is too deep to drive through. They get some bloody fierce rain here, mate."

Some of the posts were several feet tall. Muddy stains wrapped around the white paint and showed how high the floodwater had risen. It was high. Very high. I wondered if anyone had ever drowned.

I'm not sure what I expected, but when the Daintree River came into view it moved me to silence. Like an ancient, all-powerful goddess she commanded my full attention. Wide and murky, she'd journeyed to the sea for millennia and felt no need to hurry. Lush green rainforest tumbled down to the bank and overhung the water. I scanned the surface for scaly eyes and raised snouts. The only croc I'd ever seen was at the reptile park, but this was the croc's natural habitat. The Daintree was home to the saltwater crocodile—the real thing—wild and hungry.

The rickety ferry sat low in the water. It was empty, so I could see painted lines on its deck that marked spaces for six to eight cars. I hoped it would hold the weight of that many vehicles if they showed up in the morning. No lights shone from the house, so we parked the truck and hopped out. Ian walked down to the river, read the sign on the ferry, and hollered back to me.

"Too late, Rob. We missed the last bloody run. Won't run again until 6:00 AM. We fartarsed around in bloody Mossman too long. Might's well sleep the night here, eh? Let's put the truck right in front of the ramp; that way we's can wake at sparrow fart and be the first ones on the ferry."

My apprehension turned to full volume. The river was dark and eerie. Strange sounds came from the thick growth along the water's edge. This was the end of the road, so to speak. No more sightseeing. No more snakes behind glass. No more touristy boat rides. Tomorrow we'd leave the world behind and live in the jungle.

When Ian hauled out our one-canister gas stove, I was relieved at the thought of our first hot meal in days. Mushrooms, green onions, and tamari thrown into the pot with cooked oatmeal made just the kind of comfort food I needed. A belly full of hot mush, and fatigue hit me. Probably more emotional than physical.

"I'm exhausted, Ian. The last two days have caught up with me. Hope you don't mind if I turn in. Are you coming?"

"Yeah, mate. Tomorrow's going to be a big bloody day. Don't know what we'll run into. Best get some sleep."

I thought the bugs might be thick by the river, but a light breeze kept them grounded. Soft warm air brushed my arms and legs. I wondered if the air ever was cool. I tried not to think about that. I had to trust we'd find the right place to live.

Inside the truck, the heat became so stifling I could barely breathe. I thought my overworked emotions were suffocating me, but then Ian threw back his sleeping bag and sat up with an irritated sigh.

"Crikey. I'm knackered. I just need to sleep. Bloody heat in here could ripen a dead cow in ten minutes. Sorry, matey, but I'm sleeping on the bloody ground under the truck."

Ian's voice was muffled beneath the Toyota when I asked him if it was any cooler. We giggled when I told him we were sleeping in bunk beds.

"Strewth, mate. Come out here. It's heaps cooler. If it rains, the truck will keep us dry. Come on, Rob-o."

Like Linus with his blanket, I dragged my sleeping bag under the truck next to Ian. We lay with our heads poked out from between the rear tires. The Southern Hemisphere winked and shimmered with unfamiliar constellations. Eerie sounds echoed back and forth across the river. Everything felt strange and frightening. A wave of loneliness drew me closer to Ian. Maybe he also sensed it because he tried to make me laugh. Ten minutes of riotous laughter put us both to sleep.

Later, I realized the risk we took when we slept under the Toyota that evening, less than twenty feet from a crocodile-infested river. To this day I can barely think about what we naively did.

Morning mist curled around the shore's edge, in and out, to awaken every leaf with a kiss. Once the sun rose higher and hit the water, the mist shrank back into the jungle's dark depths.

"Slam!"

Somewhere behind us a screen door shut. Ian and I turned to see the ferry master approach. His long black hair was pulled back in a tidy ponytail, and wire-rim glasses made him look like a scholar . . . at least from the neck up. From the neck down he was shirtless, shoeless, and wore nothing but short shorts. He grinned and absentmindedly scratched the thick mat of hair on his chest.

"G'day. Me name's Clyde[1]. Youse waiting for the ferry, mate? Me first run's at six o'clock. Youse headed over? Spend the bloody night here, did youse? Many mozzies? No? Youse right then. I'll just grab meself some tucker, quick smart, and we'll be off. Righty-o?"

While Clyde ate breakfast, we ate fresh pawpaws and fastened everything down to ready the truck for our trip to Cape Tribulation. We had no idea what the road would be like. Clyde might be able to shed some light on it.

No other vehicles arrived for the 6:00 AM run across the river, though a tan Land Rover waited on the far shore for the return trip. I was pleasantly impressed with the stability of the ferry as we drove our truck to the far end and parked. Clyde cranked up the punt's engine, and I double-checked our emergency brake while Ian got out to pay. Visions of our truck rolling off the ferry and into the river teased my mind.

Just before Clyde pulled the punt away from the riverbank, a young Aboriginal family emerged out of nowhere and walked onto the ferry. Where'd they come from? There were no houses except for Clyde's. Maybe they camped in the bush.

While we stood at the punt's railing looking for crocodiles, the father approached us and asked if we could give him five dollars for food. Ian opened his wallet to take out some money and found that we'd used all our cash in town. We had travelers' checks and enough change to get the ferry back out if we ever decided to leave the rainforest, but they were both buried in the truck.

When Ian showed his empty billfold to the young man, the Aboriginal said, " . . . 'at's awright. You bin kind. I remember you." When I saw his wife and three kids I wished we had more money on us; the children looked hungry. They were gorgeous with their brown springy hair and huge dark eyes. They all smiled at me and spoke in their native language that reminded me of the melody of magpies. I felt frustrated that I was unable to understand them, but then it didn't matter because we all laughed, pointed, and smiled. After a few attempts at conversation they waved goodbye and walked to the other end of the ferry. They sat on the hard floor of the punt while it crossed the river.

Ian stood holding my hand while we went back to searching for crocodiles. I noticed two thick chunks of Styrofoam that hung from the ferry's railing. Each chunk was roughly six feet by five feet. Little rope loops hung every twelve inches or so on the sides.

I asked Clyde, "What are those Styro things for?"

"Bloody life rafts."

Life rafts? So if there's six to eight cars on the ferry, and each car has only two people, that's still twelve to sixteen people.

"Clyde? If there's only two rafts how do six to eight people sit on each raft?" I asked.

A roll-your-own cigarette dangled from one corner of Clyde's mouth while he slurped coffee through the other. Deadpan, he told me, "Youse don't bloody sit on it. Youse hang onto the bloody rope handles and float your body in the river."

"Oh . . . I seeeee."

My mind flashed back to the crocodile at the reptile park. He was pretty big. Big teeth. Big jaws. Big body. BIG. An image of the ferry headed for the bottom of the river flickered in my mind. Suddenly I was swimming for the raft, my hands clinging to the pathetic rope handles while my legs and torso hung submerged in deep dark water. A crocodile slipped soundlessly from the bank into the river and glided straight for my legs.

"Rob . . . Roby . . . ROBIN! Crickeys, youse crushing me bloody hand, mate. What are you thinking about?"

"Huh? Oh nothing. Sorry, Ian."

I gave up searching for crocs and just tried to act normal. Everyone else appeared normal. I figured they wouldn't run a punt across the river that didn't work . . . would they? I didn't even want to think about it. It was a bright, sunny, perfectly normal day. Everything would be fine. Just fine. While I tried to climb out of the dark depths of my imagination, Ian asked the ferry master about the road to Cape Tribulation.

Clyde explained, "When you get off the bloody ferry go straight all the way to Cape Trib. Youse got a winch? Good-o, youse right as rain then. Bloody road might be washed away in places. The creeks are up a bit. Someone told me a bloke lost a bloody Toyota awhile ago. Jumped out while his vehicle filled with water and slowly disappeared downstream. Crikeys. Stalled midway through the creek. Deadset, mate, youse wanna check your flow and depth before crossing. Watch out for the bloody sand at the end of the track. Near the beach she gets quite thick. Not much to winch off."

An inch of ash bounced around on the end of Clyde's roll-your-own until it fell down his chest and blew away. He continued.

"Most folks who use the ferry are locals, live just across the river. But every once in awhile we's get some bloody weirdos go through here. A couple of freaks went through yesterday arvo. Bloody drongos ponged so bad I stayed upwind of 'em. Might wanna watch out for 'em, mate. Just don't stop for anyone, and don't leave your missus alone in the truck. And remember, nobody stays for the wet. Not unless they's well prepared."

I reeled from Clyde's words. He certainly hadn't eased my mind. If Ian was disturbed he didn't show it. We'd already winched through leeches and mud; what could be worse than that? All I wanted was for Ian to keep his promise that we agree *before* we charged into any water or mud, down cliff faces, up mountainsides, or along ravines. Any action that caused me to gasp, made my eyes pop out, or forced my foot to stomp the invisible brake on the passenger's side of the truck *must* be discussed ahead of time.

The ferry master walked back to his controls, and I leaned close to Ian and muttered, "You don't think he's serious, do you? I mean, don't you think he knows we're tourists, and he's just having fun trying to scare us. It can't be that horrible. Can it?"

"Don't bloody know, mate. We'll soon find out. Come on. Let's go."

"'We'll soon find out.' What the hell does that mean? Shouldn't we find out *before* . . . or something?"

"Come on, mate. Let's make tracks."

Time evaporated faster than I realized. We'd already reached the other side of the river. Clyde cut the engines back and lowered the off-ramp onto the concrete embankment. With a wave, we rolled our Toyota off the ferry, and the waiting Land Rover rolled on. We were on our own.

I glanced back at Clyde and said to Ian, "I bet he keeps an instantly inflatable raft just for himself in case the ferry sinks. Yeah sure, leave us bloody tourists hanging off puny Styrofoam floaties, our legs dangling in the river like a bunch of Kentucky Fried Chicken legs. Just hanging there until some hungry crocodile comes along for a finger lickin' meal."

Ian laughed, looked at me, and shook his head. It helped ease my foreboding. With our wheels on solid ground I could afford to laugh.

We hadn't seen crocs on the riverbank while crossing, but as we pulled away from the water I spotted a lone phone booth, just like you'd see in New York City. It sat on the fringe of the rainforest 100 feet from the river in the middle of bloody nowhere.

"Last chance to make a phone call, Rob. Clyde told me it's the only phone on this side of the river and that it doesn't always work. After this there's no phone, no electricity, no running water, no bloody nothing except jungle."

"If I don't *ever* use a phone again it won't matter. I never was a phone person."

"Too right, Roby, they's only good for bloody business anyway. Me dad hates the dog and bone. People always ringing up and wanting something. Especially bloody salesmen, the ratbags."

"Sometimes I feel like it'll take me forever to slow down, Ian. I don't even know what that means yet. All I know is the only time I'm peaceful is when I'm out in Nature. I forget myself."

"Imagine it, Roby, living your whole life without bloody clocks, phones, radios, or TVs? I've *never* lived without them."

"Worse than that, Ian, I've been conditioned to cram myself into twenty-four hours, when to wake, when to work, when to eat, when to play, when to sleep, and on and on. Think about it. We're conditioned into years, when to live and when to die."

We drove on in silence, each with our own thoughts. The first part of the road was flat with thick tangled growth on either side. After awhile, the road turned into a dark leafy tunnel and began to climb. As we drove along the edge of a steep mountain, the air smelled fresh and pungent with life. Huge trees grew beside the road and allowed me to relax.

Otherwise, I'd have worried about the narrowness of the track and the vertical drop into the gullies below. Hidden deep under the forest canopy the day was cool and moist. Vines thick enough to swing on hung from massive trees. Ferns grew tall as trees, and palm fronds were shaped like open paper fans. For the first time in my life, I saw virgin rainforest.

The Aboriginals once had the whole forest to themselves, before the Europeans drove them out. It was their home. No, it IS their home. When they arrived in the rainforest, they were the first humans to look upon the giant trees. I felt myself wishing I'd been with them. I could barely imagine in the modern crowded world being the first person to see an unknown forest. Such a dream that would be. Sometimes I felt the same as the earth, overcrowded and with no untouched sacred space.

My thoughts of the first Aboriginals in the rainforest made me recall the Aboriginal family on the ferry. I vowed that if I ever saw them again I'd offer them some food. We had food in the back of the truck, but it was buried under supplies, bedding, clothes, knapsacks, and tent. That morning we were so anxious to board the ferry that we'd just thrown everything into the back of the Toyota and tied it down.

The unpaved track to Cape Tribulation wasn't as crude as I thought it would be. It was fairly hard packed, though a few patches of slick mud lured the truck sideways. Four-wheel drive ended the slide. Ian slowed the vehicle when I spotted a huge six-foot red-bellied black snake on the road ahead. The reptile writhed as we approached, but didn't seem to go anywhere. He appeared pinned to the ground but still alive. Ian stopped the truck twenty feet in front of the snake and leaned out his window.

"Hold on a tick before you get out, Rob. I'm going to grab the rifle in the back just in case. I ain't worried about snakes while we's in the truck, but I don't like what Clyde said about those bloody weirdos."

I thought I'd managed to push Clyde's comment to the back of my mind, but my stomach muscles slowly tightened.

Ian backed the truck away from the snake and hopped out to get the gun. I wasn't sure why he was worried until he hollered out.

"Somebody's been out here t'day. This bloody snake was hit on purpose. There's blokes that slam on their brakes just to rip a snake's guts open. It doesn't always kill the snake straightaway, so they die really slowly. Maybe those two weirdos did it. You know, the ones Clyde mentioned. They could have camped on the north side of the river and are on the road somewhere ahead of us."

"Bet the poor thing heard our truck coming and tried to get away."

"Too right. But the poor bastard can't move, Rob-o, not with his back broken and his guts smeared like bloody Vegemite across the road. Strewth. I don't like snakes meself, but I wouldn't do this. I mean, they's no danger to us when we's in the truck."

"Why don't you put him out of his misery."

"Not me, mate. I ain't up for touching it. I'd shoot him, but I don't want to draw any attention."

I was puzzled when he quickly got back into the truck. Unable to leave the snake to suffer for possibly hours, I jumped out, grabbed a chunk of wood, and slowly approached him. The end of his tail lifted and curved, and his jaws opened and closed. He tried to move but was unable to slither away. Arms extended, I struck him with the branch several hard blows to his head. His skull spewed open. His body went limp and still. I felt wretched doing it, but I didn't want him to suffer another minute. With the tip of my stick I turned him over. His topside was shiny coal black and his underside was as red as a Crayola crayon, stunningly beautiful. I dragged him off the road and gently set him among the greenery. He belonged with the plants and not on a man-made track, squashed by tires. I thought about the word *roadkill* and decided we should call it *humankill*. After all, we're the ones who kill them.

When I got back into the truck, Ian's face was damp with tears. As he turned over the engine he said, "Thanks, Rob-o; at least he won't suffer anymore. It's not right that he . . ." Intense emotion choked off Ian's words, but I knew how he felt and was touched by his depth of feeling. I also knew he was proud of me for ending the snake's suffering.

Although we were silent as we wound our way through the forest, I felt very close to him. The silence was only broken when we approached a washout that looked seriously alarming. The track we drove on had been cut along the edge of a steep mountainside, like a shelf. Rain had run down the upper slope, hit the road, washed away the dirt, and exposed six logs that created a bridge across a gully. Water still ran down the mountain and over the logs. True to his promise, Ian applied the brakes and we got out to check the bridge.

"It's awfully narrow, Ian. Do you think it's strong enough? Looks like someone else's tire tracks here in the mud. It's hard to tell whether they crossed or not with all this water running over the road. Maybe we'll see their tracks up ahead. But what if our tires slip between the logs and shove 'em sideways? Could the truck tip over?"

Maaaaan. This is crazy . . . like everything else we've done so far is sane.

"Come take a look, Ian. There's quite a drop here if we tip."

I inched my way to the edge of the washout and peered over. Of course, this was the only place on the mountain where tall trees didn't grow on the downhill side of the track. Slowly, I stretched out my arm as far as I could; my hand almost touched the tops of huge palm trees rooted far below. The thought of crashing down through the palms into the gully itched at my courage. I quickly withdrew my tingling arm, and Ian and I turned our attention back to the washout.

Ian walked onto the logs and began to stomp them. He didn't merely jump up and down like a normal person. He hunched his shoulders, swung his arms at his sides with fisted hands, and hopped around imitating one of his early primate relatives. I laughed my guts out when he started to scratch his armpits and grunted, "Oooh, oooh, ahhhhh, aaaah." The logs bounced but didn't crack or move. We both leaned down over the makeshift bridge to look at the underside.

"They's embedded into the sides of the bloody road pretty deep. Don't think they's going anywhere, Rob. Me guess is they must have been part of the original road and at some point the rain's uncovered them. If we hug the bloody hillside and go real slow, I think she's a goer, mate. I'll need you to be out front to direct me. You've got to make sure I stay away from this bloody outside edge. Righty-o, let's 'ave a go, eh?"

I felt guilty over my relief that I wasn't in the truck while Ian drove it over the flimsy bridge . . . but not for long. I wanted us both to walk across, but there was the Toyota, our portable home. Ian backed the truck and lined it up with the logs. He took a deep breath before he started to creep over the bridge.

"Hey, Rob-o, stand back a bit. If this bloody thing goes, don't want you going down with it. Youse too bloody close, mate. Back up, quick smart."

Ian's hands gripped the wheel, tense as eagle talons.

"Turn the wheel to the right, Ian."

"Can't, mate. I'll hit the bloody bank!"

"No. You got tons of room. Turn it. Now."

He managed to stay close to the inside edge, but halfway across I heard a loud ominous "KEEERAK." It wasn't the truck.

"Oh no! Iaaaan!"

"Yeah, I know. Out of me way, mate!"

Ian gunned the engine and leapt the rest of the way across the logs to hard ground. After that, I didn't want to think about leaving the area, not until *someone* repaired the track. I got back into the truck, and we moved on.

Thick plant growth in every shade of green dripped with moisture. Some of the plants I recognized as houseplants I'd grown in my Salt Lake City apartment, only they were ten times larger. A shaft of sunlight shown through a break in the canopy and danced across the road in front of us. Its golden beam illuminated the wings of an electric-blue butterfly. He fluttered here and there as if attached to a stretchy string, up and down on wings that spanned almost five inches.

At the rumble of another vehicle, Clyde's words raced through my mind, "Don't stop for anyone that looks bloody suspect, and don't leave yer misses alone in the truck." My eyes darted to the gun that rested on the floor alongside Ian's door.

"Watch out, Ian. There's a truck coming, and it's coming fast."

"Got it, mate. Lock your bloody door, and roll up your window."

Ian casually reached for the gun and propped it against the dashboard near his window. I knew he was tense. He swore under his breath when we went around a corner and the road narrowed to almost less than one vehicle width.

"Crikey! The road has to narrow right here. Strewth and bloody strewth." I felt Ian's alarm and wanted to keep moving.

"Maybe Clyde exaggerated," I said, as much to calm Ian as myself.

One of the vehicles would have to pull to the side of the road. There was no way two vehicles could pass on the narrow strip. Ian started to bite his fingernails down to the quick and spit them out his open window. He wiped blood from his chewed finger on his pants and said, "Bloody hell, I can't believe I forgot to load the gun, but only we know that. Hopefully the sight of it will make someone think twice. Don't act too friendly, Rob. Here they come. Crikeys! Looks like we's the ones hitting the ditch. Stupid mad wankers. They's going too bloody fast, and there's no place for them to get over."

A severely dented, mud-sprayed old Nissan rattled around the corner at high speed. Either they hadn't heard us or they didn't care. My heart raced as they skidded drunkenly to a stop right next to Ian's partially open window. Scenes from the movie *Deliverance* played through my mind as the driver gave me a slow, cocky, toothless leer. He turned to his baldheaded partner, and they both giggled like schoolboys sharing dirty jokes. My nose twitched in revulsion at the thick stench of alcohol, cigarettes, and an odor resembling rotten chicken. I almost jumped when Ian, his face still turned out the window, hands on the steering wheel, slowly moved his knee toward the rifle and casually rattled it against the metal dashboard. The toothless driver glanced at the rifle and back to Ian. Shivers ran up my spine when I realized he was sizing him up. With the full beard of a forty-year-old man, Ian looked much older than he actually was. He made a formidable opponent. Mr. Toothless made a silent decision, cleared his throat, and spoke to Ian with lazy indolence.

"Youse 'eaded to 'Trib' to camp? One of the bloody creeks is up too high for crossin'. We's already tried it this morning. How long youse stayin' this side of the river? Know where youse gonna camp?"

My hand crept to the edge of Ian's thigh and gave a hard warning squeeze. Silently, I screamed, *Don't tell him!* When I heard Ian say, "Naaaa, no way, mate. Just a bloody day trip. Meeting a couple of bloody blokes camped a quarter of a mile up. Dropped them off a fortnight ago. Picking them up t'day."

Once more, Toothless looked at the gun, then at me, then at Ian, "Youse a right lucky bloke there, mate, with a beaut little Sheila like that. Youse wanna keep a good eye on that one. Ain't none like that 'ere abouts."

Ian thanked him, slightly revved the engine, and said, "Well, mate, best be off. Don't want me mates going aggro on me."

I almost laughed when Ian said, "You know how she goes. They's me mates, but they's real mean mothers if I don't bloody well keep me word and show on time."

At first I thought they'd never move on. They had us pinned like moths in a glass showcase for as long as they wanted to hog the road. All we had was an empty rifle and Ian's muscle. I thought of my Buck knife until I remembered it sat in the back with the food. Fortunately, the Nissan rolled reluctantly forward. They were gone with a trail of inane giggles and black exhaust. Ian revved the Toyota back onto the track and told me to get the bullets out from under my seat.

"When we know they ain't going to follow us, we'll find a spot, pull over, and load the bloody rifle. Just in case."

As we drove away, my day didn't seem quite so sunny. Ian finally stopped to load the rifle and put the safety on. I got my Buck knife and put it and the gun on the shelf behind the front seat. He must have also felt the gloom because he said, "We's going to need a safe campsite where no one can bloody well see us. Let's think about it when we's looking for a place, eh, mate? We'll be right, Rob-o. No worries."

I wanted to believe Ian, but I suddenly realized I was more afraid of my fellow humans than anything I might find in the rainforest. Until then I'd only been afraid of crocs, poisonous snakes, and spiders. Ian's voice brought me out of my reverie and back to the road.

"Bloody oath, I thought they'd never shove off. Crikey, mate. That one bloke, the driver, ponged like a bloody dunny on a hot summer day. Stupid drongo. Did you see the other bloke's bald egg-shaped head? It was pointed on top. Strewth, I's seen better heads in a piss trough. Must be bloody brain damaged. If I had me a head like that I'd never take me hat off, or else I'd shave me arse and walk backwards."

"Ian, what's a drongo, and what was the other word you used? The one like a ping-pong ball? Clyde used it too."

Ian laughed and told me, "A drongo is a bloody idiot, and it wasn't ping-pong; it was pong. That toothless bloke ponged. Couldn't you smell him? He smelled like a bloody pub floor at closing time."

The laughter felt good because it chased away some of our anxiety. I told Ian, "They looked like they'd worn the same crusty clothes for years. Man, did you see the bald guy's hat before he took it off? It was shiny with grease. Looked like he'd soaked it in bear fat and slapped it on his head. Gross."

Ian loved that description and laughed even harder. Then he reminded me, "That's great, mate, except we don't have bloody bears in Oz. Probably pig fat, his own. Well, least they's leaving, Rob-o. Didn't see much tucker or supplies in their truck."

I didn't want to ask, but I had to know. "Did you see a gun?"

"Yeah, mate, they had a bloody rifle, same as us. They's most likely hunting feral pigs. Strewth. Did you see all the bloody empty tinnies in the back? Crikey. That one bloke holding the tinnie was a piss factory. His face was so bloody distorted, he looked like a dog's breakfast. Between the bloody grease, piss, and petrol, I could have thrown me a bloody match into their junk heap of a vehicle and blown her sky high. Fair dinkum, mate."

Ian was not only a master profaner, but his mastery of Australian strine was impressive. I loved it. Over the weeks I'd learned that the Aussies used the word *piss* for beer. When someone was drunk they were *pissed*. Tucker meant food, *tinnies* were beer cans and a dunny was an outhouse or toilet. Each day I understood more and more of the Australian language. I often felt like I was in a non-English-speaking country.

After meeting the two weirdos, the thought of creeks and crocs didn't seem so bad. We talked until our nerves settled. I remembered the red-bellied black snake back on the road and asked Ian, "Do you think those two killed the snake and left it to suffer?"

"Most likely, Rob-o. They's got nothing better to do."

I was glad Clyde had warned us about the two creeps. My impression of his integrity rose to a full ten.

"Hey, Rob, maybe those two blokes didn't go all the way to Cape Tribulation. Remember how they said one of the creeks was too high? We'll check it out."

Except for occasional thick muddy spots the road was pretty good, but several miles later we hit our first creek. We hopped out to face our next obstacle. Ian grabbed a long stick by the road and walked toward the stream.

"Hey, Rob, did you know Clyde told me there's bloody saltwater crocs in some of these freshwater creeks. Keep a bloody eye out for them while I check the water level."

"Oh maaaan. I thought we left the crocodiles behind."

Ian waded further into the water and hollered back, "She seems to be moving bloody fast, but she's only six inches to a foot deep. Damned slick though. These rocks are covered with algae. Crikey. It'll be like driving on ice back in bloody Maine."

I wasn't too worried about algae, but crocs frightened me. In Maine, I never had to be aware of anything. In the rainforest, it seemed I had to watch out for everything. I constantly scanned the creek banks for long scaly shapes. Every log turned into a crocodile and every vine and stick into a snake. Fear goaded me . . . crocs lurked everywhere. My emotions churned. *What if there's crocs under the water swimming toward Ian? What if I can't see 'em? What if they're behind me right now?* I dashed for the truck.

"Well, Rob-o, let's 'ave a go, eh? We'll be right. She's not too bad. I'll just have to keep her going. We'll start on the upstream edge of the track. So if the bloody current drags us downstream we'll still be in line with the track on the other side. Not many bloody trucks been through here lately . . . too much algae on the rocks."

We climbed back into the Toyota, and I asked Ian, "Have you ever driven through a stream? I mean, are you sure you can do this?"

"I's never done it, but she's a goer, Rob. It's only if the water gets into the engine, then we's rooted if she stalls. But it's not that bloody deep here. Let's go, mate."

I'd never driven through a stream before. When I was a kid I went on a lot of outdoor adventures with Dad. He took our station wagon into some rough country, but fording streams had been left off the itinerary. As the truck plowed into the water, Ian did a running commentary on the dynamics of creek crossing as if narrating a documentary.

"Ya see there's a trick to this, Rob. You can't go so bloody fast that water gets into the engine, or so bloody fast youse hydroplane. If water gets under all the tires it'll carry us away. But then we can't go too slow through deep water because then it might get into the bloody engine and stall her. She's a fine balance, mate."

I heard Ian's voice, but didn't want to hear his words. My nerves screamed at him to shut up and pay attention. At the time I didn't realize the commentary might be his stress valve. He always seemed so confident. Algae slid the truck abruptly to the right, as if a giant hand had grabbed the tires and yanked. My foot frantically pumped the invisible brake on my side of the truck.

"Can't brake now, Roby. That's just algae. Got to keep her going. Almost there, matey."

When I realized the stream started to get shallow and we were near the other bank, I breathed a sigh of relief. The dry ground felt so safe and comforting I wanted to get out and kiss it, but unfortunately my mind raced ahead.

"Do you think there's any more creeks like that, Ian?"

"Clyde said there's about four in all, maybe five. I can't exactly remember. Listen, mate, if they's too bloody high we'll wait till they go down."

"What if they don't go down, *ever*?"

"Then we won't bloody cross, *ever*."

"You promise?"

Ian laughed and said, "Strewth, mate. I don't want to lose the bloody truck or drown any more than you do. Right?"

I laughed and said, "Ian, how come you say bloody all the time?"

We both laughed and drove on. The road turned flat, smooth, and hard packed. Rainforest pressed in on each side to reclaim exposed earth. At times I became lost in the richness of the forest, intense with life. Green piled upon green everywhere I looked. Huge heart-shaped leaves wrapped around tree trunks and disappeared into the canopy. Feathery palms and patterned ferns waved long elegant arms that shimmered in the breeze. Sounds of birds, insects, and frogs drifted from deep within the greenery. But I never fully relaxed. How could I with more creeks to cross?

I didn't even know where I was going, and it really didn't matter. I hadn't researched Australia before we left. Cape Tribulation was just a vague place Hal had told us about. All that kept my life in context was Ian. I knew nothing about the rainforest or what it would be like when I arrived there, wherever "there" was. When I left America I knew only one thing about Australia; kangaroos lived there.

My mental list of Australia's deadly creatures grew daily, a little too quickly for me to be thrilled about the rainforest. I thought it was jungle until Clyde referred to it as rainforest. As a kid the Amazonian and African jungles were the only jungles I'd heard about. They were fascinating places, but safely far away from Maine. My thoughts drifted, lulled into false calm. Ian sped around the next bend and straight to the edge of a creek. My foot stomped the invisible brake.

"Another creek. Oh man alive, this one's *really* bad, Ian. It's wider and lots deeper. I can't even see the bottom."

I caught a glimpse of something in the water through the trees. The roof of a tan vehicle.

"Ian, look! Downstream. Is that a truck in the water? Can you see it? By the bend there. Holy mackerel. They musta got washed down trying to cross. They just left it there? Look at how they left the doors wide open. It's brand new. Maaaan. We're not crossing this. Are we? Ian? Say something!"

"Don't know yet, mate. Let's check it out, eh?"

"Check it out? No way."

Once again Ian waded into the water. This time I forgot about crocs and waded with him. In the middle of the creek were some large rocks. Even if the current had been mild and the water shallow, we still had to move the rocks if we wanted to cross. The current was rapid and deep. Water rose above my knee almost to mid thigh. Even Ian hesitated. Maybe the sight of the brand-new tan Toyota stranded in the river jaded his enthusiasm, for about two seconds. I knew the inevitable was about to happen when Ian started to push the rocks to one side.

Oh well, might as well help him. What else am I gonna do? Walk all the way back to Mossman? Or worse, go back to the States? And do what? When you've found your destiny you have no other life.

Fear made me ask inane questions. "Why did they just leave it?"

"What bloody choice did they have, mate? Must have walked out to get help. Probably left the doors open so the water could flow through the truck and not push it farther downstream. We's not that far from the ocean. Strewth, it could get pushed all the way to the bloody sea. Depends on what the creek's like further down. At least if it stays here they may be able to haul it back onto the track. If it goes further downstream, there's no way into the jungle to get to it."

I felt reassured when Ian scanned the opposite bank for winchable trees.

"Will the winch cable reach that far?"

"Yeah, Roby. She'll just make it. As long as the bloody engine doesn't stall, we can winch out if we get bloody stuck, eh? And if it does stall, we can at least anchor the truck to a tree with the cable so it won't drift. Aaah, we'll be right. Let's start on the upstream edge, just like we did before. We don't want to drift past the bloody track and not be able to get out of the water. Do you want to ride or wade?"

I didn't figure there'd be crocs in such fast-moving water. Clyde had told us that crocs like calm water, and this was far from calm. However, it didn't really matter because I doubted I could safely wade across. The current greedily grabbed my slim legs and almost sucked me under. I decided if Ian was going to be washed away in the Toyota, or worse, tip over, I wanted to be with him. Maybe I could help him, and if anything happened to us at least we'd be together. When I climbed into the truck, like Ian, I wound down my window, ready to jump out.

"Right-o, Roby, let's get on with it."

This time I could tell Ian was tense. He didn't say a word as the truck pushed into the swollen creek. About halfway across, water curled up over the hood like an ocean wave. It was *much* deeper than we realized. Ian gunned the faltering engine and cursed.

"Bloody strewth! She's deep. The current's got us, Rob-o. Got to slow her down so the tires grab. Deadset, we's drifting."

The truck started to float. Terror seized my heart. My mouth went dry, and I barely breathed. Water sprayed from the hood and into my side window. I wiped my eyes, reached for the handle, and rolled it shut.

"Oh no, Ian. Don't slow it so much that we stall."

Ian seemed to know what he was doing. He slowed the Toyota just enough for the tires to touch the river bottom. I relaxed a bit as the truck moved forward again. Then I realized my feet sat in an inch of water.

"Ian, the side vents! Quick, shut 'em. Water's getting in. It's up to the doors now. Damn, this is scary."

Ian laughed and reached down to close the air vent near the bottom of his door at the same time as he steered the truck. As scared as I felt, I still thought Ian was magnificently wild and brave.

"If you don't want to get wet, Rob-o, put your feet up on the bloody dash and hang on."

Getting wet was the least of my worries. Nonetheless, I hoisted my feet up onto the glove box and held onto the edge of my seat with both hands.

Naked in Eden

"We's almost there, Rob. I think we's seen the worst of it. Yup, the bloody bonnet's headed up now. We're home and hosed, matey!"

On the opposite bank, Ian parked the truck and kept the engine running to dry it out. We opened vents and doors to let water run back into the creek. After that experience I felt an enormous sense of pride and excitement, something I hadn't felt in a long time. The crocs were completely forgotten as I sat peacefully by the water and let the creek calm my insides.

Ian broke into my thoughts. "Well, mate, shall we hit the bloody road again? See if we can find Cape Tribulation?"

The rest of the creeks were shallow enough that I didn't need my invisible brake. I realized it didn't work anyway. Eventually we came to the thick sandy patch that Clyde had told us about. The engine groaned and the Toyota twisted and bucked. A couple of times we became bogged. The tires spun, and the truck didn't move forward.

Teeth clenched, hands pushed against the dashboard, I tried to remain calm. We were almost there. We couldn't get bogged now.

"You can do this, Ian, but you gotta slow her down and take your time. When she starts to bog, turn the wheel a bit like you taught me."

"Strewth! I can barely bloody control her, Rob."

"Want me to drive?"

"Naah, I'll be right. Can't risk stopping her anyway. Might get completely stuck."

He eased up on the gas and gently turned the wheel, and the truck kept moving forward. Normally, Ian had a natural ability to sense when to slow down and when to give her gas, but it had been a long stressful day. Fatigue made him impatient. Maaan, I knew how he felt. And it wasn't over yet.

Eventually the sand grew firm and packed, and we both relaxed . . . for the time being. We approached a stand of palms shaped like giant fans. It was so dense that I thought someone had planted a palm orchard. I knew they were wild because they grew right up to the road and merged into the rainforest. Palms lay dead where they'd been cut for the track to go through.

"Roby, take a look. We's finally here."

I looked through the opening made by the road. Straight in front of me spread the Coral Sea, calm aqua blue water. I could barely believe the long journey was over. Maybe this place really could be home.

Ian started to hum Cat Stevens's song, "Miles from Nowhere."

Yes, I was miles from nowhere—and finally free.

No one would bother me here. Maybe my weary spirit could unwind. I'd felt so invaded and pressured in society, as if there was never a moment's peace, nowhere to escape. No room for feelings and dreams. I knew Ian felt the same; he'd told me many times. He let out a long sigh, revved the engine, and the truck burst from dark greenery into bright daylight. The white, sandy beach held firm as Ian drove the Toyota to the water's edge. The air smelled tangy and fishy. I liked it.

I'd seen the South Pacific Ocean off and on all the way up the coast, but it usually was near a town. Here dense rainforest spilled right down to the sea. I saw nothing for miles except empty white beach, thick green rainforest, and soft-blue sea. Stinger season was at its end, so I gladly let warm water wrap around my ankles. It made me cry. I was ecstatically happy. I had no impressive plans or thoughts of what I was going to do. I didn't know and didn't care. This wild place was more than I ever dreamed would happen to me. If my destiny could lead me here, anything was possible.

We doubted many vehicles used the track, but we wanted to camp as far away from it as possible. A trip north seemed a better choice because it would take us farther away from people. The problem was we'd run out of track. Ian came up with a solution.

"Hey, Rob-o, why don't we wait till the bloody tide goes out, then drive north up the beach, eh? Looks like she's going out now. What do you think, mate?"

"Since we've been standing here the waves have gotten farther from my feet. We'll soon be able to use the beach for a road."

"Yeah, Rob, but we'll have to keep things oiled and protected from salt-water and rust. Sea spray and mist are loaded with salt."

After only an hour by the shore I could taste sea salt on my lips, and it reminded me that I was hungry. I rummaged through our gear in the back of the truck and finally found peanut butter and stale bread for a late lunch.

When the tide ebbed we drove up the coast. Rainforest creeks tumbled down the mountains and created openings in the trees, which gave us glimpses into the mysterious forest. As we came to one such creek Ian said, "Hey look, that's a beaut place. Let's suss her out. There's fresh water, trees for shade, and it's kind of sheltered."

We pulled the Toyota under the cool of the trees. Soft sand met my feet when I hopped from the truck. Bits of dried seaweed, sticks, and shells poked from the sand. As far back as we were from the day's high-tide line, I realized we stood on the remains of an even higher tide line.

"Ian, look at the shells and stuff. The tide comes way up here, or at least it has at some point. Aren't the tides higher at certain times of year? There's no way we can camp here. Some night in our sleep we'll wash out to sea. We gotta keep driving and find a place farther back from the water."

Slowly, a grin spread across Ian's face, and I turned to follow his gaze. Behind me rose a steep slope of rock and earth. It wasn't very high, thirty or forty feet. On either side grew dense rainforest. The face was just wide enough to get the truck up through the bushes and trees, but it was almost vertical.

"You gotta be kidding me. Ian? Come on, man. That's not funny. There's no way. It's not just steep; it's impossible."

"Let's at least climb up along the bloody edge and suss it out. Right-o, Rob?"

The moment I consented to suss it out, I might as well have given Ian the green light. As steep as the hill looked, if I grabbed hold of branches along its edge I could easily climb it. At the top, I was delighted to find a natural little clearing of level ground. Huge trees and graceful palms made a ring around the clearing where a scant patch of sun shone through the canopy. In that one small haven I found such peace that I forgot the rest of the world existed. It slipped away from my memory as if it had never been. In silence, I absorbed the gentle rustle of palm fronds and the soft chirp of a bird. Insects buzzed and little yellow butterflies flitted in and out of the sun. A creek gurgled off to the side as it flowed past the clearing and down the hill to the sea. In my heart I knew I'd found home. Then I remembered the truck.

Ian stood in front of a huge tree, which grew just below the crest and off to one side of the steep embankment. His eyes went from the Toyota to the tree and back again. I knew where his thoughts were headed, to the same old issue. Was the winch cable long enough?

"She'll just reach, Rob. But we's still got a problem. Even though this bloody tree is almost at the top of the bank, she's off to the side instead of directly in front of us. We need the winch to pull us straight up the hill and not into the bushes toward the tree. Well, we'll just have to make do. There ain't nothing else close enough. Nothing sturdy anyway."

I wasn't sure whether Ian tried to convince himself or me.

"Rob, no one will see us from the beach. Right? We's also hidden from the water. No one will know we's here. They won't even believe anyone could get up something this bloody steep. The tide will wash away our tracks on the beach, and we can brush off the slope with some bushes, eh?" *Oh yeah, sure. Like in the old Indian movies, we'll brush away our tracks with a leafy branch. Uh huh.* When I started to laugh at my thoughts, Ian mistook it for delight over his plan. He was so earnest I didn't have the heart to tell him what I was really laughing at.

He didn't have to convince me. "The clearing," as we called it, was definitely safe and had everything we needed. I wanted to settle there, but I worried about the truck. Ian read my thoughts again, something that occurred more frequently each day.

"Look, Roby, if we drive the bloody truck as far up the bottom of the slope as we can, the cable should reach this tree. Then once the winch gets her up there we'll have to gun the bloody engine the last bit of the way 'cause the tree isn't right at the top. Let's just hope the front wheels are over the edge by the time we get to the tree. In four-wheel drive they should grab and haul the truck over the lip. Shall we 'ave a go, matey?"

Once again, I felt pangs of guilt because I didn't want to be in the truck while we winched up the cliff face. I was afraid it might roll backwards. My extremely active and vivid imagination had worked overtime since my arrival in Australia. I envisioned a painfully taut winch cable. Then I watched it snap, thread by thread, until BOING! Our camo green Toyota broke free and careened crazily down to the sea. I loved Ian so much, I didn't want to be alive if he was killed. I'd decided I wanted to die when he did. I couldn't envision life without him. Since I'd known Ian, he'd awakened an intense passion in me. Even though it was often hard to live with, I liked myself that way. Ian kindled undying love in me. Dramatic? Yes. Humorous? Yes. All that and more, but it made life real and raw. I also liked that. I thrived on it. Nonetheless, I still didn't want to be in the truck when it went up the cliff. But I'd do it if I had to.

"Hey, Rob-o. Youse ready? I need you to be at the top to direct me."

Phew.

Ian backed the vehicle down to the water's edge, revved the engine, and charged like a mad, maniacal bull straight for the cliff. The Toyota slammed into the steep face with a jolt, rolled a little way up, and hung suspended. It was one of the damnedest things I'd ever seen. Ian eased on the emergency brake before the truck rolled back to level ground. Not sure how long the Toyota would hold its precarious position, I carefully unwound the winch cable and ran slipping and sliding up the side of the hill. I wrapped our worn piece of inner tube around the tree, then the cable over it. When I tried to hook the cable it was an eighth of an inch too short. No matter how hard I tugged, it was still too short. Wide-eyed, I watched Ian open his door and *very* slowly get out of the truck. I clung to the cable as if I alone could stop the Toyota from rolling to the sea. Sweat beaded between my shoulder blades and ran down my back as he sprinted up the side of the cliff. He grabbed the cable with his huge hands and yanked until there was enough spare to hook it in place. My gaze followed the viciously taut wire back to the truck. Ayeee, good thing it wasn't rope.

Gently, Ian slipped back into the truck, released the brake, started the winch, and slowly the vehicle crept up the hill. Fascinated, I watched it climb the cliff, at times with only three tires touching the ground.

Ian's courage and sense of adventure moved me profoundly. He seemed undaunted by the challenges we encountered. Whether we crossed creeks or winched up cliff faces, he acted as if he'd done it all his life. His face through the windshield was calm and focused. Even though he was a year younger than me, I often felt he was the elder.

I stood at the top and waited to direct him. Silently, I begged the front tires to get over the top lip and onto flat ground before we got too close to the winching tree and the end of the cable. It might be dangerous if we had to start over and roll the truck backwards down the cliff.

Inch by inch, the Toyota approached the tree and the clearing. Like a lumbering dinosaur, the front wheels struggled up and over the cliff edge. I heard Ian yell something about the tree.

"Hey, Rob, can't go no bloody farther without being pulled toward the tree."

Can't go no bloody farther? What kinda language is that?

Then I saw. We'd used up all our cable, and the truck was almost next to the tree. We needed slack to move forward. At least the front tires were hooked over the lip. We now relied on them to pull the vehicle onto flat ground.

Again, Ian gingerly stepped from the Toyota. I held my breath as he cautiously unwound a few feet of cable and laid it on the ground. While he checked the position of all the tires, he told me what to do.

"As I move the vehicle forward, I'll need you to pull the cable out of the way so it don't get caught under the bloody wheels. We won't really be using it; it's only in case the truck moves. Let's hope it don't snap if she does. Oh crikey, forgot to tell you, don't hang onto the cable for long. If this thing rolls you might not let go in time. It'd rip your bloody hands off. Righty-o?"

Rip my bloody hands off? Oh great. Adrenaline charged through my body while the truck hung there. I prayed like an ocean of nuns that it would hold and that the front tires would pull the Toyota the few remaining feet. With the winch slack, they were all that held the truck on the lip. In a whisper, I suggested to Ian that we reattach the winch cable to a tree in the clearing, but of course his reply was, "Naaahh, she'll be right, mate." I wanted to argue, but I hardly dared breathe let alone talk. My voice might avalanche the Toyota down to the sea. Besides, the trees that grew close enough to winch from were too large at the base. It would take almost a third of the cable just to wrap around one tree. We'd never do it.

Ian still had to get back into the truck to drive it. He sat cautiously in the driver's seat with the door open in case he had to jump out. I wanted to watch, and I *didn't* want to watch. In slow motion, he waved me to the side as he gently revved the engine. The front tires bit into the top surface, and one rear tire spun while the other grabbed. Slowly, in spurts of futile spinning and forward movement, the truck pulled itself over the lip to level ground.[2] I leaned against a tree to slow my frantic heart and vowed that next time I'd keep my mouth shut and settle for high tides.

At the time, I was too young to see that Ian's love for me was so complete that if I'd asked to go to the moon he'd have found a way to winch us there. He had no limitations as to what was possible.

Twenty feet from the steep edge of the hill he parked the truck and got out. With a huge incredulous grin he walked to the edge, looked over, shook his head, and laughed out loud.

"Bloody strewth!

Ian draped his arm across my shoulders, and we turned to look at our new home.

"We's finally here, Roby. And *nobody* knows where we are. Can you bloody believe it? Odd feeling, eh?"

"I kinda like it. I can finally stop the constant whirlwind that goes on around me. I have a fighting chance, Ian. The odds are more even now."

Life had squeezed in on me for so long, I was dying, but I didn't have to explain that to Ian. He knew just what I meant and how I felt. He always knew. We were two bodies with one soul.

The clearing was no more than twenty-five feet across. With my back to the sea, facing the clearing, the creek was to the left and flowed all the way down the hill, across the beach, and into the sea. At the back edge and on the right was thick forest that climbed farther up the mountain.

Except for the rough opening where we'd winched up the slope, the front edge was thick with trees that jostled down to the high-tide line. No one would spot us, not with our truck parked off to the side. Two young palms grew in the middle of the clearing and soaked up slivers of sun. A carpet of fine organic matter covered the forest floor. Garlands of tiny heart-shaped leaves zig-zagged symmetrically up the sides of trees. Curved buttressed roots twisted and folded, elegant as ribbon candy. High above my head, huge arms reached out to touch each other . . . trees holding hands. Everything dripped, moist and ripe. Vibrant green spread everywhere in wild profusion. Life competed unabashedly for every scrap of light. The rainforest knows no shame.

Although I found the forest stunningly beautiful, fear still dampened my ability to fully drink in my surroundings. I was eager to set up camp. I wanted to crawl into the truck and hide from this forest that felt so intense and overwhelming. Defiantly, beyond my control, it pushed against me, a bold palpable force, demanding to be acknowledged. It awakened cavernous emotions that lurked in the depths of my soul. I needed time to gradually adjust to its raw wildness. To fully understand this place, I'd be forced to understand myself. I'd come face-to-face with Robin. There would be no more hiding.

Ian's voice drew me from my shadowy jungle. "Hey, Roby, let's go check out the creek then we'll set up camp."

The water felt cold and tasted almost sweet. It would supply us with fresh drinking water. Two rock pools rested one above the other. Flat black stones lined their bottoms, and a little waterfall fell from the smaller pool into the larger one. I waded to the far end of the larger pool and watched bubbles float across the surface. Beneath the bubbles, crayfish inched their way toward my feet to nibble my toes. Minuscule transparent fish darted like ballerinas in unison among the rocks. On its course to the sea, the water played a symphony that reminded me of flutes and deep hollow cowbells. Dainty maidenhair ferns and delicate young palms seemed to peer over my shoulder from the edge to watch the performance with me.

Ian stepped beside me, took my hand, and said, "Well, Roby, we's far enough away from the Daintree River so's we won't have to worry about bloody crocs here. At least not in the creek. It's too bloody rocky and steep."

"Yeah, but we will have to watch out for them when we swim in the sea, especially on calm days. Like that guy said, they sometimes come up onto the beaches. You never know, they might have miniature winches strapped to their chests to haul themselves over the boulders and up the creek."

Ian and I laughed until I had tears in my eyes. I knew I was tired. I barely had enough energy to set up camp. It seemed like I'd lived a lifetime in the last two days. Holy moly! So much for easing into life. I'd been shot out of a cannon.

On impulse, I dunked my whole head in the water and drank until I ran out of breath. Somewhat calmer and more refreshed, I returned with Ian to the clearing and unpacked the truck. My stomach growled for food. Our hot supper of oatmeal and dates tasted like my grandmother's bread pudding. I was ravenous, and it was exquisitely delicious. We didn't want to attract any wildlife to our camp, so when we went to bed we threw the dirty dishes into the back of the truck. I felt relieved when Ian closed the tailgate and the cap door. I opened the screen windows on each side of the cap and we crawled into our sleeping bags. Ian's soft snores vibrated the silence within seconds. I lay and listened to the night and watched darkness push away twilight. Tiny feet scurried on the ground beneath the truck. Curious creatures came to see who had invaded their forest.

∽

From the dust of stars
A swirl of elements
Imbued with vital life
Arrives here today
Beyond retreat
Where roused, Spirit awaits

—RUSSELL HUME

three

THE OLD MAN BY THE SEA

MY EYES SNAPPED OPEN IN BLACKNESS so thick I couldn't see my hand in front of my face. I remembered I was in the truck and wondered what woke me from such drugged sleep. I heard only the gurgling stream and Ian's steady breathing. I lay in the dark and waited. Listened. Slowly, I sat up to check the lock on the back of the truck. It was secure. As I was about to lie down, a murderous screech ripped through the night.

"Blaauuuuccckkkkk! Blaauuuucccckkkkk!"

Holy mackerel! What the hell is that? It was close by, somewhere on the hill behind the truck. Like tiny insect legs, prickles scurried across my scalp and stood my hair on end. The third scream ended midway.

"Blaauc, Bla, Bl."

Then nothing. The night swallowed the sound, as if someone had wrapped their hands around their victim's throat and strangled him to silence. Wide awake, I wanted to shake Ian from sleep and tell him about the homicidal screams, but there was nothing left to hear. It could wait until morning. Ian needed sleep.

I couldn't tell if it was early morning or night. The forest canopy shut out the stars and moon, and my watch was buried somewhere in the back of the truck or else lost on the road between the Gold Coast and Cairns. I hadn't worn it in weeks. Slowly, I lay back down and tried to sleep, but no sleep remained. High-voltage fear wired my body and opened my eyes wide as fifty-cent pieces. *What was out there? That wasn't a human scream. Or was it? Did Australia have anacondas that ate large prey, like humans? The guy at the reptile park sure hadn't mentioned them.* I knew I'd be finding out before I headed into the forest.

I must have dozed off. The next time I opened my eyes, thin fragments of golden sun fluttered through the canopy. A gentle breeze arranged and rearranged layers of leaves in an intricate dance of green. I remembered last night and looked to see if Ian was awake. He began to stir, so I shook his shoulder, unable to contain my story. In the morning light everything looked so normal I wondered if I'd dreamed the night sounds. Ian's blasé response pushed my fear even farther away.

"Strewth, mate. I didn't grow up in the bloody bush. It could be anything for all I know. You sure it wasn't a bird call?"

"Yeah, a bird being murdered. Ian, if it was a bird call, it was the most murderous-sounding bird I've ever heard." I laughed and said, "They'd have to call it 'Birdis Mortis.' Look, I'm tellin' ya, I could hear its terror. Maybe we'll hear it another night when *you're* awake."

I threw on jeans, T-shirt, and socks. I no longer wore underwear. Along the hot stretches of road north it became obsolete. Ian once told me, as he merrily threw his underwear out the truck window, "Underdacks are dispensable. They's a bloody nasty and confining habit."

We kept our hiking boots in the truck at night, but I still turned mine upside down and tapped them against the Toyota before I slipped them on in the morning. I might not know much about the rainforest, but I knew that snakes, spiders, and centipedes liked to hide in dark places. A quick check cost nothing.

I hopped from the back of the truck into the morning light. The clearing glistened, as if night rain had washed it to shiny green. We shared a jar of reconstituted fruit we'd soaked the night before. The apples, apricots, prunes, and pears tasted heavenly. I'd become used to and enjoyed simple food after weeks of raw fruit and veggies.

Then we settled the basics. We kept all waste well away from water, dug a hole for feces and buried it, and left urine to the sun, wind, and rain.

When I returned to the clearing, the gurgle of water called to me. I quickly packed away my breakfast things and wandered over to the creek. At the water's edge, the air was earthy and damp. Maybe later I'd sink my whole body into one of the clear pools. It was still a bit cool in the dense shade, but once the sun rose the day would be warm.

I remembered I was near the sea. Some of my most precious memories were rare trips with Mom to the coast of Maine. These memories were dear to me because my relationship with my mother had always been strained. It seemed like arguing was the only form of communication we shared. While I washed my face and arms, I recalled the bitter cold day my mother and I walked along the beach at Reid State Park, just before I left for Australia. We really talked that day. Tears filled my eyes at the memory of how Mom opened her heart and shared some of her deepest pain. It was the first time she had done that with me, and the first time I saw her as a woman and not *just* my mother.

Mom had a lovely voice. In her early twenties she sang live on the radio in New York City. She was headed into a professional music career when she lost her parents, met my dad, married, and raised a family of six kids. She continued to sing in church and around town, but never again sang professionally. I don't think she ever fully recovered from the loss of her music career. She loved her children and gave us all amazing gifts, but my heart went out to Mom's lost dreams. It was like losing her first child. Had she been born in a different era she might have been a famous singer, artist, naturalist, or politician. Even though she had her master's degree, she was born in a time when women were expected to become mothers. They had babies, cleaned house, cooked meals, did laundry, shopped for groceries, and ran the household while their husbands went to work or established careers. Nonetheless, over the seasons of her life she played several different roles: teacher, nurse, artist, singer, seamstress, gardener, cook, local politician, and more.

I felt her pain and knew her frustration, her burning desire to live intensely and with beauty. Mom often looked out the window in awe of Nature's miracles. She inhaled natural beauty as if she could memorize every detail and imprint the world upon her soul in the event that it should vanish. When I was a child, my mother's reverence for Nature was just part of my life. I assumed all mothers were the same. They're not. I didn't know until many years later how completely her awareness had touched my life and become my own.

The morning shone too full of promise to stay melancholy. I scampered over the rocks and returned to the truck.

"Ian, I'm gonna go down to the beach, wanna come? I *gotta* see the ocean."

While I'd sat at the creek, Ian spent the time greasing the truck. He worried about rust. I waited while he packed his tools, then we worked our way down the cliff to the sea. It was more dazzling than I remembered from the previous day. I looked out at the shades of blue green water stretching to the horizon. In places it was so clear I could see the bottom. I wanted to gather the colors in my arms and wear them like a gossamer scarf that trailed behind me in the breeze. During the night, cottonwood trees that grew on the beach had thrown large yellow flowers across the sand like wedding bouquets. I noticed them the day we arrived. They were so lovely that I looked them up in my plant book.

It was a glorious day. In both directions lay sea, sand, and lush green rainforest. No people. No boats. No houses. Nothing. Hurriedly, I removed my shoes and socks and wiggled my feet into warm dry sand. Such lavish warmth raised goose bumps on my bare arms. At the water's edge, I waited patiently for the next foamy wave to caress my feet.

"Who could ask for more than this, Ian? Soft, warm air and sand, and even warm seawater. It's like a bath. Can you believe it? How did I stand Maine's cold for so long?"

I tore off my pants and T-shirt and sat naked in the shallow water. Tears of joy ran down my face and mixed with salty sea spray that clung to my lips. Ian removed his clothes and dove in. His body hung arched in the air for one second before he disappeared beneath the waves.

I was seven years old when I first tried to dive into Lake Pennesseewassee. I dove off our dock, hit bottom, and surfaced with a mouth full of sand and a bloody gash across my nose and eye. I rarely dove after that unless the water was exceptionally deep. Ian tried on several occasions to teach me how to dive, but for the moment I was content to loll lazily in the water. Each incoming wave gently stroked my body. The sea is an invigorating healer. A lifetime of dirt washed from my skin in that one bath. With handfuls of wet sand I scrubbed my entire body. Then I followed Ian into waist-deep water. We frolicked like playful seals for two hours, but the whole time I kept an eye out for crocodiles. Refreshed and tired, we waded, arm in arm, back to the beach. Less than five minutes in the sun and my skin was warm and dry. After that day I quit using soap. A swim in the sea followed by a dunk in the creek kept me cleaner than I'd ever been.

Nature's cycles set the rhythm of my days at Cape Tribulation. We woke with morning birds and slivers of light through the canopy. Sea tides set the schedule for our daily swim, and, after, we often pranced on the warm beach for hours. High noon drew us to the shade of the rainforest and a soak in the cold fresh water of the rock pools. Sometimes at dusk, I strummed my guitar or we sat and talked into the night. Eventually, my guitar became too intrusive, and I preferred the night's sounds. Evening birds and cool haunting shadows urged me to prepare for the approach of night. In the tropics, so close to the equator, each day has roughly twelve hours of darkness and twelve hours of light.

With our routine settled, Ian found our big jars and sprouting seed, and we started to grow fresh mung, garbanzo, kidney, alfalfa, radish, and other sprouts. Twice daily, we took the jars down to the creek to rinse the seed. Our sparse diet consisted of reconstituted fruit in the morning, sprouts, raw nuts, and dates or figs for lunch; and for supper we often cooked oatmeal, cornmeal, or other whole grains and legumes, and added sprouts, tamari, or dried fruit.

Some days, tropical storms blew in and whipped the sea to froth. Rain pummeled the earth with such force I barely heard the sound of my voice. The wildness of those days drew me to the sea more than ever. I swam while rain pelted my head and wind roared about my ears. It was a constant battle to stay upright as waves tossed me about. My legs grew strong and sure. Churned up sand left my skin clean and soft. Warm rain washed the salt from my body. Occasionally a few stray bluebottle jellyfish—also called the Portuguese man o' war—washed ashore after these storms. They reminded me of small cobalt blue glass globes. Although not deadly, they could inflict serious pain if their tentacles touched my skin. I had only been stung once, a few days before when I stepped on a tentacle that lay on the wet sand. Fortunately, we didn't have to worry much about the really poisonous jellyfish. Stinger season wouldn't start again until October. It was only August.

I've rarely felt so free and wild as I did on these stormy days. I treasured the tropics because, even though it stormed, everything was luxuriously warm. Ian rigged our brown tent as an awning extended outward from the back of the truck to have a dry outside sitting area. At night I loved the sound of rain on the tent and roof of the truck.

Once I felt safe and familiar with the little clearing, I wanted to explore more of the area. One morning we decided to walk deeper into the forest. We hiked a long ways up the hill behind our campsite and stopped to rest. The concentration of life in the rainforest is staggering. Everywhere life stacked upon more life. Clinging orchids. Feathery tree ferns. Climbing lawyer vines. Delicate, creeping plants with green crinkled leaves. Life shooting straight for the heavens. I closed my eyes for several minutes and tried to imagine that I'd been born blind. That I had lived in darkness and suddenly science found a way to heal my eyes and allow me to see. That when they unwrapped the bandages the rainforest in front of me was the first thing I saw. As I slowly removed my hands from the front of my face and opened my eyes, brilliant green jumped from its source and shot through my body. It was *alive* and vibrated every cell in my being. Massive brown tree trunks sprang from the earth and surged skyward with magnificent power, arms raised to praise the stars.

Maybe I hadn't *just* left Maine. Maybe somewhere along the road I died and passed into another time, a forgotten world of exquisite peace. A world in love with itself.

I glanced at Ian and saw his closed eyes open and wonder spread across his face. "It's vibrant, Rob. There's so much green it's almost pulsing. Can you feel the colors?"

It was the first time I heard Ian speak several sentences without using the word "bloody."

High above us, flashes of wing—blue, green, and red darted from tree to tree. A celebration of life. So many birds. It was like an aviary. Or maybe an aviary with a profusion of birds is what all of Nature once looked like. Joy and grief flowed up my arms and legs to arrive at my heart simultaneously. The hidden forest was home to hundreds of birds. They were happy and abundant among the trees. I laughed at their games of flirt and chase and squabbles over food. They belonged here. They were part of something and always had been. They had a home.

I didn't have a home, and hadn't for years, not a place where I belonged. Even in the forest I was an intruder in one of the earth's most private places. I wasn't part of it the way the birds were and had been for generations. I felt displaced, an outsider who didn't fit in. I didn't fit in with my own kind either. I didn't belong to anyone but Ian. We belonged to each other.

I told Ian, "Even though I grew up in small-town Maine and grew up without a TV, compared to the purity of this forest I might as well have come from an inner city. A whole throwaway society with tin cans, boxed cereal, glass jars, processed and packaged food."

Ian's response was, "We're all from there. Well, maybe a few remote tribes aren't."

"Do you hear what you're saying, Ian? It's almost as if you think that's normal. Sure, it's how most of the world lives, but it may not be right. I'm not sure why yet, but I don't think it's right for me."

"What's right, Rob? Who knows?"

I loved Ian's freethinking ways, but at times he rankled me. So I tried a different approach. I knew he loved to challenge social norms.

"Okay, I guess I can only say what's right or wrong for *me*. I just know I grew up in a society of regimented time. I've never had a break from a clock or a watch or an alarm. That's not okay for me. We even accept the term *alarm*. We use an *alarm* to wake each morning."

(**a·larm.** *n.* 1. A sudden fear caused by the realization of danger. 2. A warning of existing or approaching danger.)

Not only that, but my intelligence was measured with an IQ test full of facts and figures that had little to do with me or my most cherished dreams. Nor was there a place in the test that might reveal my ability for creative expression. The schools I went to were often abusive and depraved, basically soul destroying. On top of that, my worth in society was based on how much money I earned and what kind of car and house I owned.

Ian sat down and patted the ground at his side. With a frustrated sigh I sat next to him. Something about the rainforest affected me so irrefutably; it made me see my whole life for the lie I'd been living. I wasn't yet fully sure what that meant, but pain and confusion welled in my chest as I tried to explore my feelings with him.

"Ian, I grew up with radios, artificial light, chemicals in my water and food, artificial smells, car exhaust, and plastic clothes and shoes that were often too tight. I was left with no soul, no connection to me or the earth. I don't even know where my food came from. A grocery store, that's where it came from, and I accepted it all as normal until I stood in this forest. The cycle of life hasn't been broken here. Can you believe it? This place is still intact."

Ian glanced up at the canopy, sighed, and reached for my hand. He listened with patience and understanding while I expressed these new thoughts and feelings.

"How much have we given up without realizing it? It seems that whole parts of the human being, well, at least modern humans, have atrophied from lack of use, like muscles that atrophy from lack of exercise. After several generations will we be physically and permanently altered like lizards of the past that no longer needed or used their legs and feet so their limbs slowly shrank until they lost them and became snakes? I know that's evolution, but are we humans evolving in an unhealthy way? Maybe we have a choice. I think we do. Are we handing over our potential to machines and technology?"

I didn't miss society and had long ago given up caring whether I fit in. I didn't. But as I stood in the forest and poured out my soul to Ian, a hunger gnawed at my heart. Possessed by some new and unknown urgency, I couldn't stop the unraveling. I'd held myself in check too long. I glanced at Ian's face, and the pain and compassion in his eyes encourage me to find myself. I began to cry.

"There's so much love here. Can you feel it, Ian? It's an enchanted world. Just to be in the presence of such a whole connection, with everything in rhythm and sync, makes me aware of how disconnected I've been all my life. This earthiness is where I came from and what I'm connected to. But I haven't lived that connection for a long time, if ever. I guess there were times that I did."

Confusion made it hard to think. Even though I felt out of place, a memory stirred to life. As I sat by the giant trees, I sensed they knew me and I them. I ached with longing. In the midst of my heartache, something shifted. I started to talk with the forest, in my mind, with my thoughts.

I feel so lost. Except for Ian, I've no roots, no connection to anything that really matters. Rainforest, you were here thriving the whole time I sat at my desk in school. I didn't know such a thing could exist. No wonder I've been dying.

The potential deadliness of the snakes and other creatures scared me and made me angry, but I *still* envied life in the forest. I craved to be part of it. And I wasn't, not part of its astonishing interconnectedness. In the rainforest each life-form fed the next, all the way up to the largest tree that eventually fell and fed the earth, and fed the tiniest microorganisms that fed the worms, that fed the birds, that fed the snakes, that fed the larger birds, that fed life over and over again. The cycles of life in the forest reminded me of a trickling creek that flows into a stream, that flows into a river, that flows into the mighty Amazon, that flows into the sea, that swirls around the globe and evaporates into the sky to be reborn as tiny raindrops that start their journey anew.

Tell me rainforest, where do I fit into the cycle? Where's my place? Do I even have a place? Am I born too late? Born in a time when there are so few secret places left?

I wasn't sure what I meant by "too late." My thoughts searched the depth of my mind for some forgotten memory. As hard as I tried, I hadn't lived "wild" long enough to fully comprehend what was happening. Ian's arm curved around my shoulders as I sat on the forest floor and cried.

"I don't feel things the way you do, Roby. But often when you share your thoughts I feel them in me gut. I know what you tell me is true, mate."

As we hiked farther up the hill, we found tall green tree ferns fanned in lacy elegance. Ringed trunks of palms shot upward to seek every scrap of light the canopy hadn't claimed. The breeze shimmered the palms' feathery leaves to create a soft whir that I found comforting.

Nature created rhythm and music everywhere I turned. My body rocked and hummed to the rhythm of waves on the beach, the creek's constant gurgle, and the concert of birds, insects, and frogs.

I'd never stood next to trees so massive. As I craned my neck to the cathedral of branches above my head, a phrase wandered through my mind. I couldn't remember who wrote it, but it spoke of an ancient people who believed trees were a more intelligent and sophisticated form of life than humans. I had always adored trees and loved to rest beneath their branches and dream great dreams. But I'd never looked at them in terms of being intelligent, not until I stood in the rainforest. It was then that their towering connection to both heaven and earth silenced my insides and forced me to feel things I both craved and feared. Like the trees, I longed to sink the roots of my soul deep into the earth and raise the arms of my spirit high into the heavens. The trees noble presence commanded I awaken from my long sleep.

Either everything I've lived all these years is absolutely insane or I'm going crazy here in the forest. Which is it?

Huge leafy arms seemed to respond to me as they reached out with compassion and grace.

You gentle giants with your buttressed roots so smooth and rippled, who are you?

My book on Australian plants said true rainforest, left undisturbed, usually is open and uncluttered. Only when trees are cut down and light penetrates the forest do certain species take over. It's then that the rainforest can become a tangle of vines and jungle. We were in true rainforest. Ian and I walked with relative ease among giant trees, small ferns, and an occasional lawyer vine. Lawyer vine is a small palm with barbed tendrils that arch out-ward from its greenery and climb upward. If we got too close, needle-sharp hooks grabbed our clothes and skin. We had to stop and gently unhook ourselves before moving on. After my first "snagging," I understood why this plant is also called wait-a-while vine.

The day grew lazy with warmth, and as we hiked, I became lost in thought. Suddenly Ian let out a shriek of alarm and started to jump around. He yelled all the way down the hill and headed back the way we came.

"Aaaaaaahhhhhh, eeeeeeeooooooowww, nooooooooo!"

"Ian wait!" I screamed. "Why are you running? What happened? Tell me, damn it."

About 100 feet away, Ian stopped and looked back at me like I was half mad. Bent over with hands on knees he panted for breath and said, "Didn't you see it? The bloody snake. In front of you. I almost stepped on him. How can you stand there?"

I scanned the twigs and debris that littered the ground. About two feet in front of me curved a six-foot brown-colored snake. I froze. The snake did the same. His body lay still among the leaves, an S-shaped stick with its head slightly raised, tongue darted in and out. Ian groaned and charged off. I turned in time to see Ian dive behind the roots of an immense tree.

"Ian, where are you going *now*?"

He groaned again and mumbled something about diarrhea. By the time I turned back to the snake, it had slithered away, headed for a cluster of ferns. I walked down to Ian. The explosive sounds from behind the tree told me he wasn't done. Impishly, I advised him not to charge off into the bush to take a dump; he might run into a snake. When he reappeared from behind the tree with his face drained of blood, I regretted my tease. Ian had been such strength to me on our trip that I couldn't connect his reaction to the snake with the intrepid man I'd known so far. When I asked him if he was all right, he looked weak and distraught.

"Rob, I've got to lie down. I feel bloody crook. This is no joke, mate. That snake scared the bloody crap out of me. I'm going back to the truck."

"Are you really that frightened of snakes, Ian? You never said anything about being afraid of them at the reptile park. I assumed they didn't bother you. If you don't feel well, I'll walk back with you. Let's go, sweetie."

Ian clutched his gut as we hiked back to camp.

"Rob, will you go first and watch for snakes?"

"Sure."

"I didn't know they scared me *this* much, Rob-o. I guess I've been shutting out my fear. I'm real good at doing that. But the fact is, I hate the bloody things."

"Is it because some of them are so deadly here in Oz, or are you scared of snakes in general?"

"Bloody oath, some of them are deadly, but I just don't like snakes. They give me the willies, always have. It doesn't matter if they's big, small, venomous, or not. Snakes is snakes. I felt that way even when I was a kid. Didn't even like to look at pictures of them. It's not that uncommon. I know lots of people that are afraid of snakes."

"Yeah, so do I."

All the way up the coast whenever we had stopped to camp or chat with other Australians, sooner or later, people ended up telling us their snake stories. It seemed that Australians loved to share snake stories, the wilder the better, especially stories that concerned poisonous snakes. There was always the tale . . . "Yes, well, let me tell youse 'bout the time me uncle was cornered by one of them bloody purple-spotted, orange-bellied, fifty-foot, slimy-backed, black snakes." Even though no such creature ever existed then or now, I found it endearing that the Aussies took great pride in the fact that they had some of the world's deadliest snakes.

Nonpoisonous snakes didn't scare me at all. But the venom of several Australian snakes is extremely poisonous to humans. That *really* frightened me. If either of us were bitten we might have only a few hours to get to a hospital and lifesaving antivenom (antivenin).[1]

While Ian rested in the back of the truck, I wandered down to the beach to sit on the warm sand. I mulled over the snake incident and recognized that some dynamic in our relationship had shifted. Up until the snake crossed Ian's path, I had relied on Ian completely. This was the first sign of my independence. Waves washed rhythmically in and out. Did any of the Coral Sea end up on the coast of Maine? I thought of my mother thousands of miles away. *Mom, what are you doing while I sit here watching waves? I've traveled so far from Maine I can hardly believe I'm still on planet Earth. But I see the same moon as you. We have that in common.*

Because my mother and I often butted heads, I'd mostly grown up out of touch with her. However in the rainforest, thousands of miles away, I felt closer to her than ever. A deep unwavering love flooded my heart. Those last conversations we'd had made me wish I'd known her better. At first, Ian's reaction to the snake made me feel more vulnerable; but the more I thought about it, I realized some part of me felt surprisingly stronger. I started to understand that since Ian wasn't completely fearless I was forced to rely on myself in ways I'd never done. His weak point was a chance for me to become stronger, if I didn't cave in to my fear. I sorted through the labyrinth of my emotions as best I knew how. I thought of my dad with his impish curiosity and love of a challenge. Life had definitely become more challenging. At least I hadn't run from my first encounter with a snake. It was a good start. There was bravery in me that I hadn't known I possessed. Maybe I *could* heal in the forest.

The sea breeze grew cooler, pastel light turned to purple dusk, and the day vanished into the west. And still, I sat. I waited while the moon rose crisp and crescent against an infinitely black sky. Ian slept on. He was sick for two days and stayed close to the truck. I followed my usual routine, but also kept him company. While he rested, I studied my plant book. It was a used copy and the only plant book I could find on wild foods of Australia. The cover was torn off and whoever owned it before me had used it as much as I hoped to. There were few pictures, but the text was fairly descriptive. It wasn't as extensive as the books I'd used in the States for my classes about wild edible and medicinal plants. There weren't many books published about the wild foods or medicinal plants of this rainforest.

With my budding sense of self-reliance and my book in hand, I tried to identify some of the trees and palms that grew along the edge of our campsite. The following day I walked down to the beach and collected a few round yellow balls of fruit I'd seen in the sand. They were about the size of apples. The first inch or so was white and woody, but the center contained a pulpy substance the consistency and color of mashed prunes. I gathered up four of them and walked back to the truck. I tried to find them in my book, but they weren't mentioned. Ian suggested we might experiment and try a taste. Since some plants are highly toxic to humans, my finger was barely wet with juice when I touched it to the tip of my tongue. Delightfully sweet, it tasted a bit like prunes. After that first juice-test, I waited a day to see if there was any reaction. The next morning I woke like any other. A few days later I tried more and waited. I repeated this procedure for a couple of weeks with no reaction at all. So I ate a whole fruit with no ill effects. It became an occasional addition to our diet. After the prune-like fruit, we extended our diet to fresh seaweed stewed with oatmeal and tamari. It was gourmet food, full of good nutrients.

Ian spent even less time in the forest after "the day of the snake." I couldn't blame him. I also was scared, but I couldn't live in the truck or even the clearing forever. As weeks passed I occasionally hiked up the creek to get farther into the rainforest, but I never left the safety of the water-worn trail. It was a cleared path. I felt more at ease climbing over rocks and wading through rock pools than wandering through the bush. I believed I could spot snakes more readily, and I could easily find my way back and not get lost. Could a person really be lost if they have nowhere to be and food all around them? I didn't think so. I had nowhere to be, no time limits, no plans, no dependants. Sometimes I thought about how fun it would be to take off and walk around the world, from place to place with no destination in mind, going only where and when the spirit moved me. Someday I think I'll do that.

Ever since I'd studied edible and medicinal plants, I felt more confident that I could find food in the wild. I often wished Ian hiked with me so I could show him the incredible plants I found. However, he felt safer by the truck and on the beach, so sometimes I hiked with him north along the shoreline. We walked for what seemed like miles and swam in the sea as we went. I never suggested that we head south. In that direction lay the dirt track and the mouth of the Daintree River. People. Some part of me wanted to pretend the road and the outside world didn't exist. It was an easy thing to do so far away. I needed time alone, time to heal and find my own rhythm. But one evening Ian said, "Why don't we hike the other way and go south along the beach?" I agreed because I loved being in his company.

As we wandered along the beach, the sunset radiated orange across the twilight sky and fringed the tips of each wave with liquid gold. The moon's huge round face slowly traded places with the vanishing sun. In moonglow magic, the sea danced and shimmered like a woman in a black-sequined dress. My shadow stretched out across the sand to dance with her.

Visibility was so good we walked farther than planned. Just before a slight cove, I stopped abruptly at the flicker of a campfire a few hundred yards ahead. I hadn't smelled its smoke because the breeze blew the other way.

"Hey, Ian, look. Up under the trees. Someone else lives here. Who would live way out *here*?"

"Bloody strewth, Rob-o. We ain't the only wankers in the world, eh?"

Ian picked up at the thought that we weren't alone. It made me question how much he liked living in a remote area. Ever since he'd been terrified by the snake, I'd felt him withdraw. Was his fear of snakes making him retreat from the forest? I felt frustrated and thought about all the fears he had faced on our journey north, and I wanted him to also face his terror of snakes. Then we could do everything together.

As he started to walk toward the fire, I grabbed his hand and whispered, "Wait, Ian. You don't know who it is. Those two weirdos might have come back. Once they see us they'll know we're here and where we're camped. I mean they're bound to ask. Right? Do you want that?"

At the back of my mind, my conscience advised me to look more closely at my feelings—my hesitation went beyond the weirdos. I sensed that once I let go of Ian's hand and he walked away from me toward the campfire, something between us, something in the dream I envisioned for us would change. And it might never go back to the way it had been. My thoughts left me feeling sad and alone. I tried to ignore them, but at the same time I gently let go of Ian's hand.

Unaware of my thoughts, he turned and eagerly said, "Rob, whoever it is they must have heard us drive up the bloody beach even if they didn't see us. They must know we's still here."

"But Ian, maybe they arrived after us. Or maybe they were on a hike or asleep when we drove by. If they were sitting by a creek they might not have heard us. They might not even know we're here. Why haven't they come up the beach to look for us and visit?"

He was impressed with my reasoning and grinned devilishly. I couldn't help but giggle, my sadness gratefully forgotten. After more whispered debate, he convinced me that it might be good to have someone close by if one of us was injured. Although Ian said he wanted to be in the bush and had been driven to go to the rainforest, at times he acted restless. I got the impression that something other than his snake phobia and being far from the city agitated him. I didn't know what it was.

When we lived in Salt Lake City, Ian had spent one cold December day at work on his souped-up Mustang. At dusk he strode into our apartment, flopped down on the couch, and buried his face in his hands.

"I can't finish the work on it, Rob. It's bloody cracking me up. All me life I've done stuff I hate doing. It's why I left for America; I thought I could escape it and start fresh. But I don't seem to be doing that."

I didn't know what "it" was, but my heart went out to him anyway. As we stood on the beach, heads close together, I wondered about the powerful forces that drove Ian.

Were his needs different from mine? As I moved closer to the forest, was he moving toward something he needed? I didn't fully understand him, but my love for him ran deeper than any love I'd ever known.

"Okay, Ian, I'll go with you, but if it's those two weirdos, we go back to the truck right away. We'll have to stay up all night with the rifle and leave at the crack of dawn. I don't trust them at all. They're capable of anything."

Ian agreed and added, "Why don't we move higher up the beach and walk under the trees in the shadows? Maybe we can take a bloody sticky-beak through the bushes, see who it is *before* we introduce ourselves. How's that sound, eh?"

I was greatly relieved and even chuckled over the excitement of it as Ian and I became cohorts in crime. With great drama Ian lifted each leg really high and placed it out in front of him with pointed toes and hunched shoulders. Muffled laughter almost escaped from beneath my hand to further encourage his antics. He took a couple of furtive, slow, tippy-toed steps, then three or four really fast ones like a two-legged spider scurrying from shadow to shadow. He was so funny I had to turn my back and not watch.

We approached the high-tide line beneath the trees. As we neared the fire I saw a solitary man bent over the flames. He stood and poked at the orange blaze with a stick. We waited to see if there were others. Ian wanted to go closer and check out his camp, but I asked him to wait and watch. A few minutes passed and we heard no other voices. The man sat down in front of the fire with his back to us. We agreed his build was too thin to be one of the weirdos.

"He sure ain't got no bloody egg-shaped head. Do we go in, Roby? He looks quite set up there. Must have been here for a while, eh? Sounds like he's sharpening an ax or knife. Look at the tarps he's using on his shelter. See how he's tucked under the trees? That's probably why we didn't see him that first day we drove up the beach. What do you think, mate?"

"All right, but let's be cautious. Don't tell him where we're camped until we get to know him better. If he asks, tell him we're camped back toward the track. Even though the bushes hide us he might find us if he explored up our way."

Suddenly a lazy voice loudly intruded on our whispers.

"Well? Youse gonna hide in the shadows all night? It's a lot more comfy here by the fire."

I put my fingers over my mouth to stifle a gasp and looked at Ian with horrified eyes. He shrugged his shoulders with a might-as-well attitude and started toward the fire. I was right behind him. The man who greeted us definitely wasn't one of the weirdos. He was an older gentleman, probably in his eighties.

"Me name's Jake. How youse going? Don't mind me; I's just got real good ears, I do."

"G'day. I'm Ian and this here's me wife, Robin."

"Pleased to meet you, luv. Hold on a tick. I'll be right back, eh?"

Jake scampered off to the back of his camp and returned with two beat-up metal buckets. As he arranged the impromptu seats I couldn't help but notice what a vigorous man he was. He wore only his undershorts, and his arms, legs, and chest were very muscular and lean. His sun-browned face was clean-shaven and his sea green eyes sparkled with mischief. His smile defied the gaps in his teeth, and his thinning hair glistened white as the sun-bleached shells on the beach. Thick calluses covered the pads of his hands and feet, and his fingernails were worn and cracked. He had the hands of someone who lived closely with the land.

"Have a seat, mate. This is the best I's got for chairs. Don't get much company hereabouts. Would you like a cuppa, luv? The billy's hot, she is. Fire keeps me company, you know."

Jake grabbed two chipped teacups with delicate pink flowers on their rims and filled them with steaming tea.

"Robin, here you go, luv. Nice hot tea, eh? Ian? Watch your fingers, mate. She'll scald you, she will."

I settled onto my tin drum and hugged the cup of hot tea. It calmed my nerves and allowed me to collect my thoughts while Jake and Ian talked.

"Hey, Jake, how'd you build your donga? She's a bloody beauty. Lots of room to move about under here, eh?"

"Cut me saplings out of the forest and lashed her together with rope. No nails in her. They'd rust too fast out here in the salt air. Only tools I got is me handsaw and axe."

Something about Jake made me feel instantly safe with him. He had a soft-spoken quiet dignity. There was no cockiness or brashness about him. Although I had guessed at his age, he seemed ageless. Beauty emanated from him. Like the birds, he belonged in the forest and was part of the sand and trees and sea, as if he'd sprouted straight from the soil. Jake was content with himself.

". . . So I left me wife and the city."

I'd missed part of what Jake said, so I paid attention.

"I figure I's done me bloody part. Fought in the bloody war, built me missus a mansion, raised a bunch o' rowdy kids. Bloody strewth! I's entitled to some peace before I die."

Jake didn't sound bitter or angry, just matter-of-fact. He could've been talking about the weather.

"I love me missus and me kids, but I need a different lifestyle. Fancy things don't impress me much. They's important to me missus. That's all right; she needs those kinda things. Now me, I just need enough to live. Everything you see here is all I got. Don't even own a vehicle."

His camp was well organized and it fascinated me. Tarpaulins stretched over a grid of saplings to create the roof, and plastic flaps were rolled up at the sides and made ready-to-drop walls in case rain blew in. A pile of old Larry and Stretch paperback Westerns sat on a makeshift table. Next to it was a stack of chipped, flowered dishes. A few dented pots and pans hung from the pole that held the table up. Jake's bed was made of saplings that were raised off the ground. A worn fishing net was draped over two nearby branches.

"Catch many fish with your net, Jake?"

"Well, luv, I'll tell youse, it's illegal to fish here with a net, but who's going to see? I'm an old man who catches a few fish once in awhile. Next time I haul in a catch I'll fry youse up a few, eh?"

"Rob and me, we's both bloody vegetarians, but I'll try some fresh fish. Sounds great, mate."

As we talked into the night I wondered how long Jake had been at Cape Tribulation, but I never found out. Every time I went to ask, he'd launch into another story and I was swept away. He told us all kinds of tales and was definitely a fine talker, slow and calm, with fantastic stories. I hung on his words while he talked.

"One of me sons brought me out a fluffy little kitten to keep me company. Thought I needed it. Kitten slept right in me bed with me. One night I woke to a bloody loud screech. No kitten. I lit the candle by me bed and found a bloody fifteen-foot python on the ground next to me bunk."

Jake made a big *O* with his fingers to show us how fat the python was. "Had the kitten between his jaws, he did. Real quick-like, I jumped out of me bed, grabbed the python's tail and stuck it near the coals left over from me evening fire."

I almost fell off my seat when Old Jake jumped up and leapt toward the fire. In his hands he held an imaginary python tail.

"The python writhed like billy-o."

Jake braced his feet and jerked his arms up and down while Ian and I watched wild-eyed. Fingernails flew out of Ian's mouth as fast as a beaver chipping wood.

"Me arms near yanked from their sockets, but I hung on until he dropped the kitten and took off for the bush. Surprisingly, the little tyke lived."

I relaxed a bit when Jake returned to his seat and continued in a calmer tone.

"Next time me son came to visit, I sent the kitty back to the city." Jake chuckled at himself, but then spoke seriously.

"The forest isn't a place for cats, and I don't need the company. Plenty o' birds and such around here to keep me entertained. When that cat was full grown, even if I fed her real regular-like, she'd have killed all me birds and small mammals and lizards and such. It's their nature. Luckily, I didn't have to stick the python's tail in the coals. Couldn't have done it. Would've let him have the kitty first. Putting his tail near the heat was enough. Didn't want to harm the python, just scare him. He was a beaut ol' fella."

"Hey, Jake, I gotta ask you 'bout something I heard the first night we were here. It was a loud scream that got cut off midway. It was scary."

After I imitated the sound and told him my tale, he chuckled, shook his head knowingly, and said, "That's a bloody scrubfowl getting swallowed by a python. Some of them pythons is big bloody bastards. Up to twenty-five feet. In the dead o' night it's a funny sound, eh? The fool bird screaming away then choked off like that. Enough to make your blood freeze when you don't know what it is. Youse get used to it after awhile, luv."

Old Jake seemed calm enough about it, but I had to ask more.

"Do they eat humans?"

"Naaaw, we's too bloody big. Though they might 'ave a go at a baby left unattended. They'll eat wallabies or birds, and bandicoots, rats, and such. Youse safe from 'em, luv. They aren't even poisonous. Now, the bloody death adder, that's another story. He hides his fat ol' body under some sand or leaf mulch. Hides everything exceptin' the finger-size end of his tail, which he positions real close to his mouth. Then he wiggles it to attract small prey like lizards and mice; they think it's food. When something comes to investigate and gets real close the adder's head springs and strikes like lightning. Because he sometimes buries himself, you could step on him if youse not careful. They's deadly all right. Nocturnal too. But you won't find 'em much around here; it's mostly too wet for 'em."

"Jake, what's nocturnal mean?"

"Nocturnal means they come out at night, and diurnal means youse most likely to see them through the day. But then wild critters are always breaking the rules. They do all kinds of funny things. Sometimes in the early morning if you walk along the beach you can see snake tracks left in the sand during the night."

Jumpin' Jupiter, I'd have to watch for lizard-size tails on the way back. But wait, Jake had said death adders didn't live around here much, if at all. I didn't care; I'd still wade through the water. No, I'd walk on the wet sand. Couldn't wade in the water in the dark. I wouldn't see a croc if he was there. Oh maaan.

Jake's voice brought me back to the campfire. He'd started another story about a trip he'd taken with his wife.

"I was happy as Larry 'cause me wife was going camping with me. We was camped way out in the bush. Real dry country it was, west of here. Set up camp and everything was fine. Had a couple of beaut days, you know? Real romantic and all. Then early one morning me missus stepped on a bloody death adder."

When Old Jake stopped his story to pour us more hot tea, I couldn't believe it.

Didn't he realize his story was too intense to stop midway? Eventually, I learned that Jake was a steady, patient man. It wasn't that he liked to tease or play games with people's emotions. Life was a ritual to him, and he took his time living. He'd seen it all, done it all, traveled all over the world and now lived alone by the sea. He had no need to rush a good story or anything else. Nonetheless, I wiggled around on my tin bucket and silently urged him to resume his tale, and Ian ran out of fingernails but continued to gnaw.

"Anyway, the snake bit me missus on the calf of her leg. I was sitting at the fire like this, sharpening me hunting knife. It's a beauty, so sharp I shave with it. She'd gone off to pee before brekkie and was walking back. About twenty feet from camp she starts screaming. When I looked up there was a bloody death adder slinking off into the grass. She'd already been bitten. He probably came into camp in the night and was hidden under the sand the next morning."

Ian's eyes, now bigger than sand dollars, shot toward mine as he remembered our walk on the beach in the dark, and probably the snake he'd seen a few weeks before. Blood stained the knees of his pants where he'd bit his nails down to the quick and tried to stop the bleeding. My heart went out to him as I rested my hand casually on his leg. Old Jake didn't know about Ian's fear of snakes so he blithely continued his story.

"I bloody panicked knowing there was no way I'd get her to hospital in time to save her. We were too far out in the bush. So I took me bloody knife, grabbed her leg, and hacked a chunk of muscle out of her calf, right where the snake struck her, eh? Did it real fast-like, seconds after she was bit. She didn't even know what I'd done at first."

Ian was nearly jumping out of his skin with fear when he burst into Jake's story with a frantic string of questions. "Jake, what did you do after? Did you bandage it? Was your wife mad at you? Could she walk? Did you leave right away to go to the doctors?"

"There was no way of knowing for sure if the snake injected venom. They don't always inject, you know. But I couldn't take that risk. I washed the wound with disinfectant, stopped the bleeding, and bandaged it up. Me missus was shocked, but so glad to be alive she didn't get angry. We both knew how deadly the adder is. It was slow going, but she didn't get any snakebite symptoms and we got out. She had a nasty leg wound for awhile. Left a mean-looking scar, but she can walk normal and all."

Jake's story and his quick thinking impressed me and made me wonder if I would respond as quickly. Would I dare hack part of Ian's leg away if his life depended on it? If we were too far away from help? With no vehicle? Would it be the right thing to do? I'd have to do something. *How much do you cut out? What if my knife isn't sharp enough? Better check tomorrow. What if the snake bit somewhere else, like something you couldn't cut off? Oh man. I think if I didn't have a vehicle to drive out of the bush, I'd take antivenom with me.*

I had to stop my rampant imagination and realize there had to be an element of trust to live in the wild. I also began to suspect that if I was to live in the bush I had a responsibility to understand my world. I didn't know how I felt about the whole responsibility thing. As Jake and Ian talked on, my thoughts tried to right themselves. After hearing his frightening tales, my burgeoning courage vanished. I no longer saw my situation as an exciting challenge. Instead I sought solace in anger. It was much easier. An insidiously infantile part of me felt justified in my anger, like the world owed me something better. Why did I have to live where there were so many deadly snakes? Snakes didn't scare me, but here they could kill me. Crikey! I'd never had to be careful in Maine. There was nothing poisonous there. I didn't have to watch out for anything. I just cruised through the woods wherever I wanted. Everything seemed so deadly or just plain awful in the rainforest.

It felt good to mentally spew. Silently, I counted off the things I had to watch for. As if the higher the number the more justified my anger. *Snakes, spiders, ants, leeches, and feral pigs. Let's see, what else? Cassowaries, jellyfish, crocodiles, ticks, and probably more that I don't yet know about. Makes me want to kill them all. All those evil, deadly snakes and every other lethal thing.* As I stopped to catch my breath, I was shocked. I wondered where such volatile feelings had come from.

All I knew was that I felt very edgy. I couldn't see how I'd ever be able to relax in the rainforest. I'd have to watch where I put my feet and hands and where I sat. I'd have to check my shoes and clothes for spiders and scorpions, my hair and body for ticks and leeches. Why was it so hard to be careful? I didn't want to have to be conscious. It felt exhausting. Why hadn't we just stayed near Ian's family in Melbourne?

I related to Ian's fear. I dreaded the walk back up the beach in the moon-light. Ian and Old Jake talked about his war adventures while I tried to come to grips with my emotions. The dialogue played itself out in my head, and I was shaken at the anger I felt. On some level, though, it fascinated me to see a twisted and spoiled part of myself, a part that found justice in anger. I wasn't angry at Jake. I had merely reacted to his death adder story.

Why did I feel love and reverence for the trees, and hate and disgust for the snakes? Was it because the snakes were deadly or was it something more? What did I really fear?

Jake's voice caught my attention again.

". . . Yeah, it's mighty savage, mate. Youse have to watch out for it. Tomorrow morning I'll show youse what it looks like, eh?"

Old Jake's words penetrated my secret thoughts right on cue. Was he still talking about the death adder? Did he intend to show us one in the morning? I had to ask, "What's that Jake? What do we have to watch out for now?"

"Just the bloody ol' stinging tree, luv."

Deadly plants too? I was still trying to deal with the snakes.

"Farther south, the Aboriginals call it Gympie Gympie or stinging tree.

You know, those big fuzzy, heart-shaped leaves you see around here. Grows close to the beach or places where the sun gets in. You touch 'em or brush against 'em and she burns like bloody billy-o."

Again I was impatient and asked, "It goes away doesn't it? Kinda like nettles? They contain formic acid like an ant bite, but it goes away, right?"

"Noooo, it's not the same. Been stung by nettles. I think it's related to nettles, but they's *nothing* compared to the stinging tree. Not sure what causes it. Might be silica spines that have some type of poison in them. But it doesn't go away, luv. At least not for a long time. Here on me arm I got a small patch that's played up for bloody months. Every time I take me bath it burns. Sometimes it burns like bloody billy-o for no reason. Change in temperature. Things like that. I'd hate to have a big patch on me skin. Don't think I could stand it."

Crikeys! And I'd wandered around the bush like an ignoramus. I remembered seeing a six-foot tree near the beach with huge heart-shaped leaves covered with fine hairs. My study of wild plants of the United States had made me cautious. I listened as Jake continued.

"When the early pioneers pushed their way through the bush they didn't know anything about it. They'd take off their bloody shirts in the heat, hack away with machetes, and end up getting stung by a stinging tree. I've read accounts of blokes blowing their brains out with pistols 'cause the pain was intolerable."

I was terrified that such a plant existed. This was too much in one night. I'd have to get my book and look it up.

Old Jake wasn't done talking.

"Sometimes when the settlers took their horses through the bush they'd run smack into a bloody stinging tree. Pain burned unbearably. Poor horses would blister up real bad and even go crazy. Run wild until they broke their fool necks on trees or jumped off cliffs. Had to shoot 'em sometimes just to put 'em out of their bloody misery. Same with dogs. Some blokes who got stung poured kerosene on their skin and lit it with a match, burned the spines out of the skin. More recently some blokes took a blowtorch to the stung area. Did the same job as kerosene. At least when the burn healed there was no more pain."

Oh charming. A bit of kero, a blowtorch. Of course. Why hadn't I thought of that? Old Jake saw my look of horror and said, "Eh, luv, youse just gotta learn to spot the stinging tree in the bush; that's all. No different from learning to stop your car at a red light. You'll be right. That's why I's telling you 'bout it. Nature has her ways of slowing us down and making us think about things, eh? It's best that way. Snakes and stinging trees stop us from crashing through the bush like a mad bull in a china shop."

Ian tipped back on the edge of his drum, then rocked forward, back and forth, riding his anxiety. Jake continued.

"Naaah, mate, she's not too bad, but youse want to watch out for her. Can't take it lightly. A long time ago I heard about this bloke who camped out here with his girlfriend and some other couples. They got to horsing around, playing Adam and Eve and such. This bloke stripped down and grabbed a big old leaf to cover his donger. Turned out to be a stinging tree leaf.

Ian rocked faster and faster. While he chewed his fingernails, Old Jake talked on.

"Well, I'll tell youse, he jumped around clutching his crotch and screaming about being on fire. His mates had to hold him down while they took a blowtorch to his bloody donger."

CRASH!

Ian fell off his drum and landed on his backside in the bushes. Jake burst into laughter, slapped his knee and said, "Eh, mate, I's just funning youse. No worries. No one's going to torch your donger, Ian."

We all laughed our guts out. I felt relieved because Jake was kidding. Relieved until he said, "Story's true except for torching the guy's donger."

Jake looked at his crotch, shook his head, and said, "Poor bloke getting stung down there. Imagine that? And *that* ain't something you can cut off."

I don't think either Ian or I wanted to imagine much of anything at that point. Jake's fire died down to glowing embers. Fatigue tugged at my body, probably more emotionally than anything else. I couldn't imagine how I'd process everything Jake had told us. Maybe I wouldn't. I knew the old man didn't mean to scare us. It was the reality of the bush, and that was that. But we sure kept both eyes open for snakes in the sand as we walked back along the beach to our camp. Thankfully, when we crawled into the truck exhaustion overrode fear and we slept deeply.

In the shade of these trees
The ancient voice of love
Resonates my senses
Ignites awareness
And calls me into being

—RUSSELL HUME

four

Goin' Troppo

WITH THE ARRIVAL OF OLD JAKE in our lives, the pattern of my days changed. He wasn't intrusive in any way, and he never came to our camp or bothered us, maybe in part because we lived so far up the beach. So we walked up to visit him. Jake seemed the most content human being I'd ever met. I wanted to absorb everything he knew about the rainforest. It astounded me when he told us that the rainforest of Cape Tribulation is one of the oldest tropical rainforests on earth, roughly 100 million years old, millions of years older than the Amazon.

Upon meeting Jake, my relationship with Ian shifted in stages. No matter how much I loved Ian and no matter how interesting Old Jake's stories were, over time I became dissatisfied sitting around his camp every day. In my own way, I grew as restless as Ian. I'd come to love Old Jake, but I didn't want to sit around his campfire anymore. Talking about someone else's life was too much like watching television. I wanted to live adventure. Although I still feared the forest, a beguiling force summoned me to its secret depths. As weeks faded into months, Ian continued to hike up the beach to visit Jake but I began to hike up the creek again.

We often take things for granted when we're young. When I went to the jungle, I anticipated that we'd explore the forest and live the adventure together. That's what we'd been doing until Ian almost stepped on the snake and became sick. But it didn't continue that way. The more independent I became, the more Ian relied on Old Jake's company, or maybe I became more independent *because* of Ian's friendship with Jake? Or maybe things happened exactly as they needed to for us *both* to grow?

Deep in my heart I wondered if I'd lose Ian one day. Not his love; I'd never lose that. But our interests and needs changed, and I worried that he might someday return to the money, the city, and the fancy way of life he'd known before he met me. I was being drawn in a direction that made me adventurous and hungry for relationship with the rainforest. I thought Ian and I had to do everything together and have all the same interests. I even thought that with time he would change his mind and join me in the forest. I was wrong.

Regardless of all that, I had powerful inner battles taking place. Mother Nature lifted the lid off my Pandora's box when I entered the rainforest, and a host of characters, scenes, and dramas played themselves out. The forest owned me, although I didn't yet know it. Ian appeared more and more removed from the green world around him and said it didn't speak to him the way it did me. Maybe he was right. Maybe his destiny waited for him elsewhere.

I didn't understand his battles at the time, but I began to understand some of my own. A black cloak of fear hung heavy over me, never far away. It draped about me, cold and damp. I grappled with hate and anger at all the "deadly creatures" in my new world. The thought of being bitten by a poisonous snake was more than I could handle. I started to understand how people filled with great fear could hate and kill *anything* that frightened them. Angry at the world, that's what I was. I believed I had no control over my life. That belonged to someone else, not me. A war raged inside and tore me apart. Most days, I had little peace.

One morning, driven by frustration because Ian was at Jake's and I was fed up with my own fear, I abandoned my usual safe path up the creek and marched off into the bush. I didn't know where I was going, and I was too upset to care. Before I realized it, I arrived at the place where Ian and I had sat many weeks before. Oddly enough, when I entered the circle of trees my fear was forgotten as I sat on cool, bare earth. The forest was more breath-taking than I remembered. Everywhere I looked, green trees, ferns, and vines burst radiantly forward, weaving and intertwining, unable to contain themselves. I felt the forest growing, *heard* it growing, inching forward as cells multiplied and crept across the ground, up the trees, and through the leaves to golden sunlight. Life at last!

The chattered conversations of early-morning birds had died down, but I still heard their activity in the treetops. Unripe figs plopped to the ground near my feet, rejected by parrots and pigeons that fed in the branches above my head.

I'd hiked into the rainforest to try and sort through my fears, but in the company of the trees my mind wandered, aimless and dreamy. The longer I sat in the circle, the more the light began to diffuse and grow soft. I shook my head to clear it, but the leaves continued to blur into glowing green. I could've sworn I heard music, the exultation of a thousand angels. Time and memory slipped away. I forgot myself in the awareness of another "presence." Ecstatic fingers of life reached from the trees and tentatively explored my face and arms. These curious beings stretched out long, luminous tentacles that gently wrapped themselves around me. A voice drifted through my mind.

"Trees are highly aware beings. We desire to make contact and to *love* you, Robin."

What kind of magic is this place? Either I'm going insane or . . .

The trees interrupted my thoughts. "No. That's not true, Robin. You are not going insane. You have been insane and now have a chance to heal."

I've been starving on a meal of death. We have wars and crime when there's love like this in the world? We're not connected to this anymore. Were we ever? Is everything I've lived a lie?

Mother Nature began her work of stripping away the fabrication I'd called "my life." She spoke directly to my innermost self, and the human-animal within me heard her voice, pricked up its ears and grew restless. It crawled around inside me, seeking a way out, an opportunity to express itself. It rebelled against the muck and mire of my domestication. The contrast between who I really am and the role I'd tried to fill in society was so great it was beyond understanding. The trees guided me.

"Robin, your cultural story will decompose here in the forest. Let it happen. We offer you a blank tablet. No one here will reinforce your old story or reality. We will not shame you back into place. Your cultural reality is incongruous and means nothing to us. Here among the trees you can explore and evolve. Write whatever story you want; no one here will tell you that it is not true."

I gotta be brave and listen to my heart. At some point I'm gonna have to act boldly with daring and courage, even when it doesn't feel normal. Even when I'm scared.

Surrounded by emerald green leaves and surging brown tree trunks, the world I knew vanished. New emotions and possibilities seeped in and eagerly nibbled at the confines of my old reality. The "presence" entered my mind and spoke again.

"You do not need to die, Robin. You are merely ravenous for life. You have suffered gravely from years of disconnection. You must pull yourself out of your autistic state[1] by exposing yourself to as much life as possible. If you don't, then you *will* die. Remember, there are many worlds and many realities, and they are forever changing."

Autistic state? What are you talking about?

"You know it well. You know what is wrong. You can feel it in your body, and have felt it for a very long time. Think more about your life, Robin. You will remember. Trust it."

I thought about what the trees said, and I remembered the painful memories of my childhood that had come to light when Ian and I had driven north up the coast of Australia. Memories of my repetitive rocking, my inability to make eye contact, my fear and anxiety, my difficulty in accepting change, my desire to be alone and not be held, my learning disabilities in school, and other social handicaps that had isolated me all through grade school and junior high. I remembered how society had closed in around me until I was so overwhelmed and squeezed that I had to escape somewhere quiet and green, or else I'd go numb. Voices and sounds were too loud, information came at me too fast, and I became easily over stimulated. I didn't know how to maintain a sense of self around other people. I gave up my sense of self so that I would appear like everyone else, so that I would survive. I sold my soul so that I might fit in, and I did, but that didn't make me whole.

When I left high school, I felt confused about my place in the world and could no longer remember who Robin *really* was. I'd see someone standing at a grocery store checkout or at a party, and something about them would impress me. It might be the way they dressed, behaved, or what they did for a living, and I'd think to myself, *So that's what I need to be.* For a short time, I felt as if I had a sense of self, like I had it all figured out. I knew who I was and what I would do with my life—that is until I met someone else who impressed me equally as much but in a different way. Then once again I'd say to myself, *Okay, this is who I am. Now I've got it.*

I might change "selves" five times a week. In a group of people expressing thoughts, ideas, or feelings I might change selves five times during that gathering. The internal chaos I experienced was almost more than I could handle. The room swirled around me and nothing anchored me. It was enormously unsettling. I wanted to know who I was.

In the years prior to rainforest life, the "chameleon syndrome," as I later called it, took its toll on me. The autistic state I'd lived in all my life had left me without a sense of self, especially since high school when I finally learned to act "normal." Most of the time, the way I survived and appeared normal was to emulate other people, but it never felt real.

In the forest it was different. Although I was still scared of the rainforest creatures, there was peace and quiet. I could start to feel and experience Robin, whatever that entailed. Often in the beginning, the only deep emotion I felt other than fear was a singular emptiness. Sometimes not even that. Some days I felt numb, no feelings at all. I had to just wait. I preferred emptiness because I could *feel* it, and it was *my* emptiness, something of my own and not an emulation of someone else. Emptiness birthed longing and made me cry. I occasionally glimpsed the possibility that I might eventually grow strong and clear and know myself in the rainforest. I still didn't know how to be in society, and the contrast between Nature's wildness and society's domestication was so drastic that it confused me. I could be one or the other, tame or wild, but not both. I didn't know how, not yet.

I'd been given much to think about. I leaned my back against a curved tree trunk and pondered this new insight. I sat alone, a single dot of female humanity deep in the Australian rainforest. Millions of years of untouched silence washed over me. The roar of it pulsed through my ears and woke primitive rhythms in my heart, rhythms long ago denied. Stolen.

When I found my way "home" that day, a beautifully raw and highly intelligent world awaited me. Unabashed. Unashamed. Ancient peace, still and undisturbed, gave birth to spontaneous healing. Rocks, trees, and plants vibrated with energy. Life burst through every cell, vein, and structure. I knelt on sacred ground and wept.

I'd been brainwashed. I'd grown up perceiving only the earth's wild places as sacred. I thought that was normal, and how it had always been. Where there is a parking lot, there was always a parking lot. Right?

No. Once trees, wild plants, native grasses, waterways, birds, and other animals lived where the parking lot sits. All the earth is sacred, every inch of her.

My new awareness made my throat tighten with pain. I could barely breathe. The earth beneath a tarred parking lot, a toxic waste dump, a stump-riddled forest, and the center of a city filled with concrete, asphalt, and millions of people is also sacred. Sacred and wounded.

Do we justify our destruction by believing that only certain places are sacred? As long as we have a few national parks, wildlife refuges, and zoos we're okay. But are we? If we were to consciously feel in our guts what we're doing to the earth, I don't think we'd feel okay. I don't think we could stand the pain.

Terrible hurt and anger overcame me. My unfolding had only begun, and I didn't yet know how to assimilate that much emotion. However, I could cry. Tears begged me to sob. Grief ran down my face and onto the earth.

It occurred to me that one day humanity might erase the hallowed place I sat upon. I didn't want to think about that possibility. Not when I'd just found heaven. Although I now understood how fear could motivate someone to kill what they fear, I still couldn't comprehend how anyone could touch heaven and destroy it. Again, the voice spoke words far too wise and beautiful to be my own.

"Robin, if you truly see this place, you cannot destroy it. But when eyes no longer see and hearts no longer feel, it is easier to destroy."

I sat upon the forest floor and raised tear-filled eyes to the tops of the trees. Suddenly I felt as if part of me became the trees, as if transported to the tangled canopy. I saw myself through their ancient eyes of wisdom. From that grand height, I looked down upon the forest floor and saw a young woman who sat alone, a pinpoint of humanity hidden among miles of verdant green. She seemed totally unafraid and deeply in love with the rainforest.

Is that me I'm looking at? It can't be. I'm too afraid of everything. She looks peaceful, as if she belongs.

As I sat, the breath from those gigantic trees gently fanned my face, and I heard their voices as one.

"Robin, you have not arrived at this remote place by mere chance. You have been drawn here for a reason. We have stood as silent sentinels for countless centuries. When our shoots were cracking through the soil of Mother Earth you were only a spark of light, a part of the great universal cosmos.

"Even now, you are a tiny child curled at our ancient buttressed feet. We are very old, and silently we have watched the world's passing. In that time many beings sat at our feet. Most lived harmoniously with their mother. They walked gently and with reverence, their impact so slight, no more than the passing of a shadow. To make contact, we did not need to reach far to find loving hearts. But for some time now things have changed. Your kind no longer comes to worship the giant trees.

"You have arrived here from a world that cries out in disharmony and pain. Whether you know it or not, you are seeking solace, Robin. You have come here to heal."

I didn't know it, but the trees were preparing me for things to come. Something familiar and tender filled me with tears, as if I'd been here before, born for this one single moment of truth. My life rode on a wave of profound change. I was exposed to and absorbed wisdom far greater than my own. The rainforest beckoned me beyond my control, and drew me irresistibly in search of its mysteries. The trees continued to talk with me, and for the first time in my life I began to seriously consider the meaning of intelligence.

"Robin, trees are alive with breath and emotion. When you stand next to a tree, even though you may not know it or feel it, that tree is aware of you, more aware of you than most people are. Trees communicate, even over great distance. We love. You are the one who has closed off your beating heart."

The flux of my life flowed rapidly after that and demanded my full attention in every moment. I didn't go to the trees because I knew they'd talk to me; it just happened. I heard them. Realities shifted and surfaced to light much too fast to express in a journal, but I never forgot their powerful voices.

"To be around trees for any length of time is to heal. But you have forgotten how to listen, Robin, not only to your own beating heart but to the living world around you. You are the one who has not heard when the trees speak."

I felt shocked and humbled by their request to be treated with respect, to be seen and loved. But what life doesn't exult in love? I knew of no such life.

I'd never listened so completely to a tree. They're incredibly stoic and gentle, capable of unconditional love in its cleanest form. For all of our callous and uncouth ways, they harbored no animosity, only tender sorrow and more love than I'd ever felt in my life. Trees have a timeless patience, a virtue I wanted to learn. In the presence of their grandeur, I felt like an unruly and recalcitrant child, ashamed of the behavior society had taught me and I wore as my own. Ignorance and arrogance toward other life forms were the norm in the culture I'd grown up in. Beneath the swaying branches of the trees, my back supported by solid trunk, contrast lent me insight. And yet in my disgrace, I also felt gentle compassion for myself and humanity's desperate plight. Emotions and insights swirled in and out of my awareness, one after the other and all at once. I'd never thought about these things in such a complete way. I almost felt as if I was a tree.

The heat of day had long passed and taken with it late afternoon. Insects tuned up for their evening symphony as I headed back down the hill to our camp. Enough light seeped through the canopy for me to find my way, but I knew it wouldn't last. No matter how enchanting my day, I grew tired and hungry. I hadn't eaten all day, and I was still uneasy in the forest at night.

As I approached camp, magic jumped from my shoulders like silver fairy dust to land on the trees and watch my disappearance down the hill. Sad and confused, I suddenly realized the spirits wouldn't follow me to camp. They wouldn't venture near my truck and the world it represented, a world that even I feared.

Tears stung my eyes because living in the rainforest had turned my life "real" very fast. I couldn't hide from myself in the same way I'd been able to in the outside world. In the forest I felt raw and exposed under the watchful and all-knowing eyes of the trees. I sensed they desired to know me, the real me. I didn't know why I wanted to cry or how to tell Ian my feelings. They were beyond words. When I reached the edge of our little clearing, a wave of empathy tapped me on the shoulder from behind and filled my heart, as if someone much older had reached out to comfort me. The voice spoke one last time.

"Robin, the rainforest will teach you everything you missed and all you need to become a whole and complete woman. Be patient. Trust."

Do I dare let that happen? Can I be that brave? Could life be that real?

Emptiness met me at the clearing so I walked down to the beach to find Ian hunched over a book tipped toward the last rays of light.

"Whatcha reading? Can you even see in this light?"

"Barely. It's an old paperback of Jake's, an American Western about these two blokes named Larry and Stretch. Stretch is tall and thin and Larry's short and stocky and has lots of bloody muscle like me."

Ian grinned and flexed a bicep. I rolled my eyes and he chuckled.

"Bloody good reading, Rob-o. Jake's got dozens of 'em."

My thoughts and emotions skittered around and found no settled or comfortable explanation. Was I going insane? I'd gone from Jake's stories of stinging trees and death adders, to the love of the trees, back to my husband who sat on a remote Australian beach reading a paperback Western. What planet had I landed on? This was too much. There appeared to be no reality at all in the rainforest. Everything seemed haywire. Or . . . was I haywire? Either way, I had to get a grip, find some level of normalcy before I could eat or sleep or do anything, so I told Ian about the trees. Fascinated, he listened to all the details. He struck me funny that way, afraid of the snakes, but totally intrigued by the trees, leeches, insects, and the battles of life and death that took place on the forest floor, right near the truck. Often I found him in the camp clearing on hands and knees with his face inches from the ground. When I walked closer, I'd see that he was watching an ant that carried a leaf or insect many times its own size. Or maybe a wounded spider or worm that fought for its life. Ian would watch them for hours, like a scientist on a research project.

Once I discovered him with an injured bee in the palm of his hand. Ian feared snakes but had no fear of bees. I didn't fear them, but I couldn't handle them the way he did. They landed on his hands, arms, or face, and it never ruffled his calm, as if people handled bees every day. He could pick a perfectly healthy bee right off his arm, set it on the ground with his fingers and never get stung.

Light vanished from the beach, so he dog-eared his paperback and we hiked up the hill to the clearing. By now I was more tired than hungry, so I skipped supper and climbed into the truck to lick my wounds. I needed sleep. Ian ate some fruit and crawled in after me.

"Hey, Roby, I forgot to tell youse, Old Jake invited us to have bloody homemade damper with him tomorrow's lunch."

"I've been in the forest so much lately, Ian, I haven't seen Jake in ages. After a day like today it would do me good to see him."

The next morning I spent in camp with Ian and caught up on chores. While he told me about damper, we walked to the creek to rinse our sprout seeds.

"You'll like this bloody damper Jake's making us for lunch, Roby. It's pan-fried bread that's really crispy and hot. You put lots of golden syrup on it. That's thick bloody syrup, like honey, only it's made from sugar."

"Boy, it's been months since we've eaten anything like dessert. You'll be in heaven, Ian."

"Too right, mate."

I hadn't eaten much of anything hot for some time, so hot bread sounded pretty good. While we waited, we aired our bedding and cleaned out the truck and greased it. When I stumbled across the camera, I thought it might be nice to take some pictures. Unfortunately fungus had eaten the film on the Canon's lens. When I gazed through its viewfinder the world looked foggy. Sooner or later fungus and mold invaded everything. I noticed that items in the truck that I touched with food-sticky hands had my moldy fingerprints on them a few weeks later. It was not a good idea to read a book while eating. Eventually the sides of the pages were covered with gray, moldy fingerprints. We had packed dozens of cans of crystallized desiccant, and kept a can with each food item. After discovering the damaged lens, we decided it was a good time to check the cans and replace any that needed it. As thorough as we were at doing this, neither of us had thought to add extra desiccant to the camera case.

After we finished with the truck, I grabbed some of our dried figs for Jake, and we climbed down the cliff to the beach. The day glistened, clear and sunny. With plenty of time to meander, we chatted while we examined shells.

Jake was tending his fire when we reached his camp. We never lit fires, but instead cooked on a gas stove the size of a coffee mug. We'd use it until the gas canisters ran out, and since we ate most of our food raw that might take forever. Two tin-bucket seats sat ready for us when we arrived at Old Jake's. I knew he was glad to see me.

"How youse going there, luv? Hear youse spending your time in the forest. Watching out for bloody snakes? They's no real worry if youse careful where you step? There's more to see in this jungle than youse can poke a bloody stick at. You might think some things are downright revolting 'cause something is always getting eaten here, but that's the way of Nature, luv. You get used to it after awhile. Spend some time in the jungle and youse bound to see all kinds of things. You'll even find yourself wanting to protect or defend some creature that's getting eaten, but it's always best to let Mother Nature take care of herself, eh?"

Smoke billowed from the frying pan when Old Jake poured in the cooking oil, something I hadn't used in months. Rising bread dough sat in a blue-enamel bowl on Jake's makeshift table. When I asked him if he used yeast, he laughed.

"Strewth, luv, I'm not *that* kinda' cook. Use self-raising flour. It's heaps easier. When youse next go to Mossman, fetch some there. Oh, by the way, youse staying while the ferry's out?"

Met by blank stares from Ian and me, Jake continued. "You do know that the ferry shuts down for a couple of months? Ferry master hauls it out of the river for repairs. If youse needing anything best make a run to Mossman. Once that ferry's out, only way in and out of here is by bloody boat. Might want some more tucker and such if youse staying through the wet."

Questions flooded my mind, but I couldn't get past my anxiety over a trip to town. Once Jake threw out the bait, I figured Ian would jump at it. His restlessness had increased over the months. He loved to use the truck and winch, but even more, he loved to spend money. Oh noooo. We'd have to go back through all those creeks, over the washout and catch the ferry across the river. Jumpin' Jupiter, we'd also have to get the truck down the hill to the beach and then back up again. I couldn't go through it.

After Jake told us about the ferry, two questions cut through my worry. How did he know the ferry would be taken out? What month was it?

I didn't even know the day of the week. We didn't have a radio, clock, or calendar, and I hadn't seen any in Jake's camp.

"Hey, Jake, how'd you know 'bout the ferry?"

Jake grinned and said, "Inside secrets, luv. One of me sons came out the other day. Brought me some tinned goods and other supplies. He told me. Now me, I'll stay here 'til I die. Got no need to be headin' to town. So, youse staying through the wet?"

When Ian said, "Most bloody likely," I almost fell off my bucket at the readiness of his reply. I quickly approved his choice. "Ian, I agree with Jake, I don't need a trip to town. Takes too long. If all this rain keeps up, the creeks will be high. We've got tons of food. Let's stay here. *For years. Forever.*"

I could have kissed Jake when he said, "Yeah, me son said one of the creeks is way up. Bloody old Holden stranded in the middle of the water. Some bloke just up and left it. What else could he do? It's not the first time it's happened. Imagine it though; some wanker trying to drive a bloody Holden car all the way out here, and with them creeks up. Might's well have driven a Mini Moke. Oh well, takes all kinds; that's often how life works. Makes the world fun, eh?"

Jake glanced at me and quickly winked one sea-green eye, then looked away just as quickly. Had he said that for me? Did he know I didn't want to leave? Was there really a Holden car stranded in the creek?

Jake wouldn't meet my eyes again, but it didn't matter. A great weight floated from my shoulders when Ian shrugged and said, "Sounds good to me if we just sit tight, eh? My oath, I ain't too interested in moving the bloody truck off the hill and back through all those creeks and washouts. Did your son say anything else about the road?"

"Like I said, the creeks are way up. Guess there's quite a bit of mud on the track too. I'll just sit tight. Got no use for the bloody city. Simple things is all I need."

Thank you, Jake.

Ian completely trusted Old Jake's judgment and clung to his words like a child with a shiny quarter. I suspected that Jake knew it. I decided that he also knew I didn't want to leave. Did he recognize in me a kindred spirit who also wanted a simple life? Did he think I was starting to love the forest? Was I? At that exact instant, Old Jake lifted his head and looked straight at me, the way my dad did when he was letting *me* know that *he* knew what I was thinking. When Ian turned to Jake, the old man looked away from me and casually spread bread dough into the hot crackling frying pan. Oil popped and spat. It stung each time it landed on my bare legs. I moved my tin bucket back, and Jake tossed me a tea towel to wipe away the splattered oil. Before we left our camp to go to Jake's, I'd cut off a pair of my jeans for shorts. On the beach or by our camp we went naked, but on the rare occasions I went with Ian to Jake's, I wore a T-shirt and shorts.

Sticky syrup ran onto my chin and fingers as I wolfed Jake's damper. The rich sweetness made my teeth throb. My mug of hot tea washed down the whole mess, but only increased the pain. I wasn't used to hot liquid. I usually drank air-temperature water from a glass jar we kept by the truck. When I hiked, I filled my belly before I left and drank slowly from the creek throughout the day.

Midway through a bite of damper, Jake said, "Did I ever tell youse 'bout the tour bus? Believe it or not, Robin and Ian, during the drier months some of these dumbarse tour operators from Cairns manage to get their buses all the way out here. They spread a blanket on the sand and have 'em-selves a nice ol' picnic. Doesn't happen often or last long, but they always do it right out there."

Jake pointed to the beach in front of his camp and stabbed the air three times as he said, "Right . . . out . . . there."

Shocked, I asked, "In front of your camp, Jake? Don't they think you might want some privacy?"

"Bah! That lot wouldn't know privacy if it sat on 'em, luv. Noisy tourists leaving their trash everywhere, yellin' and carryin' on. Invadin' me camp, taking pictures like it's some sorta bloody caveman display in a museum. You know, exhibit number five: primitive man. Strewth, shoulda charged ten dollars a pop, eh? Fortunately, they can't get through when the creeks are up. But even in the dry season they must be hard up for cash to come way out here, or else they's bloody wankers. Aaahh, they's bloody wankers anyway."

I was flabbergasted that tour buses could make it that far into the bush. But Jake had said the dry season. I tried to get over my shock and focus on his story.

"I sat here one morning just tending me fire when suddenly I heard the rumble of a distant vehicle, not just an ordinary four-by-four, but a loud engine, like something big headed this way. A few more minutes and here it comes, an old beat-up bus, sputtering and lurching its way along the shore. Something about LUXURY RAINFOREST TOURS was painted on the side of the gray metal heap. Between the splattered mud and rust, I couldn't read it all."

Jake threw back his head, cocked up one corner of his mouth, and let out a "phhft" of disgust, like he didn't even care what was written on the bus.

"Luv, that groaning old bus came to a sudden stop a hundred yards in front of me bloody camp. Even with the ignition turned off, the engine popped and hissed and kicked up a fine old rumpus. Let me tell youse; it's a weird experience to see a bus way out here. Might's well have been a space-ship full of little green Martians arrive on the beach, eh?"

I knew exactly how Jake felt. It was beyond bizarre, like one of those otherworldly experiences people have on drugs. Ian was still shaking his head in disbelief.

"Now you two listen up while I finish me yarn here. The middle-aged bus driver removed his sunnies with the flourish of a bloody 'merican movie star and swung open the bus door all in one deft movement. He acted so arrogant you'd of thought he was Moses come to part the Coral Sea. Those tourists tumbled outta that bus like a bunch o' colorful confetti and stood waiting while the wanker driver and his young son spread a blue blanket on the hot sand. Next to it they opened a huge white Esky full of tucker, you know, sandwiches, cold drinks, and such. The driver hollered out, 'Teatime, mates,' and I sat here watching them scuffle and fight for space on the blanket, until the drongo driver yelled, 'Hey, let's not be gettin' bloody sand all over the tucker, eh?'"

Caught in Jake's spell, I completely forgot where I was until I saw Ian lean forward. Old Jake chuckled to himself as he continued his tale.

"Those tourists were hot and thirsty, real hungry from the long ride out here. They didn't even stop to look at the sea. Strewth, might's well been sitting on a sidewalk in downtown Sydney for all the time they took to appreciate their surroundings. They was just settling happily into their nice little tea when three blokes appeared out of the bush next to me camp. Those blokes marched straight down the beach to the tour bus with a live twenty-foot python. Arms a jerking up and down as that snake wriggled and gyrated. Mr. Python didn't take too kindly to being manhandled."

Jake slapped his knee and hooted with laughter. His eyes widened as he grappled with an imaginary snake. A twenty-foot python. It *really* hit home that monster-sized snakes hung out in the same forest I hiked in. And we slept with the tent and truck wide open. At least they weren't poisonous, and they weren't really fat like an anaconda. Jake had said an adult human would be too big to eat, but they might have a go at an unattended baby or little kid. So I figured they weren't too much of a worry. Nonetheless, it was a dreadfully long snake.

I quickly glanced at Ian. His mouth hung open catching flies. Jake's eyes glittered with tears of laughter. He jerked his chin at us and said, "Best pay attention, luv, so's you don't miss me yarn."

"So we's got a blanket full of city folks just starting their tea when along come three blokes with a squirming twenty-foot python. They walked right up to those tourists all innocence and smiles. The lead bloke says, 'Take a gander, folks. He's a right beaut specimen, eh? Really friendly sorta snake this one. Ain't even poisonous, nothing of that sort. He just bloody suffocates his food before he eats it. You know, mates, he's gotta eat just like you city folks.'"

Jake clapped his hands and howled with laughter.

"Gasps rippled through the tourists, luv. The snake was huuuuge. The first bloke said, 'Yeah, mates, this 'ere reptile swallows his tucker whole and alive, head first, bones, hair and all, then gives birth to a bloody Pommy.'" Jake laughed so hard over the Pommy line that he started to hack and spit.

"Luv, I'll tell youse, he shoved that fat python right into the tourists' faces, telling them, 'Ave a feel, mate. He's 'armless. Here 'ave a go, eh? Come on. Don't be shy.'"

Ian bit off another fingernail and I gasped when Jake said, "That ol' python lunged out and snapped his jaws, biting air, and all hell broke loose. You talk about a wild fracas; poke a stick in an anthill and you'll know what I mean, luv. The bloke who held the snake's head jumped onto the blanket and cajoled the passengers to touch his prime specimen. Ian, you shoulda seen it, mate. The bloke holding the snake's tail wiggled it right up close to the crowd and said, 'Aw come on, mates. He's 'armless. He's a rare beauty, eh? Youse might never see 'nother like 'im. Come on, be a sport, 'ave a feel. Youse don't want to 'urt his feelings, eh?'"

Tears of laughter rolled down Old Jake's face, and even Ian was laughing in between nail biting. At the back of his mind he was fretting about twenty-foot snakes.

"I'm telling youse, those local blokes acted all innocent as if their feelings were hurt because no one wanted to pet their python. They thrust that slithering snake right into the crowd, directly in front of two middle-aged women. That did it, mate; those tourists went over the bloody edge. All those ladies in flowered dresses and blokes in proper leather shoes started screaming and cursing."

Jake jumped up and began to mimic a woman running in heels, wobbling in the sand and clutching an imaginary skirt.

"They shoved each other trying to get away from that squirming reptile and onto the safety of the bus. There was hats and hair flying every which way. Sandwiches got dropped and a big ol' orange pawpaw got squished across the blanket. Sand was spraying this way and that, and above all the racket that wanker of a bus driver started yelling, 'Back onto the bus. Everyone back onto the bus. NOW!' I'm telling ya, that bloody tour guide was frothing at the mouth. He snatched up the empty Esky, threw it onto the bus, and in all the chaos forgot that their food and drink still sat on the blanket."

Jake stopped to catch his breath. Each bout of laughter ended with a long wheeze and a fit of coughing. His thigh turned red where his hand slapped his bare leg. I laughed so hard I started to pee my pants, and his tale was far from over. When Ian said, "Bloody strewth, mate. Those three blokes were crazy as a hat full of arseholes," I had to agree with him.

Old Jake put up a hand, trying to tell us to hold on because he had more to say.

"Those threes blokes tried to climb right up the steps and into the bus, python and all, and then WHAM! That bus driver pulled the lever, snapped the door shut, revved the old engine, and tried to peel out. You ever seen anyone try to peel out on sand? Through the windshield I saw his red-eyed rage. He gnashed his teeth to stubs, mate, and shot flames at the three snake handlers. Mad as a cut snake, he was. Good thing he didn't have a gun. He'd a shot all three of the blokes and the snake too. Probably shot me just for laughing."

I'd heard that stuff like that happened in Queensland, that it was a good ol' Wild West bar brawl, anything-goes place. I couldn't decide if it was risky or ridiculous. Usually it was both.

"Wish you'd seen it, luv. That ol' bus rattled and rocked as the driver floored the gas, pedal to metal, and ground the engine in frustration. Tires spun and sand sprayed. Those wide-eyed tourists stared from the bus windows, watching the three wily inciters of mayhem clinging to that wiggling python while blissfully devouring their abandoned sandwiches. I damned near carked it laughing when the tourists pounded on the windows as they watched their lunch disappear. Mad as hell, they were. They still had a long, hot ride back to Cairns without food and drink, but not one of them dared get off that bus. The driver wasn't afraid of the python, but he knew if he opened the door even an inch those blokes would haul that pulsing mound of flesh clean onto the bus. I sat here praying they would. I bloody well wanted to see a twenty-foot python furiously slithering among a busload of panicking passengers. Now that would've been a bloody bonza event."

"What happened next, Jake? Did the tourists leave? Who were the guys with the snake?"

"Well, luv, one of the blokes piled the food and drinks into the middle of the blue blanket, gathered up its four corners and threw the loot over his shoulder like Santa Claus with a sack full of presents. Then all three blokes muckled onto Mr. Python, waved to the tourists, and trudged happily into the forest, laughing all the way. No one followed. The bus slowly vanished south down the beach. I was sitting here still cackling like a crazed chook when I heard another engine coming from the opposite direction. That was me three mates' Toyota."

Your mates? You knew them?

Jake saw my surprise, winked at me, and kept talking.

"They'd returned the python into the bush and were headed back to Mossman. They drove toward me camp laughing and hooting, hanging out the windows with long-armed waves. Right out front here they slowed down just enough to drop a big blue bundle of tucker on the sand. I heard one bloke yell, 'Anytime, mate. Anytime.' Ya see, luv, some of the local blokes from Mossman don't much take to tourists either. Besides, there's not a born Aussie who can resist a spot o' mischief, eh?"

Jake hopped up and indignantly placed his hands on his hips and paced back and forth a few times.

"Bloody tourists gettin' me all riled up when all a bloke wants is a bit o' peace. So, me mates offered to cause interference for me. The three of 'em came out here to camp a couple of nights before the tour bus arrived. Set up camp a few hundred yards north of me. Hid their vehicle in the bush by the creek up there. When I told 'em 'bout the tourists ruining me privacy, they decided to have 'emselves a spot o' fun, eh? They'd heard this bus might try to head out here even with the creeks up. Bloody driver's a stupid bastard. Anyway, me mates searched the hills for a big ol' boy, a python long enough to send the smart arse tourists fleeing back to the city."

Jake doubled over with laughter and told us the rest remained confidential. "Can't tell youse their names, or such, but had to share the yarn with you, eh?"

"I can't believe this place."

Old Jake cocked his head at me and said, "I know, luv, we's a strange lot o' ratbags, eh? There's an expression us Aussies use here in the tropics. Kinda' sums us up. If youse here long enough, sweet as you are, luv, most likely it'll happen to you too. We say, we's gone *troppo*, or a bit bonkers from the life here—the heat, humidity, and such. Kinda gets to you after awhile, luv. Thing is, by the time it does, you don't care. Youse already bloody troppo. You know, crazy, sick in the head."

Jake lifted a gnarled finger and tapped his head knowingly. His shrewd green eyes glittered with vitality. I didn't understand how he could talk about going crazy. He stared past me and out to sea to enjoy a private moment of beauty.

"Life's hard here, luv. At least until youse used to it. There's mozzies and ticks and all the bloody rotten mold and fungus that gets into your supplies. During the wet, there's enough rain to wash youse out to sea. You never really dry out, you just go a bit silly in the head, eh? No worries. It's not like youse the only one. We's all a bit troppo here in the far north. Don't fight it, luv. You can't make sense of it."

Jake handed Ian a small bowl of self-raising flour, and we departed with hugs and full bellies. Ian left with visions of tomorrow's hot damper breakfast. I left with a gut ache. Whenever we'd stopped in a town on our trip, Ian had bought a loaf of bread and some local honey and ate the whole loaf in one sitting. He loved it almost as much as ice cream. He chattered away excitedly as we walked, which made me happy. As long as we didn't have to leave the forest and go back "out," I'd eat damper for the rest of my life.

Reliving the antics of Jake's story made the hike back to camp go fast. We walked across hard, wet sand, always watchful for crocodiles, until we got to the cliff face. Then we gingerly crossed the sand to the high-tide line and very slowly climbed the hill. It grew dark so I walked cautiously. Ian's fear of snakes made him want to run for camp and the truck, but I yelled after him, "Go slow. There could be snakes." He went steady after that. Next time we walked in the dark, we'd take the candle lantern and matches.

We crawled into the Toyota, stripped down, and within seconds Ian's snores drowned out the night sounds. I envied his ability to sleep instantly. As usual, I lay awake for some time. Mozzies hummed somewhere outside the screen windows by the thousands. Why hadn't any mozzies come in through the open cap door? When I strained to hear them they sounded like they were up in the canopy. As I listened, their whiny buzz turned to an odd chatter of voices like a radio. Then the number of voices increased until I heard music *and* voices, and then different languages. I recognized French, German, and what sounded like Russian and Chinese. And there were others I didn't know. The sound got so loud I couldn't stand it any longer, and I woke Ian.

"Hey, mate, wake up. Ian, wake up."

"Strewth, you okay, Rob-o? What's up? Can't you bloody sleep, mate?"

"Listen, Ian. Can you hear voices and music? It's like twenty radios playing at once."

"Rob, I can't hear anything but a ton of mozzies. Bloody strange they's not in the truck."

"That's what I thought at first, but then the more I listened the louder the sound got, then it changed to voices and music. I'm going outside to see if there are any mozzies."

Ian followed me out of the truck. We sat quietly on the log by the Toyota, and the voices and music were still there. I described what I heard and Ian listened with an open mind.

"Maybe youse hearing bloody radio waves. It could have something to do with atmospheric pressure or the lack of disturbance here. It is possible. You do have extremely acute hearing. Remember the bloody night we slept on the bank of the Daintree River? You said you heard the ocean. Strewth. That's quite a ways away. I could barely make it out, only a couple of times. But for you it sounded loud."

"Ian, not one mozzie has come near us. They're not even out tonight. It cooled off this evening, and they don't like that."

We crawled back into the truck. I tried to go to sleep, but I still heard music and voices. I told Ian I wished I had earplugs, so he lit the candle, rummaged in the first-aid kit, and pulled out some cotton. I rolled it up, stuffed it in my ears, and mercifully the sound lessened. At least it wasn't in my head. It had to be external. We knew Old Jake didn't have a radio. Even if he did, he was too far away, and I wouldn't have heard so many stations at once.

That night I dreamed glorious music floated from the trees to me. I could hear it in my dream, expansive and wondrous, unlike anything I'd ever heard. It lifted me out of the truck, through the canopy, and into the stars beyond. Surrounded by music, my body turned to fluid, and I rained down upon the earth. Where I fell, new young trees sprouted from the brown soil. My dream shifted, and I sat before a warm, crackling fire. Old Jake's face loomed in front of me, and I heard his words.

"It's the oldest tropical rainforest on earth, Robin." He laughed and said, "Almost as old as me."

Suddenly Jake's face changed, and I saw a group of trees standing in front of me. They spoke to me in one voice.

"You are out of touch with the ways of Mother Earth. Your life is restricted and blinded by fear. Fear of what you don't understand and cannot control. You have not acknowledged nor accepted your death."

I don't like what you're saying. What do you mean I haven't accepted my death? How do you know? I'm not going to die . . . am I?

The trees ignored my indignation and remained silent. I awoke to Ian's voice and tears on my face.

"Hey, Rob, wake up. Youse having a bloody dream, something about dying. Youse right now. I'm here, matey. Go on back to sleep."

"Yeah, okay. It's just a dream."

Ian fell asleep in minutes, but I lay awake for what seemed like hours. I hadn't told him that my dream troubled me. It would take a bit to sort it out, maybe time and daylight. The dark night held powerful energies full of ancient spirits and dreams.

Morning came but sleep took a long time to drift from my body. When I woke, Ian sat on a nearby rock eating a jar of fruit and reading his Western. As I climbed out of the truck my dream came back to me. I also remembered the radio voices and music I'd heard. It was a disquieting night. Ian looked so calm. Didn't any of this affect him? Were we even in the same rainforest?

An urge to be close to him with his paperback Westerns and matter-of-fact ways made me spend the day in the clearing instead of the forest. Alone in the rainforest, I'd dwell too much on my dream. I wasn't ready to look at it. I sensed the forest waited for me, as if it knew of my dream. I needed a break, at least for one day.

The handful of books I took with me to Cape Tribulation sat in the truck for months, except for the plant book. I had my snake and bird identification books and one book on Australian mammals. That was it. It seemed a good morning to haul them out and have a browse. My book on Australian snakes intrigued me. It was a tattered, used copy, and someone had pasted a great article about snakes in the front of it. The article stated that all snakes lack eardrums, but they aren't completely deaf. They just can't hear airborne sounds in the way that humans do. Many herpetologists believe the ancestors of modern snakes moved underground a long time ago, where the ability to detect airborne vibrations was not required. Over time, they lost their eardrums. Snakes today retain some parts of the inner ear, and their body substitutes for eardrums by transferring low-frequency airborne sounds and ground vibrations to these remaining parts.

I grew excited when I read that a hiker should carry a walking stick and tap the ground while traveling. Most snakes feel the vibration and leave the area. They can pick up the vibration of someone walking on the ground better than they can someone who is running. It amazed me that such a simple bit of knowledge set my mind at ease. Snakes weren't entirely the unknown horror that they previously had been. I still felt wary, but I'd just learned what I could do to warn them of my approach. It was extremely exciting.

I started to read about the snakes in my area. Were they nocturnal or diurnal? What type of disposition did they have? What did they eat? The answers to those questions gave birth to awareness, and I began to gradually relax. Simply to know that they are cold-blooded (ectothermic—Greek for "heat from outside") and seek patches of sun in the cool morning, and shade in the heat of the day, gave me a better idea where to watch for them. I started to piece together a picture of the lives of the poisonous snakes in the rainforest.

The few times I stayed around camp, Ian and I ate our lunch of sprouts, nuts, figs, and dates down on the beach. Sometimes we soaked dates and raw oats in water to make a sweet pudding-like paste. It tasted unexpectedly good. Our nuts wouldn't keep much longer in the heat. Rancidity was always a concern. We both grew to recognize the foul taste of rancid nuts after a couple bouts of slightly upset stomach.

It's remarkable how well equipped we were when we went into the forest, but I forgot one of the most basic things. My needs as a woman were few—no makeup or hand creams. The humid climate kept my skin soft. No detergents, shampoos, deodorant, or toothpaste. Toothbrushes and floss, yes. Seawater made great toothpaste and gargle. No painkillers, no drugs, recreational or otherwise (including antibiotics), no eye, ear, or nose drops. None of the medicine cabinet "junk" we often can live without. The one thing I ran out of was my supply of tampons for my menstrual cycle. There were a few left in the truck, about four.

The day I stayed in camp with Ian and read, I started my menses. Since there were only four tampons left I stripped off my clothes, grabbed my lunch, and walked down to the beach. Ian followed behind, as naked as me. I sat on a rock in the mouth of the creek, where it flowed across the sand and into the sea. Cool creek water trickled over my feet and ankles while I ate lunch and bled. Ian was completely unfazed.

"Wow. Youse not going to use a bloody tampon anymore?"

I laughed out loud when he said "bloody" because it sounded so absurd in context with my cycle. My glib reply made him laugh.

"No, I'm not gonna use a bloody tampon. I'm not even gonna use a clean tampon. But at night I'll lay on that old orange towel. That way I won't stain the sleeping bag."

"Strewth, that's cool, Rob-o. Just come down here every month, bleed, and rinse. So what if the blood runs down your legs. It doesn't bother me. It's bloody natural for you to bleed. There's nothing gross about it. You could spend the day resting in the sand and sea, or sit on your rock in the water and read."

I loved Ian for his innocence. He responded with exuberance over things that many people found uncomfortable. He sat calm as a tropical breeze and ate his lunch while I bled. My belly tugged and squeezed to be rid of my monthly blood.

"Ian, maybe when my cramps get bad I can come down here—if it's a sunny day—and lay my belly on the hot sand to ease the pain."

"I think that's a beaut idea, Rob-o. How about after tea I'll dig a shallow trench and cover you with warm dry sand?"

I propped my head on a packed sand pillow, and while I watched the grains run through his long fingers he covered my belly. My monthly cycle became a ritual as old and natural as the tides of the sea and the cycles of the moon. It was a time to rest and heal. A time for Ian and me to ramble our thoughts in and out of each other's mind. Other days, he read his Westerns and I read my field guides. I was intensely curious about my new world. Everything I read raised ten more questions. That had been a major problem in school; I asked too many questions.

Strength received a frown. Girls weren't supposed to be strong. Weakness was often accepted (expected?) of young women. Certain forms of ignorance were encouraged, and emotions met with uneasiness. A teacher once told me, "You *must* learn to contain your feelings, Robin. One should never get overly emotional."

I was not only passionately emotional but extremely inquisitive. I hungered to know, "Why do the planets revolve around the sun? But what is gravity? Why does it happen? What makes flowers grow to be different colors? Why do stars flicker?"

I learned to be quiet or be ostracized. Another teacher once said, "There's no need to ask so many questions, Robin. It's a waste of time. Only the really smart kids have to know that stuff."

I didn't think it was "stuff." Those questions and possibilities made the world vast and intriguing. They still do. Nevertheless, in school I was often told not to ask questions. Far worse, in fact criminal, I was told that I wasn't one of the "really smart kids."

To believe that the young do not feel deeply, desperately, and wondrously is a grievous mistake.

Ian loved my questions and knew much about the planets. Often on clear nights we sat on the little cliff leading down to the sea, beneath a vast dome of stars, our arms and fingers entwined. I asked him questions for hours, late into the night, for as long as he had answers. I asked him questions until we ran into the unanswerable, inexplicable mysteries of the universe. That was magic.

As I lay in my sand bed next to Ian on the beach, I thought about my parents and how much they'd taught me to love Nature. I was blessed to grow up with a freethinking father and a very bright mother. They loved Nature's splendor intensely and wished to share it with their children. My father often came home from a long day of work and begged me to paddle the length of Lake Pennesseewassee with him or hike to the top of Streaked Mountain. Mom rarely went a day without commenting on the whiteness of snow, the brilliance of fall leaves or the soft pastels of spring trees. She loved to call us to the back door and say, "Snow's coming. Can you smell it?" To this day I smell a snowstorm on its way. I remember a mother who walked barefoot with us across the lawn just to feel clean wet grass on our bare feet. What I missed in school, my parents gave me. Their reverence for Nature and its grandeur is one of the greatest gifts I've ever received. It profoundly influences my life.

While we need to reestablish our kinship with Nature, billions of us can't go traipsing off to live in the wild. That time is past. We are too many and our fragile wild areas too few, but we can appreciate Mother Nature right in our city parks, and in our own backyards by growing trees and gardens, or feeding the local birds, or growing a flower or house plant on our window-sills. We live in a world of tremendous beauty and bounteous life. We must take time to experience Nature with each other and do it without our snowmobiles, jets skis, mountain bikes, and motorboats—all of which can keep us from hearing the voice of the wild. Can we leave our machinery at home and simply walk into Nature with gentle feet and open hearts? Can we learn to have a loving and protective relationship with Nature so that she is here for generations to come? It's harder to destroy that which we understand and love. Given the opportunity, children instinctively have a great love of Nature. They have keen minds and are hungry for exploration and adventurous play. Their spirits thrive on magic and mystery, and Nature is *full* of magic and mystery. We may pass this way only once . . . maybe? Regardless, while we are here there is much to learn and experience. We must live life as if it were the last, our only. Maybe it is.

I shared these thoughts with Ian on the days I sat on my rock in the mouth of the creek and bled. He usually sat on a nearby rock. They were intimate, poignant days. Our voices followed where our thoughts wandered. We talked about all kinds of things, and while we talked we painted on flat stones with colorful pieces of shale: orange, red, and yellow.

How many Aboriginals sat right here and drew their stories on this stone?

In the timelessness of these days, I began to process and share my rainforest experiences with Ian, both my fears and triumphs. Though he rarely ventured into the forest, pride lit his face when I shared my adventures. Love filled my heart because of Ian's steadfastness. Always a sympathetic and unflappable listener he sustained my rebirth as I gradually awakened from my cocoon of death.

Shadows ran long and thin across the beach, and our thoughts turned to food. I sat up and brushed the sand from my belly. A rinse in the creek and I felt ready to climb the hill and make supper. Just as Ian gathered my books, I glanced up the beach and noticed a young woman emerge like an apparition from the rainforest. She was as naked and brown as me, about my age. Her hair sprang from her head in a tangle of matted black curls. When her stride brought her closer, I noticed she wore a green fanny pack. She responded to my stunned but friendly wave and trudged toward us at a lazy pace. No preamble, no introductions, she just started to talk as if we knew her and had been waiting for her to walk out of the bush at that exact moment.

"Just walked part of the Bloomfield track. The damned leeches are thick as thieves. Got tired of pulling 'em off. Finally gave up and let them drop off when they were done feeding. Too wet and too many leeches to keep going. Decided to head back. Is the old bloke still camped down the beach? Told me I could stay with him a day or two on me way back through."

A zillion questions demanded attention, but I only managed one.

"Where's your tent and clothes?"

"Got a piece of plastic and a sarong in me little pack."

Where the hell had she slept? There was nothing between Cape Trib and Bloomfield, and Bloomfield was miles and miles away. At best, it was only a walking track. She told Ian she'd come from New Zealand and then asked if I was a "Yank." As quickly as she'd arrived, she waved and took off down the beach to Old Jake's for "some tucker." She disappeared at a trot into the proverbial sunset and left me with a thousand questions dripping from my lips. What did she eat? She couldn't have fit more than a few nuts or a candy bar in her pouch. On impulse I hollered after her, "What did you eat?" I thought she hadn't heard me until, "I didn't" floated back on the night air. Don't ask me why but tears of joy and admiration sprang to my eyes. I wondered if that's how Ian felt about my adventures. But she was *really* brave. She'd had leeches clinging to her ankles, slept under a sheet of plastic, and had gone days without food. Something about her set me free.

All the way up the cliff Ian had a grin on his face. He seemed exceptionally happy as he hopped onto the tailgate of the Toyota.

"My oath, don't know why you're so bloody shocked over her behavior, Roby. A few more months and you'll be just like that, running bloody wild. You wait; I already see it coming. Youse changing, Rob, and fast."

"No way. Not that much. She's *really* brave, or else crazy. I haven't figured out which. Damn it, Ian, I don't even know which I am."

"Hey, Rob-o, that reminds me, we got some bloody sarongs here too, somewhere in the truck. I'll find them. We can wear them tomorrow."

That night I dreamed of a young New Zealand woman with wild hair and a green fanny pack. She walked toward me in slow motion down the beach. Suddenly she changed, and I realized I knew her. I recognized the long-limbed walk and the oval face as my own. My hair grew wild and full of debris. Dad's hunting knife hung on a belt around my waist. Stunned to see myself outside of myself, I stood motionless and stared at the other me until she gently stepped forward and into my body. I felt her inside me.

The twitter of early morning birds seeped through my dreams as I lay in the truck and tossed and turned. As I struggled to awaken, I felt disoriented and couldn't remember where I was. What were dreams, and what was reality? Or were they the same? Had I only dreamed about the New Zealand girl or did she really happen?

I woke to find my red sarong draped over the tailgate of the truck. Without a thought I hopped from the back of the Toyota, wrapped the red cloth around my torso, and hiked into the rainforest to pee. After my business was taken care of I kept walking without thinking about it. Halfway to my circle of trees, I felt something lightly crawl up my leg. Two flat dark ticks raced toward my knee. Revulsion made me react with lightning speed. With a flick of my finger both ticks shot into space. I found them on a piece of bark that lay on the ground. One struggled to turn itself over. His legs frantically kicked like a baby on its back. Feeling sorry for it I reached for a twig and turned it over, and it headed straight for my feet. Did movement draw them to me? Quickly, I jumped out of its path and sat on a rock after I checked it for ticks. It was bare. No snakes behind it, no spiders, no ticks. It finally dawned on me; I'd gone off without socks and boots. I was naked except for the sarong. What had possessed me to take off without my shoes and pants? Anything could get me now. At first I decided to go back and get my shoes. But then I realized I was already halfway there. Maybe I could just be careful and watch where I stepped. Parasites got under my clothing no matter what I did. At least naked, I could see them and brush them off. Snakes were another thing, but then I remembered how my book said to tap the ground with a walking stick so that the snakes could hear me coming. Near the piece of bark lay a good-sized stick. I checked to make sure the two ticks hadn't hitched a ride before I picked it up. No ticks. It was a bit too curved, but long enough. I'd find a better one later.

With great care I wound my way among the trees while my stick tapped the ground. For the first time, I saw intriguing life everywhere. I actually began to observe the things I thought I feared. Columns of ants moved like diminutive armies over major obstacle courses. Spiders and beetles scurried under dry leaves that my feet avoided. Fifteen feet ahead a small yellow-bellied snake cautiously slithered behind a buttressed root.

I let him be. Two brown stick insects stood side by side, camouflaged on the tip of a branch. Lime green cicadas and grasshoppers darted and buzzed ahead of me as if to announce my arrival in the forest. "She's coming. She's coming. Hide. Quickly!"

As I searched the ground ahead for anything that might bite or sting, I suddenly realized that I had to be aware like the rest of life in the forest. I was the insect that watched for the snap of the bird's beak, the bird that watched for the slow slither of snake, the stinging tree covered with deadly spines to ward off those who would dine on juicy leaves. If I wanted to survive, I too had to be conscious.

I arrived safely at the circle of trees. My heart trembled as I sat on the bare earth and exhaled a long shaky breath. I felt like I'd walked through a minefield, but if I wanted to live naked in Eden, I had to confront my fears. I didn't know it then, but that day I chose to face my fear of the unknown. The minefield I tiptoed through lay mostly in my imagination. It had little to do with the rainforest and its supposed monsters. The rainforest was my new teacher, and this was the first day of school. And me, without an apple.

I feel so alive. I've never had to be this careful or aware. I've lived a flaccid life. It's disgusting. For the first time in my life, I feel challenged, and I'm excited about it. But can I do it alone, without Ian? Mmmm . . . maybe that's the only way any of us face the unknown.

The trees responded to my new openness with a stronger voice. "You are not alone, Robin. You never were. Fear thrives where there is little understanding and no true wisdom. You do not need to die. You can choose life. Part of your destiny is to face this forest with your eyes and heart open. Soul and destiny are closely linked. If you dare take risks, dare let your soul journey into unknown depths, you will encounter your deepest, most authentic self. You will live your destiny. Therein lie dreams you cannot yet imagine."

I still had the long hike back to camp, but this time I would walk with my heart open. I'd see more than my fear.

~

Night has left the forest
With the moistness of its kiss
And upon morning's breaking
The moment of trust arrives
When the decision is made
You open
And the earth receives you

—RUSSELL HUME

five

THINGS EATING THINGS

WHAT'S IAN'S HAIR DOING IN MY FACE? Wish he'd move over. I just need sleep. Half asleep, my hand brushed at the nuisance and touched something warm and alive. Dainty feet scurried across my mouth, over my nose and eyes and got tangled in my hair at the top of my head.

"Iaaaaannnn. Wake up! There's something in my haaair. Quiiiick! Light the candle."

Ian woke instantly. He sat bolt upright, eyes wide open, and said, "Don't move."

It took me a few seconds to adjust to the candle's bright flame, but through squinting eyes I spotted the monster.

"Oh look at him, Ian; he's so cute."

A fat little rat had untangled himself from my hair and sat on the plastic jerry can at the opposite end of the truck. His soft red brown coat shined so clean it looked like someone had washed him and "air-fluffed" him dry. He appeared about half the size of a house rat, and his tail curved around the jerry can spout, long and sleek. He didn't move other than to sit back on his haunches, rest his "arms" on his plump belly and intently peer at us with liquid black eyes. Whiskers, fine as fish line, twitched forward and back. He looked smug and unafraid. I half expected him to giggle, like a rotund little elf.

We waited to see if he'd leave through the open cap door. Instead, he sauntered back into the truck toward me, as if we knew each other. Ian lunged forward, clapped his hands, and Mr. Rat again scurried to the end of the truck, but not outside. He sat for another two minutes and eyed us with keen curiosity, then darted over the tailgate and disappeared in his own good time. We burst into laughter and went back to sleep.

"Mouse Without a House," as Ian called him, came to our truck many other nights. After the first few visits, even though I felt the tickle of "Mouse's" whiskers and the patter of his delicate feet, I never fully awoke. Mouse became as much a part of the night as my dreams. I think he slept some nights curled into a little furry ball in my hair. Teeny tiny mouse snores accompanied Ian's raucous snores and my deep sighs, a little chorus of sleeping life. Later I learned that he was some type of melomys, the local native mouse. He never bit us and never chewed on anything in the Toyota. Mouse appeared to be truck-trained because he never left a calling card.

Morning came with gray clouds that hung so low in the sky they merged with the salty mist that danced in ghostly swirls along the shore. The birds sang, but not with their usual excited chatter. Everything hung heavy and hushed, the prelude to a storm.

We sat and talked while we ate our fruit.

"Hey, Rob-o, why don't we go get some bloody coconuts t'day? Old Jake told me about a place just beyond his camp where coconuts grow right on the beach."

I always disliked hiking south, closer to the outside world, but coconuts sounded mighty good. So after breakfast Ian grabbed our machete and we trudged down the coast. We found the coconut trees on the high-tide line, right where Jake said they'd be. They were tall coconut trees, taller than I expected. Undaunted as usual, Ian clenched the machete tightly between his teeth and scrambled up one of the nut-loaded palms. His bare feet curved around the tree trunk while his hands gripped the trunk above his head. He reminded me of an inchworm as his hands pulled upward and his feet followed. Hands, feet, hands, feet, up he went.

I stood below, well out of harm's way, but still my mouth was tightly pursed and my teeth painfully clenched. A machete is no light hunting knife. I worried he'd drop it and cut himself, but he made it safely to the top, twenty or so feet off the ground. One at a time, the coconuts landed with a dull thud in the soft sand.

I first saw green coconuts in Mexico. The tops were chopped off right through the husk and into the shell. With a straw inserted into the small opening they make a refreshing drink. When the nut is in the green stage the milk is sweet and full of enzymes. The meat is gelatinous and thin. Scooped out with a spoon and eaten raw, it has a mild pleasant taste. Coconuts with brown husks don't have much juice, but they have thick nutty-rich meat.

We could cart only a few coconuts back up the beach to the clearing. We must have looked hilarious with our sarongs removed, stuffed full of coconuts and slung over our shoulders. It became a ritual to hike south every few months and gather a "handful" of coconuts. They were a refreshing and hearty addition to our diet. Green coconut milk poured over raw oats and dates, left to soak, makes a sweet and tasty meal.

The next morning I rose early and found the expected storm blown out to sea, but its lingering fog left the day hot and muggy. I decided to hike into the forest to escape the heat. The air barely stirred under the canopy, but its cool dampness soothed my hot skin. I spent the day with my trees then started back to camp at dusk. Partway down the hill I saw a dark lump on the ground, about the size of a large house cat. I thought it might be a piece of wood or bark, but it moved, which drew me cautiously closer.

Although I hadn't yet seen a bandicoot, I recognized him as a long-nosed bandicoot from a picture in one of my books. A bandicoot is a marsupial (mammal with a pouch) that looks similar to a giant rat with a pointy nose, red brown fur, and long thin tail. They're fabulous diggers and have a rear entry pouch so it won't fill with dirt when they dig. Compared to the photo in my book this one seemed fairly big, so I didn't move too close. I knew almost nothing about bandicoots and worried he might try to bite. Then I noticed something odd about his behavior. He lay half on his side as if unable to walk.

As I slowly moved closer, his eyes stared directly into mine. Fear lifted him onto his feet, but he didn't advance. Bandicoot's hind legs gave out. He collapsed onto his belly with his front legs bent under his chest and his two useless hind legs splayed out behind him. Slowly, he uncurled his front feet, dug his long claws into the soft earth, and tried to pull himself to safety. *Dear God, how far has he gone like that? And now I've scared him by moving too close. Poor little bugger.*

I quietly stepped back a few feet so he wouldn't feel threatened, but he still desperately tried to crawl forward. My heart ached because the movement must have caused him excruciating pain. With each pull his eyes closed and he slumped in defeat. I wanted to reach down and help him, but I didn't know what to do. Had he been cut or torn open, I could have stitched him together with my sutures, except I saw no blood or wounds. Tears of sympathy ran down my face as a soothing voice rose past the lump in my throat to comfort Bandicoot.

"It's okay, little fella. I won't hurt you. What happened to you? Did you fall or did something grab your legs and break 'em? There's no teeth marks. Maybe you're sick. Poor little guy."

At the sound of my soft voice, Bandicoot seemed to relax. He stopped his hopeless clawing and lay on the earth to rest. Half on his side, he opened his eyes to look at me. Very slowly, I crept closer on hands and knees, and with gentled voice I crouched down beside him. I wondered if bandicoots ever died of old age. He didn't look old, but I'd never seen a bandicoot, let alone an old one. He didn't have any white hairs or sagging muscles or jowls, if old bandicoots even have such things. Maybe pythons eat them long before they arrive at a natural death. Although being eaten by a python can be a natural death for a bandicoot.

I still pictured a wise, old, silver-haired bandicoot huddled in a ball under an ancient fallen tree, as both tree and bandicoot slowly decayed into the earth. It was a captivating reverie, but even hidden away from large predators, small predators like ants, maggots, and beetles would eat a dead bandicoot long before it decayed into the forest floor.

He could hardly move, and yet his alert eyes never left mine. He didn't seem afraid anymore; instead I sensed he tried to communicate with me, reach me. Could that be possible? He was a bandicoot and I was a human, and we'd never even seen each other before. I was clearly startled when I became aware of the beseeching intent in his eyes. I couldn't look away. I sat spellbound as he poured the intensity of his entire being down into my gaze and through my soul, as if he transferred everything he knew into me. He pulled thoughts and memories from forgotten corners, and for a fleeting second the wisdom of the earth passed before my eyes. I felt the history of all life inside me, millions of years of my own genetic memory and evolution.

Bandicoot, do you know me? I feel like I know you. You're aware of everything I'm feeling, aren't you? I can see it in your eyes. It's as if you're waiting to see how I'll respond to awareness. You're so small, but size has nothing to do with wisdom or knowing; does it? How do I permanently connect to that mystery? Bandicoot, are you as intelligent as me? What is intelligence anyway? I'm ashamed to say that a large brain doesn't necessarily give my species more wisdom, and certainly not more compassion.

Even in death, Bandicoot lay upon the earth more alive and connected to "the mystery" than me. Under his insightful scrutiny, I felt completely disconnected. Once again, the contrast between what I'd lived and what I now experienced made me feel anger and grief. I was forced to ask questions. How much had I forgotten? How many lies had I believed? Had I buried truth? The part of the story I'd been told all my life was only a fragment of the whole tale, and I began to see the cultural half-truths for what they were. The lie I'd been living lost its transparency. I started to understand that I'd grown up with an outlook on life that had little to do with my animal origins and connection to this living earth, and nothing to do with the woman I really am.

Bandicoot's silent demand that I witness his death, rekindled wild primitive hungers buried deep inside me. I wasn't sure how he had allowed me to experience his connection to everything around him. In flashing seconds of light, I became his awareness. *I understand now, Bandicoot. The more in touch I am with the living world around me, the more alive and aware I am. Possibly more intelligent? Bandicoot, how do you speak directly to me? That's what the trees do. They speak without speaking. But it's more than that. They know my thoughts and feelings.*

Why do we consider animals and plants dumb? What am I saying? We often don't consider anything. That's the problem. It seems we spend a lot of time studying Nature, but very little time learning *from* Nature. Maybe we've become a *logi-stic* society. We put "logy" at the end of a word (*bio-logy, socio-logy, theo-logy*), and it becomes "the study of" instead of "friendship with," like *fellow-ship, relation-ship,* or *bio-ship*. I like that. It puts us ALL together in one big ship, as equals. Is it safer for us to study life rather than experience it? Be it?

Bandicoot whimpered, and I reached down to stroke his fur, but his thoughts stayed my hand.

"Please do not touch me. It will only make the pain worse, and I want it to stop."

I could've wrapped him in my sarong and taken him back to camp; however, I'd made Ian promise me that neither of us would feed nor interfere with the wild creatures. I couldn't break that promise.

"You cannot take me or any other beings from this place, Robin. You can only take what you learn; that is yours. That, and the bond you create with us."

Bandicoot's words humbled me, and I remembered what Old Jake had said.

"Best let Mother Nature take care of herself." I knew Bandicoot didn't want me to carry him to camp, but I wished to prolong his life. Then I could avoid the reality of death. It could have been me who lay on damp earth and clung to vanishing wisps of my rainforest world. Who would witness my passing? A part of me tried to shut out what I *knew* he was about to tell me.

Suddenly, I was drawn away from my thoughts when I realized an audience surrounded us. They'd been there all along, but now I felt their attention focus intensely on Bandicoot and me. When I raised my eyes I saw green and brown energetic beings step from the tree trunks. Well, they didn't really "step"; the Tree Beings seemed to slowly stretch away from the trees until they separated from their trunks and stood free. I watched them extend gently forward to form a circle around Bandicoot and me. Adults, children, and elders, green and brown forms gathered around us. Up until that day, I'd only heard their voices. Now they had faces, and they moved as if they had arms and legs. They were a family of living trees. I almost could have named every one of them, they seemed so intensely familiar. I knew without a doubt that each one had a complete and individual personality and soul. Just like you and me. They were fully alive and knowing beings who could move, think, and feel. Like Bandicoot, they knew everything about me.

"We have taken this form, Robin, because you are now ready to see us. You are ready to believe what you feel and know in your heart."

As if in the midst of a dream, I watched them tenderly approach with heads and arms tipped in compassion. Their love lent swift, piercing contrast to my entire life.

"Robin, it is a great tragedy that many humans no longer converse with the natural world. Your ancestors did, but now most humans see it as simplistic and primitive. As if it's not real or possible. As if we are not real. How did you become so removed from the rest? Do you even realize what has happened?"

I can hardly grasp what I'm hearing and seeing. If this is what life is REALLY like, and I've not been living it, no wonder I've been so ill.

I burst into tears because of my loss. A life of disconnection. Society had severed my connection to spirit and soul. The horror of it chilled my blood. If I didn't heal I would continue to contribute to the severing, not only my own but the collective.

I've swallowed it all. I've gone along with the lie that, as a human, I'm separate and above all other life. I've believed I'm superior, more intelligent, and more spiritual when really I'm the most ignorant and destructive animal on earth.

The circle of Tree Beings moved closer as if to validate what I was seeing. In the past when I'd heard the voice of the trees, I'd never consciously thought I could respond to them and be *heard*. Now I *knew* they heard me and waited for me to acknowledge their presence. I sensed their anticipation, and instead of panic, I felt unusually safe and protected. An ancestral memory sought voice of its own volition. Thoughts and feelings rose from somewhere deep inside me and spoke to the trees.

You knew I'd come to this place. How? Thousands and thousands of miles away, and you've been waiting for me. I can feel it. Your souls are as real as mine.

In that moment, I remembered once reading that animals and plants don't have individual souls and that they're *merely* part of one immense collective soul. The writer believed that only humans are blessed with individuation.

If we took time to listen to our fellow beings, whether it's a tree, rock, or bandicoot, we'd feel their unique and individual souls. If there is a collective soul, aren't we all, humans included, part of it? Are we as separate as we'd like to believe?

The trees responded to my thoughts. "If you do not believe that you are part of the collective soul then you have given yourself license to be unaccountable. It is one of the great human self-deceptions."

Does our sentience make us unconscious?

The trees' love felt unlike anything I'd ever experienced with my own species. The rainforest breathes with living spirits. Animals, plants, and rocks emanate eternal, brilliant intelligence. The life around me seemed so familiar; I felt I'd always known it and it had always known me. I'd merely forgotten my legacy of love, my connection to all things. In that moment of reacquaintance, I remembered what home felt like, or was it heaven? I decided they are one and the same.

Although I could no longer see the Tree Beings, I knew they were there, watching and listening.

I spoke to Bandicoot as I would a dear friend. "Bandicoot, all you've known is this place. But the world I come from isn't the same as here. At times it's a society without soul, without emotional depth and vitality. Have we torn holes in a fabric woven by God? Maybe if we don't have to see how aware you all are, then we can more easily destroy you. But you are us, and we kill ourselves. Is it too late? Have we completely annihilated our connection to the rest of life?"

Thoughts jumped around in my head like hot oil in Old Jake's frying pan. Splendor lived abundantly in the forest, and again I faced death. This time, I found beauty in it. Each thought raised more questions. I found no answers. Only more mysteries.

In the rainforest, life and death are vividly real. Everything has to eat. Everything has to watch out for something else all the time. How do they enjoy life? Do they ever get to play? Or is it always day-to-day survival? I lived in the wild, and I had to be aware of all kinds of things. Yes, the forest was teaching me that awareness is essential for healthy and sustained life.

Lost in thought, I absentmindedly brushed at an itchy sting on my leg, then another and another. I glanced down and saw my legs covered with dozens of black ants. They stung my feet and ankles and crawled up my calves and under my sarong. In a blur of red cloth I unwound the sarong, tossed it aside and ran my palms up and down my legs to brush away the ants. Engrossed in Bandicoot, I hadn't noticed that I squatted on a trail of ants headed for my wounded friend. Had they come to check me out and discovered Bandicoot? Or did a scout find him, go back for reinforcements, and I just happen to be squatting on their return route?

I never thought the ants might try and drag a whole bandicoot back to their nest. Not until I watched in dismay as they formed chains. One ant gripped a twig rooted in the soil. Then they formed a chain as each ant linked wire-thin legs to the ant in front until the last ant gripped Bandicoot's fur with his pincers. A whole bandicoot would be a lot of food to move. Maybe they'd tear him apart and carry him back in pieces. They'd still have to work for hours to do that, maybe days. Is that what Bandicoot is afraid of? He already knew well what I was only starting to learn, the rainforest is no place to be wounded. Mother Nature cleans up after herself. She wastes nothing.

Bandicoot lay helpless, covered with biting insects. Ants swarmed toward the limp, brown body, seeking exposed flesh. He opened his eyes again and pleaded with me. Instead of listening to what he tried to tell me, I frantically stuck my walking stick into the ant trail. Back and forth with the stick I stirred the ants to a frenzy. I swatted with a leafy branch at the ants that clung to Bandicoot. Tears blurred my vision, and a faint whimper escaped from the wounded animal. I ignored the ants on my legs and brushed the ground around Bandicoot with my branch.

Bewildered ants scurried in circles, anxious to find their attacker. While they regrouped, I knelt and tried to decide what to do.

Dead and wounded ants lay scattered everywhere. Glass-thin bodies curled into minute balls of agony, minus legs and antenna, split open abdomens, crushed and still alive. They were *only* ants, but I swore I heard their *whimpers* of agony too. They looked so fragile. Hair-thin legs kicked in every direction as they tried to right themselves and escape.

Amid my tears, with thumb and forefinger, I crushed to death as many of the severely wounded as I could find. Maybe an absurd act, but one I had to do. I loathed suffering of any kind and had harmed them only to end Bandicoot's torment. Instead, I'd caused more suffering and done *nothing* to end Bandicoot's pain. I burned with shame. The smell of formic acid stung my nose, and from somewhere in the forest a voice spoke.

"Robin, the ants are not evil, merely hungry. The dead and wounded are their food. You eat. So do the ants. They are the janitors of the rainforest."

Are you telling me that the exquisite beauty in this forest doesn't exist, that it's really a world full of death? If I'm killed or wounded and can't move, this seething mass of life will eat me dead or alive?

"Robin, beauty in the rainforest is always real. But so is death. Yes, it can eat you down to the bone. Down to dust. Life in this ancient forest does not deny the existence of death. It cannot afford that luxury. If you are to live fully and value *any* life, you must first value your own. To do that you have to acknowledge death. Embrace it and understand it. That is the way of the wild. If you do not approve, go back to your disconnected world. No one will make you stay in the forest."

I wasn't done raging.

There aren't any rules, are there? There's nothing. It's all a sham. Or are you testing me by taking me from the loveliness of the trees to the death of this wounded bandicoot?

"This is no test, Robin. It is not about you. This simply is life. Whether you are here or not, this is how the real world lives and has lived for millennia. It frightens and offends your fragile ego because you are disconnected from your source. Why do you think you are dying?"

I didn't know what to say to that. Spread about the ground in front of me was the aftermath of war, a carnage of tiny crushed ant bodies and one wounded bandicoot. My limp-legged friend rested while the poor ants carried off their dead and dying. They even eat their own.

A few minutes later, the ants reorganized and formed chains around Bandicoot. His breathing had grown shallow and rapid. He probably wouldn't make it to camp alive, even if I broke my promise and carried him back in my red sarong. His dark eyes stared directly into mine. Bandicoot spoke to me one last time. This time I had to listen.

"Hear me, Robin, and do not be afraid. Please end my torment and kill me now. Do this for *me*. The ants will still have their meal, but I will feel no pain."

My hand with a mind of its own reached for a flat gray rock and slowly hid it behind my back. Bandicoot stared at me, waiting. How could I kill him while he watched me? His bite no longer worried me, but I didn't want him to see the rock slam into his small, furry head. I had to move quickly because ants approached by the dozens and already ringed his eyes, like cattle at a water hole.

I squatted away from the ant trail on the opposite side of Bandicoot and with my gentlest voice I tried to soothe my dying friend. Our relationship had grown beyond marsupial and human. We were two souls who communicated in a way both foreign to me and completely innate and natural. I told him things I'm sure he knew better than I did, but it was all I had.

"It's all right, little guy. You're safe and so beautiful. I love you and always will. I won't forget you. I promise."

Bandicoot's eyes slowly closed at the sound of my soft voice. The ants hung on as I slammed the gray rock into his fragile skull. Tears and splattered blood ran together down my face. I was shocked at how little resistance his skull offered, how easily shattered the boundary between life and death. In detached awe I watched some part of Bandicoot's spirit rise and join with mine.

I left the ants their meal, picked up my red sarong and walking stick, and wandered down the hill. The gray rock remained clutched tightly between fingers, stained with blood and formic acid.

Less than a mile up hill from camp, I found the creek. Daylight crept from beneath the forest canopy and left it to the dark of night. With the absence of artificial light in my life, my night vision grew extremely sharp with each passing month. Several hours after dusk, the forest turned to shapes of jet black. I didn't worry as long as I could easily move among the trees and tap my walking stick as I went. Even though I left camp almost every day, I hadn't yet been out all night. Ian might worry that something had happened to me. I hoped he'd stay late at Old Jake's as he often did, then he'd be too distracted to worry.

I rested on a flat rock that overhung the creek and let the babbling water drown the echo of Bandicoot's whimpers. In the dark, moonless night the water appeared black and oily. I didn't want to go back to camp. Something changed in me that day. I grew so far beyond myself, I didn't know if I'd ever be able to get back inside the confines of my body. Or if I even wanted to. Naked and alone in the dark rainforest, I felt safer and more myself than ever before. I wanted to lay my body upon the rainforest floor and sob until I dissolved into soft earth. The ancient life around me actually knew how to love, and was loving me as I sat on my rock and cried.

Somehow bandicoot blood, crushed ant juice, and tears of grief flowed together and set me free. My soul became so huge and infinite that I lost myself in the life around me. No longer separate, I drifted in all directions into the forest. I merged with giant trees, ancient rocks, birds, frogs, and wallabies. The fingers of my soul reached far into the infinite and touched the face of God.[1]

How can I be so many places at once and feel more whole than I've ever felt in my life? I could be lost in such beauty forever . . . and never wish to be found.

The gentle trees spoke, "Robin, let your tears run freely. All life comes from tears. You were carried nine months in the salty ocean of your mother's womb, an ocean not unlike your tears, not unlike the vast seas that swirl around planet Earth and bathe her flesh. Your microbial ancestors dwelled in an ocean of tears long before they evolved and crawled onto land. You do not bind up your laughter, nor should you your tears. They will cleanse and renew your spirit. Surrender yourself to anguish and passion and joy, and lust so intensely you forget yourself in the sheer experience of being alive."

I gave my tears to the creek, and she carried them to the sea. Cold water cleansed the death from my hands, while my soul soaked up love and forgiveness from the trees and stars and infinite universe.

Hours may have passed, maybe only minutes. Perhaps I slept and dreamed it all. When I opened my eyes, I thought I might still be in the midst of a dream. Across the creek, the earth glowed luminous white green, like the light of a hundred pulsing fireflies clustered together in a moment of stillness. It was enchanting. The more I gazed at the glowing light, the darker the forest grew and the brighter the light became, until it appeared to swell and pulse.

The night grew cool so I draped my sarong over my shoulders and waded through black water to the other side of the creek. I clung tightly to the gray rock, worried I'd lose it. Tomorrow I'd return it. When I reached the opposite bank, I again tapped my walking stick to warn nocturnal snakes of my approach. Two feet from the ghostly glow a familiar pungent smell tickled my nose. Fungus. The glow came from luminous mushrooms. I'd read about them but had never seen their fairy magic until that night.

Everything was beautiful and bursting with life, so peaceful. Yet everything fought to stay alive. *Is it possible death isn't what I think it is, something terrible and finite? Maybe death is a simple passing through a door into another reality or awareness. A passage down a hall to another room.*

I tapped my way down the hill and wandered into camp. Ian sat under the tarp reading by candlelight. He didn't see me. At the edge of the clearing, I stood behind a tree and immersed myself in his beauty. Legs, solid with muscle, stretched out in front of him and crossed at the ankles. His face tipped toward his book. Candlelight shone on his high cheekbones and thin straight nose.

You've no idea how handsome you are. You're romantically beautiful and entirely masculine.

His golden hair, streaked from hours in the sun, had grown long and curled about his neck. Half his face was hidden under thick, shiny beard. I loved his beard, but missed seeing his square jaw. Shadows cast from his long, thick eyelashes made them appear twice their length.

I stepped from behind my tree and softly spoke his name.

"Ian?"

"Thought I heard a bloody tapping noise." Relief chased anxiety from his face. "Bloody strewth, Rob-o, am I glad to see you. Crikeys, it's late. It's been dark for hours. I yelled a couple of times, mate. Didn't you hear me?" "No. I was sitting on a rock by the creek. The water must have drowned you out. I might have dosed off for a bit. I'm sorry. I know you're worried. I would be too. You look tired, so why don't we talk about it in the morning? I'm really glad to see you. Got lots to share, but it can wait till tomorrow."

"Rob, just tell me one thing, are you okay?"

"Oh I'm fine; it just seems like I've cried all day long. It's a miracle in some ways. I'll try and explain it to you at brekkie. You wanna go to bed?" Ian was great. As long as he knew I was okay, he was happy. He had every reason to be concerned. I'd been walking barefoot in the dark with venomous snakes and other potentially dangerous forest creatures. In the morning, we'd have to come to some kind of agreement. I knew he worried. Each day I grew more wild. And more sane.

As we crawled into the truck, I thought about my experience earlier that evening when my soul had left my body and merged with the forest. That night Ian and I made love, and my soul again left my body.

Ian was a wonderfully intense man, extremely passionate and deeply emotional about everything. He was born with a wild, untamed nature. We both were. That's one of the things that drew us together. With Ian, love-making had little to do with technique or performance. Those things had no meaning to him or me. Loving happened instinctively and was motivated by breathless desire and beauty. It stirred our souls to life. We didn't set out to make it that way. It just happened. It's who we were together. Lovemaking was languid and sensual, a deeply moving experience that often lasted hours and always left me changed and healed.

That evening, as bone and flesh dissolved, I lost all physical form and could not find arm or leg, hand or foot. I became a mass of spinning atoms that spun faster and faster and turned into weightless, boundless energy. I had no control over mind or body, nor did I want any. I forgot myself in the love and ecstasy, and as swirling atoms spun outward I let go.

Suddenly the entire Milky Way galaxy lay spread before me. I floated in the midst of its millions upon millions of stars that made up a vast organism, a physical body comprised of revolving atoms. I felt its knowing and awareness. It knew me. It was *loving* me.

Through the eyes of that vastness, I looked upon myself and saw a smaller galaxy of whirling stars tenderly nested within the larger galaxy. In my own way, I existed immense and infinite as the Milky Way. Billions of stars shaped my body, and I was loving them. Were they loving theirs?

I was infinite within the infinite. I journeyed into worlds beyond this one, into dimensions I hadn't known to exist. Ian felt both my wild beauty and his own. His warm tears fell upon my face. Not one word was spoken.

I swam in a deep immutable river where all life swam with me, so motivated by love and ecstasy that swimming was effortless. Life compelled, with no choice but to live . . . and live . . . and live.

While he quietly slept I lay in his arms until just before dawn and thought about the rainforest and how it was changing me. As each day passed, the forest unraveled the old fabric of my life and wove a new and tougher substance in its place, one so organic and energetic that it demanded my full presence.

I could barely comprehend the mysteries of life and death I discovered in the forest. My awareness changed rapidly, and although I tried I could barely convey the changes to Ian. Many stories went untold. However, my connection to him existed beyond the short time we'd been together. My path wasn't his, nevertheless he understood my consuming relationship with the forest as if it was his own. He always understood me, not just what I said or felt, but who I am. Like the trees, he just knew. He eagerly listened to my tales and insights. More important, he encouraged me because he knew that my time with the trees was essential for my survival.

Through the night while I lay beside Ian, I made a choice. I decided that I would not live in an autistic state; it no longer needed to be part of my reality. It would not exist in the new story or dream that I chose to create. I would completely open myself to life and let my body, mind, and spirit heal. *Do I dare be that powerful? That responsible? Yes, I do.*

As the gray of early dawn colored the sky, my mind wandered and I finally dozed. In my dream, I stood before wounded Bandicoot and crushed ants. A faraway voice echoed off the trees and spoke to me. I tried hard to grasp the strange words.

"There are no rules in the rainforest, Robin. No right or wrong. No good or bad. It is not your place to judge. Your rigid rules and feeble education, your 'should' and 'supposed to be' do not apply here. You are not in charge. The forest takes care of itself. This is a different realm than your disconnected society. The lessons you must learn in the forest differ from anything you have ever been taught. A whole other set of laws apply here, the laws of the universe. Be aware and learn without judgment. Respect all life. Do not kill *anything* unless you need to eat or defend your life. Stay alive. And stay free."

Tumultuous thoughts tossed me about until I awoke. I listened to Ian's deep breathing and tried to sort through my feelings. In the forest, life is stark, raw, and vigorously alive. I was the outsider here, the one who had been lost and out of touch with the natural world. My life had been stunted by fear and ignorance.

What happened to our relationship with earth? How did our species lose daily intimate contact with her? Rain on bare flesh and wind through our hair, sometimes cold and life-threatening, sometimes miraculous and life-giving. What happened to the gathering of food on hands and knees, fingers stained with berry juice and brown root? From womb to grave, our bare feet rarely touch the living earth. We've lost the season-to-season nourishment and with it our attunement to Mother Nature, our greatest source of love. We fly to the moon, and yet we're farther away from the stars than ever before.

As my thoughts wandered, I remembered how one of my schoolteachers told me and my classmates, "The human race is now at the pinnacle of advancement." The word *advancement* automatically implied everything better and good.

Since my meeting with the Tree Beings, something changed in me. I had merged with them and felt them inside me, all around me as if I was now part of them. Maybe I always had been. In my mind, an unused door that hung on rusted hinges slowly creaked opened. Wisdom burst through the gap with lightning speed. I tried to keep up. I could hardly grasp how adrift I'd been over the years. I'd amputated myself from the natural world, the world I originally came from.

No matter how scientific, educated, or advanced we become, our whole society appears unconscious. We seem to accept our separation from other species as an established reality. We talk of finding intelligent life on other planets, and yet we rarely recognize intelligent life on our own planet. It's all around us. Until we learn to treat other species with respect, I hope we never find life on other planets. Heaven help them. "Hey, you guys, if you're out there, run for your lives!"

With these insights, I began to appreciate how visionary my parents were. They took all six of their kids into the beauty of Nature: camping, hiking, and canoeing. But even with my parent's gifts, there were times I perceived the natural world as a painted backdrop. When my hands and feet didn't touch leaves and rocks and water and earth, the things that children love, when long days and months were filled with books, desks, artificial light, bare walls, and sitting still, disconnection occurred. I still had to go to school; it controlled the greater part of my life. It was then that Nature hung at the rear of the stage—a mere prop—while I carried out the petty drama of my so-called real life. On the stage of society, my performance was pitiful at best. Fortunately, in the rainforest I recognized the gifts my parents gave me, especially the time we had spent together in the woods. I was able to draw on a reservoir of inner strength and courage, and managed to confront my fears and not run from the forest. I'd been given a love of Nature when my parents traded our TV for the outdoors, and that love would include the rainforest, no matter how afraid I became.

I remember arriving home from school one day to find the family TV gone. I ran crying to Mom in the kitchen, "Mama, where's the TV? How come it's not in the living room?"

Mom calmly said, "Daddy will explain when he gets home. Why don't you go in the backyard and play? It's nice out."

At that age it didn't mean a lot when Dad said, "You're watchin' too much TV. And I don't think it's healthy for you."

My sister, older brother, and I kicked up a royal ruckus over no more TV. But it was soon forgotten while helping Dad build an ice skating rink in the backyard, forgotten while camping and fishing on Pickerel Pond, forgotten while hiking up Streaked Mountain, Patch Mountain, and Mount Washington, forgotten while he taught me how to ski, swim, and handle a canoe.

One spring day of my senior year in high school, Dad and I paddled the length of Lake Pennesseewassee. Mayflies lay on the water's surface by the thousands. Trout fed in a frenzy on their delicate bodies. Dad scooped a handful of lacy-winged insects from the water and asked, "Did you know that when mayflies hatch they live for only one day? Isn't life amazing?" Then, out of the blue, he said, "Robsy, I took the TV away from you kids because I wanted you living life, not watching it."

In the rainforest, I came face-to-face with old memories and unexplored realities. I felt punched in the gut with more truth than I thought my thin body could experience, but I did experience it. Furthermore, I had no desire to stop Nature's unveiling truth. I was finally in an environment where meaningful information was communicated to me in a clear and solid way, and I wanted to take it in. Observations and questions passed rapidly through my mind. I had to pay attention.

How much of our illness, physical or psychological, is a result of our disconnection and its manifestations? Are we so completely isolated that we no longer identify or empathize with other life forms, with our "Mother"? Ourselves? Maybe I'm not the only one who has lived in an autistic state. Could it be that "civilization" is autistic? And we don't even know it. If autism is being withdrawn or cut off from "Mother" or "Source," emotionally detached, unable to really feel or see or hear her presence, unable to interact or communicate, performing repetitive movements and compulsive routines, unable to be aware of other people's feelings, then our relationship to planet Earth has become an autistic one.

Without realizing, I instinctively began to repattern my nervous system using the rainforest as a template. How immense and loving my Mother was. In the forest close to her wild heart, I clearly saw the extent of my "taming." In the outside world I had lived like a zoo animal that lives out its life in an existing sort of way. Maybe some species approach a modicum of contentment, but for others the "wild memory" never goes away, and once removed from a relationship with Mother Earth they die a lonely, grievous death.

One of my earliest memories of the death of wildness was when Dad and I once drove along the bank of the Androscoggin River in Maine. I was probably seven years old, and I remember putting my hand over my nose and asking, "Daddy, why does it stink so bad? How come the water's so brown?"

"Oh, I think it's from paper and textile mills. They're polluting the river."

"What's polluting?"

"Oh, that means they're probably dumping waste from the mills into the water. It makes it dirty and smell like that. But look at her, Rob. She's still beautiful. Hundreds of years ago, Indians paddled up this river in their birchbark canoes. They'd have traveled 'round that bend right there. Can't you almost see 'em? I can. Just think how clean it musta been back then before the mills were here. You could have drunk the water. Not anymore. Probably doesn't even have fish in it now. Too polluted. We've destroyed all the wildness."

I leaned forward to look out Dad's window, and through his eyes I saw what the river might once have looked like. When he said, "Boy, wish I'd been alive then," his longing pierced my heart, lodged deep inside and resurfaced years later in Australia.

The rainforest blazed a trail of truth through my mind and bit-by-bit, like pieces of a jigsaw puzzle, I put together a whole picture of my life. From that picture arose a new awareness that brought a different kind of anger. I poured out my hurt and anger to the trees. I knew they listened.

This rainforest is more civilized than anything I've ever known. As a child, all the big rivers I saw were brown and frothy with putrid foam. Nothing lived in them. They were sewers, toxic veins running through Mother Earth. That can't be healthy. But it has been that way for as long as I can remember.

Although the sight of the contaminated Androscoggin disgusted and shocked me as a kid, at the time I just thought, *This is how things are.*

It wasn't until Dad painted a picture of the original people traveling a pristine waterway full of fish that I consciously knew we were capable of being unkind to the earth.

My torrent of anger set free a flood of questions.

Have we grown used to a high level of disconnection? And are we . . . addicted . . . to our disconnection? Have we unknowingly slipped into a seemingly blissful twilight hour never to return? As the day ends will we end with it? Can you hear the bells toll? They sing, "Awaken, awaken."

I'd unleashed a monster and wanted to rant. The trees would not stop me. Initially my angry behavior disgusted me, but then part of me was fascinated by the outpouring. I even wondered if we had traded healthy anger for complacence and violence. Had I? Musty rooms in my mind were being opened to air out dust and decay. It was a good thing; anger brought forth my awakening. Regardless of its purpose, I couldn't stop it.

In a state of detachment we cut down trees that take decades, sometimes hundreds, even thousands of years to reach the sky. Gone in minutes. We never know them or treat them with respect, but then we often don't treat each other with respect. We create wars. We commit genocide against millions of people. We destroy air, water, and food, and slaughter innocent animals. What things have we come to accept in our day-to-day lives without thinking of the repercussions? Is this who we want to be? We ask why children are filled with rage. Why they rebel. Why they have no respect for their elders. We're not respecting them; we're destroying their world.

Slowly, my ball of anger unwound to its very end of shock and despair. Shortly before full light, exhaustion ended my raving and I fell asleep. Once again I dreamed. I always did. Rust-colored pine needles carpeted the ground at my feet. I wore white and blue tennis shoes, something I didn't wear anymore. I bent to remove the shoes so I could feel soft brown needles beneath my bare feet, but my hands couldn't reach the laces. Splashes of yellow buttercups grew among the trees. The woods were silent except for soft whispers of wind through pine. Warm sun made the day gentle and golden.

If only I could lie at the feet of the trees and dream with them.
When I couldn't find my body, I wept.
Please let me rest on this bed of warm pine needles. When I die, scatter my ashes in a grove of whispering pines, and I'll be at peace forever.

Dreams are funny things. They jump around and take me many places at once. I try to follow and learn. One moment I felt serene, and the next moment the trees were gone, replaced with stumps and burned debris, and I felt very uneasy. Then just as quickly they reappeared, and their towering trunks had no lower branches. They'd been sawn off. The trees grew straight and tall, without limbs. Suddenly the earth spun beneath me, around and around, a blur of brown and green, flashes of sun and yellow flowers. A sudden stop. Brown trunks radiated in straight lines, neat rows in every direction.

No lower branches? Straight rows? That's weird.

Then a voice said, "Robin, you cannot die here because the trees won't be here when your time is up. They are crop trees."

I'd never heard the term *crop trees*, but I instinctively knew the pines would be hacked down, dead bodies piled onto a logging truck, taken to a mill—a slaughterhouse for trees—and run through a screaming saw. Butchered and sold for lumber.

Do the trees know they're gonna die?

The sound of my crying finally woke me.

Exhausted, I crawled out of the truck and told Ian my dream. Somehow it made my time in the rainforest of Cape Tribulation more precious. Once again, I began to grasp that there were greater fears than venomous snakes. There were humans.

By the time I finished breakfast, I'd grown to accept the ants' job of cleaning the forest. They too are entitled to eat. We do. Except most of the food we eat suffers intolerably before it's slaughtered or harvested. We kill even when we're not hungry. We kill out of fear and greed. Sometimes we don't know why we kill. Or that we have killed.

As I hiked up the creek to return my gray rock to its home, I thought of my conversation with Ian that morning. We agreed that if we went to Cairns I would learn about snakebite treatment. My book showed how to use ACE bandages (long stretchy bandages) to bind the puncture area and the whole limb to slow the spread of venom, and then how to attach a splint. At best, we had only two ACE bandages. Eventually, I'd need four or five of them. Ian also suggested that we should purchase a loud police whistle. Since I hiked quite a distance most days, I doubted he'd hear it, but he thought it might guide him to me if I didn't return. I dug my blue fanny pack out of the back of the truck, put the two bandages and my dad's hunting knife inside, and strapped it around my waist. We did what we could for the moment and then had a serious talk. As I explained to Ian the need to be really aware in the forest, he gave me a sidelong glance, shook his head, laughed, and said, "You bloody thrive on that. Don't you?"

I laughed and said, "Well, yes, I'm beginning to. The more conscious I am of the *rainforest*, the more conscious *I* am. Having to be more aware makes me feel intensely alive. I don't wanna ever die, Ian, but if something happened to me in this forest, I'd rather die here taking risks and *really* living than die a hundred years old never having lived. I'm happy in the woods. Some things still kinda freak me out and scare me, but you're right, I thrive on the challenge. I guess I'm like Dad in that way. Besides, I'm beginning to see that there's really very little to fear in this rainforest. I think almost all of the dangers have been in my imagination, kinda like a social paranoia that I've swallowed. It's got to the point that I'd stay in the forest, at least for a while, even if I didn't know you."

Ian looked pleased, sad, and wistful all at once. It didn't occur to me at the time that he might feel like he was losing me, not to another man but to my love affair with the forest.

He shook his head and grinned. "Strewth, Rob-o. You're the bloody smartest person I know. I see how much you've changed, mate, and how fast. Fair dinkum, you could do about anything. Nothing would surprise me anymore. Really proud of you, Rob-o. Just promise me you'll be bloody careful, and if you think you might be out after dark let me know, eh?"

Ian went quiet for a bit, and his eyes looked inward. I waited. Whenever he divulged an inner fear or secret he grew still, trying to decide if he wanted to share or not. He once told me that it was never a matter of trusting me, only a matter of whether or not he could face his feelings.

"It's weird, Roby, I think I got me fear of snakes from social conditioning too. I'm only starting to realize that I've always been afraid of them, bloody *terrified* of them. I couldn't even tell you that at the reptile park. You kept asking me why I was so quiet. Well, I freaked seeing all those snakes. Sometimes when I get scared, I just shut it all out. Most people I know are terrified of them too, so I didn't think my reaction was odd. But I'm starting to see that in most cases my fear isn't about snakes. Though knowing that doesn't make it go away."

"Give it time, Ian. And I want you to know that I'll be really careful. Okay? I wanna stay alive. I'm beginning to learn that being in the forest is much safer than being in a city. It's actually very safe. Hey, did you know that I know how to whistle?"

"What do you mean by that, Rob? Don't most people?"

"No, I don't mean that kind of whistling."

I stuck the index and middle finger of both hands in my mouth and let loose an ear-piercing blast. When Ian plugged his ears, I laughed. We decided that until I had a police whistle my fingers would do.

Ian's earlier words of high praise touched me deeply as I continued up the hill. His love followed me into the forest and went everywhere with me. I contemplated his fear of snakes and found it interesting that even though he remained afraid of them, he didn't judge them in the way that I did. The snakes weren't evil or revolting to him; he was simply terrified of them. He taught me that sometimes fear and judgment could be two separate things. Unlike my initial reaction to the basic laws of Nature, Ian placed no judgment on the snakes or the life-and-death struggles he witnessed in the forest. After the past few weeks I'd learned that revulsion didn't exist in the rainforest. It existed only within the context of my conditioning.

Mother Nature doesn't judge, that's a human thing. However, she sure knows how to look after herself. She's a tough but fair old taskmaster, and I began to fall in love with her blunt and unforgiving laws. I finally knew where I stood. There was no guesswork, nothing twisted or vague, nothing complicated about Nature. I liked that. Sure, I had to be aware if I wanted to stay alive, but I was starting to like that too. It meant I had to be responsible for my actions for the first time in my life. Society had easily allowed me to be irresponsible.

As I meandered farther uphill between the trees, I began to recognize that my fear of death had started to change in the forest. Close to the earth, the thought of death didn't feel dark and alone, not like it had in the outside world of institutions, metal, and concrete. "Alone" didn't mean that others wouldn't sit with me while I died. Alone meant that I might not be part of something safe and intensely familiar, something greater than myself that had *always* known me, and I it. Something that *loved* me. In the past I'd often thought my death would be empty and soulless, as if only darkness remained when life snuffed out. No returning home. No peace. In the forest, I learned that was not true. I also knew that if I had to, I'd always fight like a demon for my life. I desperately wanted to live, but if I did die in the forest I would not die alone. Here with the trees, death would be such a part of life that I would merely be going home to the love that created me, the love that we all *are*. It wasn't death that I had feared, but my disconnection from Mother Earth and the infinitely compassionate Spirit of Life.

Lost in thought, I quickly arrived at the place where I'd left Bandicoot. I found the indentation in the earth where the gray rock lived. It fit perfectly. I patted its smooth round surface, like a friend. All the rainforest sighed with relief at the small stone's safe return. It had traveled millions of years to that exact spot. Who was I to change its path?

No signs of Bandicoot remained other than a few drops of dried blood from his crushed skull. No column of ants marched back and forth like the day before, only an occasional lone ant. We had no rain through the night or that morning to wash away fresh tracks, but the soil always felt damp since we were in the midst of the wet. When I squatted closer to the ground, I saw a faint drag path in the dirt where something hauled Bandicoot away. It seemed inconceivable that the ants could have dragged him off, but there were no dingo (domestic dog) crosses or feral pig tracks, no python slithers in the soft earth. Most snakes, including pythons, usually eat their food live, although not always. I tended to think it wasn't a snake that took him, but I wasn't sure. A pig, dingo, or goanna might have had a go at Bandicoot, but there were no tracks. Bandicoot might have been torn apart and chewed, except there was no new blood. No skin or bones.

On hands and knees, I followed the drag trail two feet uphill then a foot under some young tree ferns, to a pile of good-sized rocks, a bit of debris across a rock, and then nothing. The rocks fit snugly together and left no caves or holes.

Had the ants dragged Bandicoot to their nest and down a hidden hole? If so, how did they get Bandicoot inside? Did they dismember him? Could they do that in less than twenty-four hours? What about his bones and fur? Maybe a kite or eagle or other carrion eater had taken him? But I couldn't recall having seen them under the canopy. And what had made the drag marks?

With my nose to the ground, careful not to disturb anything, I took a slow trip around the rock pile in search of tracks or signs of disturbed soil. I started where the drag path left debris on a rock and disappeared. With my face down at soil level I spied an opening underneath an overhanging stone. It remained protected from rain. A neat undisturbed pile of ant tailings lay at the mouth of the dark hole. It appeared just big enough to haul a flattened bandicoot through, but there were no drag marks in front of the entrance. Maybe the tailings were fresh and covered the drag path. I knew Bandicoot hadn't hauled himself there with a smashed skull.

From a safe distance I looked into the cavity. If anything hid in its dark interior, I couldn't see it. The desire to know niggled at me so strongly that I contemplated sticking my hand in the darkness, but it was a perfect place for a snake to curl up and rest. I cursed when I didn't have a flashlight or match.

There was another remote possibility. A couple of stout branches hung about two feet above the rock pile and ran parallel to the drag marks. It *might* have been possible for a huge python to dangle some of its length from the branch, grab Bandicoot, drag him along the ground for a bit, then lift him up onto the branch and swallow him whole. It's possible the python lay draped in the tree and watched the whole time I sat with Bandicoot. He could have grabbed him right after I left. In fact, he *might* have been in the process of killing Bandicoot *before* I arrived and scared him off. He could have waited until I left and then gone back to his meal.

Snakes are strong, solid muscle. I'd seen them do unbelievable feats of daring. Ian and I once saw a yellow-bellied snake climb a twenty-foot branchless coconut tree. How did he do it? When the fronds drop off palm trees they leave small ribs all the way up the trunk. Mr. Yellow Belly very slowly zigzagged his way, rib-to-rib, up the side of the coconut palm. After we found several coconuts with round holes in them, we knew why he'd gone up there: to eat the rats and mice that ate the coconuts. He smelled their trail and climbed the tree to hide and wait. As the unsuspecting rodents sat down to dine, so did the snake. Isn't life extraordinary?

The Bandicoot riddle went unsolved. While I sat beside the rock pile, I realized I could live a hundred years in the forest and never know all her secrets. However, if I remained patient and observant, I would see things so remarkable and rare that I might only see them once in a lifetime and never again.

The intimate life of the rainforest sparked keen curiosity and left me vibrantly alive. As I hiked back down the hill to the beach, a new exciting possibility came to light. Maybe I wasn't dumb and lacking curiosity like I'd been taught in school to believe. I began to suspect that I might have capacity for infinite intelligence. Doesn't all life?

A secret smile curled across my face, and my bare feet danced along the forest floor, lightened by joy and hope. Somewhere, Bandicoot knew.

Surrogate life shatters in the crush of corporeal reality
Exposing the raw process of living
Shocked out of judgment
Embracing the unashamed honesty of existence
I come to know love

—RUSSELL HUME

six

THE WAY OF THE EARTH

A RACKET OF WIND AND RAIN JOLTED ME from sleep. Our tent, which had been stretched like an awning from the back of the truck, wildly flapped about. One side had come loose and the aluminum tent pole banged against the truck. We'd need stronger poles driven farther into the ground. I woke Ian, and we hastily tied everything down, closed the cap windows, and put our gear into the truck.

Down below on the beach, the sea raged like a thunderous monster. The canopy above the clearing wasn't as thick as most of the forest, and we weren't as protected.

The storm didn't bother me because I was used to storms and had been through worse. However, a dream I'd had just before waking clung to me like a fortune-teller's prediction. I'd started to see my future, and it left me inspired but uneasy. The future wasn't something I yearned for, not yet. All I wanted was to be in the forest. If I passed the day with Ian it might dispel my mood, except I didn't want to spend all day in the truck.

"Hey, Ian, do you wanna go for a hike with me? We could walk along the beach."

"Naaaw, not me, mate. Too wet and windy. Maybe a cyclone's coming. I ain't even going to Old Jake's t'day. Why don't you crawl in and read with me?"

"I feel too restless to read."

I was annoyed with him and hurt because he didn't want to walk north up the beach with me. He lounged contentedly in the back of the truck and read his Larry and Stretch paperbacks. Most days, I easily accepted that he didn't want to adventure with me. I loved my time alone, but that morning I wanted his company.

I stood naked in the rain by the tailgate and watched him read. He looked so content, snuggled in the truck. Nonetheless, I still hoped my dejected face would change his mind. When it didn't, I still decided to go for a walk. It might help with my churning emotions. For the moment, I needed to forget about my dream and the future. All I had was the present.

Life's funny how it works. Leaving Ian in camp that day and going out into the storm on my own required that I accept and experience the uncontrollable elements of Nature. That included the weather, Ian, and my own emotions. There was something humbling, even reassuring knowing that as a human I was not the greatest force on earth. There existed forces far greater than myself that would either push me into more heightened awareness or kill me. Daily, I chose awareness.

Head bent to the wind, I trudged north up the beach. Waves crashed on hard sand. Sea and grit stung my eyes and skin. Unleashed energy smashed into my chest and evoked wild exhilaration. The gale's ferocity crushed my agitation. In disregard to my sensibilities, Mother Nature force-fed me the soul of the storm. Pumped full of power, I thrilled at the howling wind and squealed with delight as it buffeted me in circles, forward and backward. I didn't mind; I *wanted* to eat the life of the storm. I felt like a grizzled old sea captain standing on the deck of his schooner, weathering a man-eating tempest. No safe harbor for me, matey. I'm sailin' straight into the belly of the whale.

Never again would I complain if Ian didn't hike with me. I'd grab every opportunity to experience such wildness. Yet as I looked across the tops of the thrashing waves toward the horizon, I couldn't help but wonder if someone was out there sitting in a life raft. Lost at sea. Alone. My heart wrenched at such a possibility. The sea is a vast place to be alone. *If you are out there, I'm thinking of you. Don't give up hope.*

The Great Barrier Reef lay out there, and beyond her coral ridges lay open sea. It would be rough water. As if to protect the Daintree Rainforest, the reef sat like a guardian off the coast and usually prevented large crashing waves from touching our beach. I remembered reading that she stretches over 2,000 km (1,242.8 miles) along the east coast of Queensland, from Bundaberg to the tip of Cape York. The world's largest living organism, she can be seen from outer space. Enormous swells crash upon the reef and lose momentum before they continue on to gently lap the shore of Cape Trib. Although the waves at Trib weren't the mountainous blue-green curls of Kirra Beach farther south, during a storm they often writhed tumultuously, full of sand and seaweed. Their frothy tops heaved as passionately as naked lovers. The wind beckoned, and the sea followed.

My eardrums ached and each blink of my eyes ground sand beneath my lids, so I turned away from the sea and disappeared into the trees. Beneath the canopy, the wind blew less ferociously. Rain didn't bite my skin the way it had in the open. It ran in rivulets down tree trunks and lazily dripped off leaves. The relative quiet calmed my nerves and allowed the ache in my ears to subside. I knelt on the earth to rest and catch my breath. I wanted to worship in the greatest cathedral ever built. As I praised the life I'd been given, I felt how earth's superb beauty must have moved early humans to spontaneous prayer and worship. I had once read that it was *only* the hard times that moved people to pray, but in the forest I experienced something different and knew it to be more than that. As my relationship with the earth deepened, prayer was a natural response to her beauty, mystery, and love.

Nature had become my church, different from the church I'd known in my youth. I remembered, as a little girl how I wore my patent leather shoes and white socks to Sunday service. My toes hurt, crammed into the stylish point. The rise and fall of the minister's voice floated above my head while I doodled on my pad of paper, feeling as cramped as my toes. My sister and I giggled at the hushed formality of the affair and how our slightest whisper echoed off the high ceilings and drew indignant scowls. The dead animals draped around the collars of women's coats fascinated us, and the see-through veils that hung off the front of frivolous hats seemed glamorous. The men reminded me of tidy rows of penguins in their dark suits, white shirts, and bow ties.

My only memory of Sunday school was the smell of musty rooms, stale air filled with disinfectant and old, yellowed floor wax. Sitting on hard folding chairs made me restless. One Sunday, without notice, we stopped going to church. On a drive one day to pick up bread for Mom, Dad and I passed the white, steepled building. I asked, "How come we don't go to church anymore, Daddy? Why do you read to us from the Bible and those other books?" Dad called them stories of human courage and inner strength. "Why do we stay home and talk and read every Sunday morning?"

"Well, Robsy, one day I realized that you don't have to belong to a church to be close to God. God is everywhere."

"Even in this car?"

"Yup, even in this car."

"Even in the *baaathtub*?"

Dad chuckled and said, "Yup, even in the bathtub."

Over the years my father's "Sunday readings" came from the Bible, *The Power of Positive Thinking* by Norman Vincent Peale, *The Teachings of Don Juan* by Carlos Castaneda, and others. I remember stories of how prayer changed people's lives, accounts of people who had overcome illness, drugs, alcohol, pain, and poverty. As a child, I found it tedious and booooring, except for the occasional *Guideposts* adventure story where someone became lost in the wilderness and prayed for guidance and strength. As an adult, I started to appreciate Dad's desire to influence his children's lives in a positive way.

I thought of all this as I knelt in the rainforest. I hoped Mom and Dad were doing okay. I gave thanks for my time far away from the rest of the world, my chance to heal close to Mother Earth. It was changing my life.

Under the trees, birds and frogs boldly challenged the wind and rain. I don't know why, but I waited for something more. It came. A slow groan and creak, like the breaking of a thousand dry bones, fragmented my thoughts. A loud riflelike crack ripped the air as a huge elephantine tree snapped from its mooring. Leaves rattled, branches bent, and birds screeched their outrage at the unexpected disruption. The tree slammed into the earth with a thud I felt through the soles of my feet. Excitement shot through my body. This was a spectacular event, something akin to a tornado or an eclipse. I raced through the forest, chasing a memory of sound. I found my fallen giant with its broken trunk, like a great splintered claw.

Wary of green tree ants, snakes, and centipedes, I clambered over the arms of the fallen tree and searched every reachable branch for bird's nests, staghorn ferns, and wild creatures. With my ear to the trunk, I listened for hollows filled with native "stingless" bees. There might be honey. I found the weak spot that ended the giant's life, a rotten place in the trunk—maybe an old lightning strike. Vines entangled in the branches stretched upward to the still-standing trees. The moment the tree timbered, all things green and alive would compete for the glistening rays of light that shone through the hole in the canopy. The plants knew where their source of sustenance came from, and they knew they had competition.

I left my memories of Dad and the fallen tree behind and hiked farther uphill. I came to another large toppled tree, probably felled by the mighty hand of some other storm. Its titanic trunk had turned spongy and was partially covered with velvet green moss. The opening it would have left in the canopy had long since closed. I sat on the ground beside the once-living body and gently ran my fingers over its mossy softness.

There wasn't much activity around me. Except for frogs, everything hid under log, leaf, and rock, anywhere away from the torrential rain. Some of the water droplets were so fat that one drop would easily drown an ant, beetle, or spider. Heavy rain had pummeled the earth off and on for weeks. Lashing, wet wind bent the tops of palms and tore out their green hair. Naked trunks stood as solemn reminders of Mother Nature's formidable force. That summer I finally made friends with the rain. In warm tropical air with only my naked body, I had nothing to keep dry while I hiked among the trees. Day after day and week after week, rain sang to me in primitive rhythms. The scent and feel of rain seeped deeply into my soul until I forgot I was Robin and thought I was Rain. Constantly, day and night, the patter of billions of falling drops kissed the canopy. Enveloped in their song, my love affair with the forest became an intimate solitary experience. I felt reborn into another lifetime. I definitely stood on planet Earth, but little else of me or my old reality remained the same. Yet each day I felt more familiar to myself. I remembered who I am. I'd never be able to go back, not ever again. Even if I physically returned to Maine in a boat or plane, I would never be the same. Something had changed forever.

I dwelled in peace, excruciatingly sweet, flawless in its completeness. Each day and many nights, I soaked up the rainforest's offering of love. I was nothing more than forest. Through wind, fog, and rain, I saw life more clearly than ever before.

Life is astoundingly intelligent. No. . . that's not right. Life IS intelligence. No wait . . . intelligence IS.

I lived so close to the tiniest ant and the most towering tree that I witnessed intelligence (the IS) in motion, millions of years of evolution and refinement of life. Did you ever think about evolution and how it happens? That summer and summers after, I did. In the rainforest many species were in the midst of evolution. Some species sprouted legs, some shed their legs, others shed tails, still others adapted to plentiful rain and low light. Some species appeared to have perfected their evolution, like the saltwater crocodile. They're the only living members of the class Archosauria, the ruling reptiles of the Mesozoic Era. Their ancestors first arrived on earth 200 million years ago, *before* the extraordinary dinosaur age. They were alive when Tyrannosaurus rex, the earth's most daunting predator, roamed the planet. Crocs are *still* here. They survived the breakup of the continents. Their genetic blueprint is so tough and dynamic that they survived the ice ages of the last 2 million years when sheets of ice periodically covered the earth. Early humans and crocodiles were driven to the equator's lazy warmth to survive.

As my concept of Nature expanded, I recognized that every atom has its function. Everything has its place in the unfolding of life; human, insect, pine needle, rock, and water are unique and each contributes to the other. Even the estuarine crocodile, who on extremely rare occasion eats a human being, is millions of years of perfection in the making.

I remembered something Old Jake had told Ian. "Crocodiles have traveled millions of years down the evolutionary highway to be threatened by extinction in the last sixty years, all due to bloody human greed. Millions of years down the drain for a few rotten bucks. Makes you bloody sick, eh?"

Sixty years? That's a blink of an eye in the history of the saltwater crocodile. Wildlife the world over struggles daily to survive. The planet is currently in the midst of an extinction so extensive that it's the sixth most serious threat to life on earth during its entire history. We've irrevocably altered the face of our environment for millennia to come. We humans tend to believe we're impervious to just about everything, but mass extinction is not a new thing. It has happened before and will probably happen again. What's unique about the current extinction? It's being caused by one species. Humans. Will other beings one day talk about us the way we talk about the dinosaurs? Humanity? Is that too kind a word for how we humans treat our fellow beings? Humane. I associate that word with a gentle, thoughtful, and protective nature. Are we humane?

We've walled ourselves off from wildlife, shut ourselves safely in our houses, offices, and cars—our boxes—so we aren't attacked or eaten. We domesticated other species, and in the process domesticated ourselves. We've almost completely removed ourselves from the food chain and are finally safe. But is there a new threat? Could the very thing we once did to survive as a species now be killing us? Could we be killing ourselves because we are no longer in touch with the wild world? A world that we are inescapably bound to and need if we are to survive physically, emotionally, and spiritually? Would a compassionate relationship with our wild brethren, one that is benevolent, honest, and of mutual purpose, help us value their necessary place in our lives? We are seriously flirting with extinction. Perhaps such a relationship, handled with care, would help us *all* heal and survive. Thrive? Maybe we would protect and cherish their existence and our own more fully. We might feel more whole and alive.

Can we revive a dormant memory, a longing and respect for this sacred vulnerable planet? Can we reach the basically good facet of our humanity that still clings to the heart and soul of life? Maybe we can walk more softly and treat our fellow beings and ancient earth in a more loving and conscious way. Can we walk in a way that lends spirit to humanity?

Life is always making choices to protect and heal itself, to further its survival and thrive. It would cease to exist if it stood still. The entire planet is an impressive experiment in process. In the rainforest, plants, animals, and insects jumped off the pages of this living textbook and revealed themselves to me with obvious clarity. I flourished in an amazing classroom, only this one was without walls. I needed simply to watch, listen, and learn.

I started to understand that each species evolves a unique "knowing" or way of gathering information that serves them in their environment. For example, the huge towering fig trees knew to evolve buttressed roots that stand on top of the shallow rainforest soil. In this way they can suck up nutrients close to the surface and also escape rain-saturated soil. The roots are not only tall—some a meter or more above ground—but they also fan out horizontally and often ripple, which gives the tree added structural support. Another example is ants that work as a team and form chains for strength and leverage. I found it fascinating how they send out scouts that look for food or watch for approaching dangers to the colony and post sentries at the colony entrance. Some ants even carry out a sophisticated form of agriculture when they "farm" aphids for the sticky, sweet sap that aphids secrete when eating certain plants. This is done in much the same way that we farm dairy cows. Stick insects also enthralled me because they have evolved to appear like the twigs they cling to when they eat their leaves. Everyday I saw dozens of examples of evolution. Every form of life seemed to offer a slightly different expression and experience for the intelligence that flows through all things. That is all things. I fell passionately in love with a Universal Intelligence that forever pushes the boundaries of its own existence to discover who and what it is. Sometimes it seemed that life evolved by chance, but more often than not it appeared to evolve by some type of choice, by making choices in response to its environment.

My thoughts raised another question. Would the "knowing" that humans evolve and the choices we make serve us in the environment in which we live (create)? I didn't yet have the answer. I suspected the more a species is connected to and aware of its environment, the more numerous, more dynamic, and healthier its choices.

Mother Nature kept me off balance just enough to nurture my growth with an open mind. I lived so close to death while surrounded by ecstatic life. Death slowly became my advisor, urging me to live. I came to know death well. It not only leaned over my shoulder and lurked in my body, but I saw death in the forest every day. It wove its way in and out of life until the two were inseparable.

It reminded me of the strangler fig. A fruit-eating bird eats the fig, and when it defecates, the seeds are deposited high in the fork of a tree where they germinate. The new seedling sends roots downward, through the air to the ground, which wrap around the trunk of its host. The roots rapidly grow thick and woody and become well established in the soil. Soon the host tree is completely encased in a latticework of strong roots, some as fine as my finger and others as big as my thigh. I saw strangler's roots that looked like human arms wrapped around their lover, one tree embraced by another. This deceptively loving embrace eventually brings death to the host. The crown of the fig rapidly grows to keep pace with its roots and eventually overshadows its victim's crown. With its light cut off and strangled by a web of roots, the once-healthy host tree slowly dies and rots away to become nourishment for other life.

One of the most stunning sights I saw in the forest was a hollow strangler fig. Its host had completely rotted and left the fig's latticed trunk in its place. When I peeked inside it was like looking through a loosely woven basket. That fig had to be one of the tallest trees I've ever seen. Strangler figs are among the tallest trees in the rainforest because they start their life high in the canopy.

With more to see and learn than ever before, I grew faster than a weed. Some days I laughed aloud at the miracle of my freedom. It must have been divine guidance that led me to the rainforest of Cape Tribulation, and divine intervention that plucked me from the pits of hell and shoved me through the gates of paradise. I felt so happy I abandoned myself to the forest and its rhythms. I no longer needed a calendar. Unused travelers checks from the States still lay locked in the glove box of the Toyota. Boredom never plagued me. Nor did I miss clothes, jewelry, dishes, or furniture. I forgot about fancy food, restaurants, stores, magazines, books, and movies. Some days I forgot to eat. My body relaxed in the blessed absence of TV, telephone, and electricity. More amazing to me, I didn't pine for human contact. In fact my deepest darkest childhood fear—being alone—melted away. And I no longer felt a need for Ian to go with me into the forest. I knew he eagerly awaited my return to camp and would want to hear about my adventures and insights. I smiled to myself as I thought about him snuggled in the truck reading.

He will be especially eager to see me after spending a rainy day alone. But I'm not quite ready to return.

I continued to sit by the spongy old tree, lost in a green trance. Drumming rain on the canopy increased to a thunderous rumble and awakened me from my bliss. Above my head, drips off leaves grew fatter and rivulets ran faster down tree trunks. In the peace of the forest, my thoughts again strayed and memories surfaced, sometimes painful, sometimes joyous, but all precious. This time to reflect allowed me to understand my troubled heart, as well as claim valuable gifts I'd been given. Nature has a way of healing wounds of all kinds.

As I sat in the rain, I remembered a dream from the night before last about a hike I'd taken with Dad when I was sixteen years old. It was exactly like the events of many years before, except I began to see my father through adult eyes and wisdom.

In the dream, Dad arrived home from work one spring evening. He'd just come through the screen door when he begged me to climb Streaked Mountain with him. I loved the woods, but I felt irritable and tired because I had to study for final exams. I hated school. Mom wanted me to help with dinner, and the laundry needed folding.

All the way up the mountain Dad consulted his trees-of-Maine identification book. He found damned near every tree in the book on that mountain, except one. And he was determined to find that last tree.

"I know she's here, Robsy. We'll just go a bit farther. If we don't find it we'll head back down."

And just how far is a "bit farther"? I wondered. I was hot, hungry, and frustrated. Homework looked mighty good. But Dad loved the woods and strode ahead impervious to my teenage impatience. It seemed as if finding that last tree would make his day complete, make him whole after a long day at work doing things he didn't really want to do.

We finally reached the bare rocky top of the mountain. Dad halted about a hundred yards in front of me and began to laugh and chatter with excitement.

"I'll be damned! Knew she'd be here, Robsy. Just knew it. By God, come look at this."

I begrudgingly trudged the few remaining feet and stopped short right behind him. The sight before me wiped away my smug superiority and replaced it with open-mouthed awe. Dad stood perfectly still. In front of him grew a conifer tree, its trunk softly lit in the warm orange glow of the setting sun. The bare rock shone rosy pink from twilight rays. Dad's broad shoulders and serene face made me want to cry. I didn't. We stood silently. Lower down the mountain a hermit thrush fluted its haunting call. Dad turned and smiled, his face lit with the rapture of a child before a Christmas tree.

"Oh, Robsy, my day is perfect."

In that one moment everything made sense. It wasn't something I thought about, but I felt it. For the first time in my sixteen years of life, I saw Dad as just another fragile person doing the simple things that made him happy.

The memory of my dream drifted over me and tried to settle. Once again, my hand had crushed the soft moss on the decaying log. I brushed away my imprint and slid Dad's hunting knife from its sheath. I absently ran my finger gently along the sharp blade, then shaved white flakes off my thumbnail. It was a strong knife; in camp I'd used it on coconut meat, fruit, seaweed, wild ginger, rope, wood, wire, almost anything. I'd carried the knife into the forest for several weeks, but it had been with me longer than that.

When I left for Europe at eighteen, I wanted to take something of my parents with me. I never thought to ask my father for the knife. Nor did I feel that I'd stolen something from him when I took it from his cedar chest full of bow-hunting gear and slipped it into my suitcase. I wanted a part of him with me. I slept with his knife under my pillow when I traveled alone through Europe. I don't know if I would have used it to protect myself. Maybe my father's spirit kept me safe.

Even a continent away, I felt his presence as strongly as if he sat next to me by the spongy, old log.

Through tear-filled eyes I spotted a long branch, perfect for a stirring stick. I hadn't yet used Dad's knife for whittling so I gave it a try. My thoughts peeled away years of memories as my knife peeled away thin strips of bark. Round off the end and taper the handle, chips of wood like bits of memory lay curled at my feet. I recalled the year I left home and traveled through Europe. I thought I might be pregnant. After much anguish and despair, I went to my father for help. It was a crisp autumn day full of blue sky and orange leaves. I'd spent the afternoon on Lake Pennesseewassee, alone in the canoe. It seemed there was more water in that old green canoe than in the lake. I had no tears left to cry. I thought my life was over; my great dream of travel and adventure would be lost. I'd saved my money for four years, and instead of college I'd chosen to see Europe. Although I feared being alone, anything was preferable to more schooling and small-town Maine.

My mother and I were like many other mothers and daughters of that day who rarely talked about sex. Sex and bodily functions had been a taboo subject in the culture I grew up in. I don't blame Mom, because she gave what she could and more. One of the reasons I love and understand her is because we shared the same hurts and faced the same challenges. She grew up in a time that repressed and used women, repressed the natural and uninhibited beauty of the human body and shunned the topic of sex.

That summer, like a few other summers, I'd gone to New York to visit some friends. A young man whom I'd known from previous visits, lived on a nearby farm. He had fresh, outdoor good looks, and as he was a couple of years older than me, I was fascinated by his more mature ways. I also was naive about my body and sex, even more so a man's body. The memory of my first time was depressing and lonely. It's the typical story of a dark night in a parked car on an empty dirt road. I was physically close with another human being for the first time in my life, and I felt frightened and alone in the days that followed.

A few days later my young man said, "You know you're not a virgin anymore."

Why are you telling me this? What does it matter?

His words, and the way they were said, hurt so deeply they shocked me into silence. I didn't think to say, "So what? Neither are you." Instead, something sweet and poignant rose up and clutched at my heart. Something innocent and defiant demanded the experience be treated with respect and cherished, no matter how amateurish.

All I could say to his comment was "Yes I am." When cutting laughter and the words "No you're not. You'll never be a virgin again," slapped me in the face, I knew we were miles apart. For me, whether my damned hymen was intact or not wasn't what made me a virgin. "Virgin rainforest" that's what Old Jake had called the forest, a 100 million years of life mating with life, and it's still virgin rainforest. As old as this living earth is and as much as we've raped her, she'll always be the virgin earth to me. I guess I saw virgin as beauty and wholeness of life. Wasn't I still those things? But I think I asked too much of another youth bewildered by the same social pressures and value systems as me. We both were inherently good people; most people are. Had I known him in a different time and place, I'd have loved him deeply, but the ability to love was lost in the getting by.

I left New York and returned to Maine and our cottage on the lake. During the week before I headed to Europe I felt terribly isolated. My dark secret cut me off from the rest of humanity. However, that tear-filled day in the canoe turned out like I never could have expected. As I paddled into the small cove by our well, I spotted Dad walking up the path to the cottage. He saw me and stopped to wave. My lungs gripped my ribs, braced in terror. How could I tell him? What if he got angry and yelled at me? What if he made me feel bad? I didn't know if I could do it. The canoe's keel left a trail in the wet sand as I wearily hauled it onto the beach and dragged myself on wooden legs up the path to my father.

The closer I got, my heart raced.

Thump. Thump. Thump.

I can't do it. I can't tell him.

"Dad, I might be pregnant."

Strong warm arms wrapped around my back and drew my head to his broad chest. Scratchy green and black plaid wool rubbed my face, the familiar smell of leather arrow quivers and cedar helped me sob like a small girl. For a long time we said nothing; he just held me. When he finally spoke, simple, kind words righted my world. "It'll all work out, Robsy. You're okay."

Dad handled it perfectly. He made no recriminations. No lectures. No degradation. No "How could you?" No "You should have known better." He asked practical questions, and we made decisions. I had two weeks before my cycle started and less than one week before I left for Europe. The nurse at the hospital told me to wait the two weeks to see if my menses started on schedule, "Then you can decide what you want to do."

"What about Europe?" I asked Dad. "Do I cancel my flight and wait here?" "You have a round-trip ticket, so why not go? If your cycle starts, you'll be where you want to be. If it doesn't, then call me and we can take it from there. You can always come home, Robsy, anytime."

On a dark autumn night, my parents drove me to the Portland airport to begin my journey to Paris. Mom's tears ran freely down her face and glittered from the oncoming headlights. Her warm hand held mine tightly when I reached for her between the front and back seats. At the airport Dad double-checked that I had the list of phone numbers he'd given me. They were people he knew in Europe whom I could contact if I needed a place to stay. The three of us huddled together in the terminal, holding hands, oblivious to everything but each other. People spilled around us like water that flows around rocks in a stream. I clung to my parents while we laughed and cried.

As I look back on that night, I have no doubt of their love for each other and me. I saw the eye contact, the silent messages they exchanged. "She'll be all right, won't she? Will you miss her? It hurts, doesn't it? But we gotta let her go."

Had that been my daughter, would I have been so brave? I don't think so. A few days after I arrived in Paris, familiar tugs and cramps pushed unused blood from my womb. I called Dad immediately. I don't remember much of the brief conversation. However, I do remember the letter I received a week later. I read it over and over until it was worn and tattered and permanently etched on my heart.

Dear Robs,

I am here in the dental office alone tonight. All the girls and your mother have gone home. I stayed late to write you this note. I jumped up and down with joy over your good news. Today I am celebrating your cycle. In your honor I wore all red to the dental office. I am wearing red pants, a white shirt with little red turtles on it, a red tie and red socks. When everyone, including your mother, asked me why I wore all red, I told them it was a private celebration. I can't tell you what you should have done or should do in your life. I have made too many mistakes in my own life. But if I can ever help you, please let me know. I am proud that you are my daughter.

Love,

Dad

Sitting in the rain, sheltered in the forest's love, I sobbed as I remembered the letter and how gentle my father had been. Often I couldn't tell if I cried with the world or the world cried with me. Huge tears flooded my eyes and fell onto my hands as I carved the stirring stick. I cried about Dad and Mom and my life. They were good, healing tears, cleansing tears. That's the way of Mother Earth; she absorbs pain and heals wounds.

Paris seemed so long ago. Here I was, years later, in the rainforest whittling a stirring stick. I didn't even know what month it was, let alone the day. It must have been well past December. Probably February or March. That made me twenty-six. I'd lived lifetimes inside of lifetimes. With no sense of time in the forest, life passed in a dream state. I lived several parts of my life at once because time was not linear. It was fluid. The loss of time is an awesome thing. It might distress some, but it allowed me to catch my breath and let my body relax. Every day felt like "Septembuary." In my life outside the forest, there had been either too much or never enough time. Time poked and prodded until I could no longer think, feel, or question anything. I spent my days worrying about being on time. What a great way to control masses of people.

At Cape Tribulation, not only did I lose all concept of time, but also distance became a malleable and changing substance until it vanished altogether. Maybe because I lived so far away without phone or mail, I became aware of another type of communication, one that rendered distance, time, and death meaningless. My soul's connection to other people, thousands of miles away, and even to childhood places, grew fiercely strong. In my longing and desire to love, I gathered up souls and drew them close into my heart. Through timeless space, I renewed bonds with my parents, ancestors, and friends, both living and dead, that would last well beyond my lifetime. Bonds that were as ancient as the earth and more familiar than my own voice.

My stirring stick was almost done, but the closer I got to finishing it, the harder it was to whittle. The wood's surface became more slippery with the increased rain. I should have put the knife away, but the rhythm of each cut soothed and mesmerized. I grew up with knives and bows and arrows. When Dad was young, he was one of the best bow hunters in the state of Maine. That was before they made high-powered bows with pulleys and sights. He used to set up archery courses with bales of hay and teach us how to shoot a bow and arrow. He was a strong believer in safety precautions and would have cringed had he seen me using the knife in such heavy rain. When red rain ran down my hand and dripped onto my feet, I knew it was too late. It happened so fast, I didn't at first feel the cut. I panicked at the sight of so much blood. The whole end of my index finger was sliced through the fingernail, across the pad on the other side and back to the nail. It was cut down to the bone, almost all the way around my finger.

The blade's edge was embedded in bone. When I jerked the knife away, blood pulsed from my finger and squirted into the air. Horrified, I grabbed my red sarong and wrapped a corner of cloth around my finger. It was useless. Blood soaked through the fabric in seconds. When I stood, the movement made blood pump twice as fast, so I sat back down and raised my arm above my head. I was several miles from camp, and I felt scared. Some part of me laughed when I thought about putting my fingers, blood and all, into my mouth to whistle for Ian. So much for that. How much blood could I lose before I passed out? I wished I'd carried sutures with me; I'd have stitched it up right then and later soaked it in saltwater so the end wouldn't rot off.

In my panic, a voice snapped through my head. I'm sure it was my mother's. She could sometimes be all business in a crisis, or at least the kind of crisis where one of us kids was hurt. Dad performed oral surgery every week, but he often panicked when one of his children was injured. That's when Mom became rock solid and dished out orders. You could be cut in two, and she'd be telling everyone to shut up and calm down. "Get me this. Get me that. Hold this. Put that there. Everything will be fine. I'm sure you'll live to pester me another day."

Sometimes mothers can be the best healers in the world. That day I felt my mother with me and heard her voice, "Oh for God's sake, Robin, calm down. Do you want to save your finger or not? You *can* deal with this. Your panic is a conditioned reaction. Don't abandon your body when it needs you the most. Use your brain, girl. It's not just there for daydreaming."

Suddenly the voice changed and was older than my mother's. It was the trees speaking. I listened.

"If you panic, Robin, you become like a parent fleeing a burning house, leaving their children to die in the fire. Gather your courage and give your children direction and reassurance. Most parents would no more abandon their precious babies than fly to the moon.

"When you are injured, you frantically look for someone else to deal with the injury. In some cases this *is* necessary. But you lose power when you panic, because you disrupt what happens naturally with what you *think* you need to do. When you stay calm, your heart will beat slowly and steadily, and your blood will not pump from your body. Allow your injured finger to realign its torn cells and disrupted energy patterns. Your body will respond and heal."

I'd grown accustomed to the sight of cut flesh when I assisted Dad in oral surgery, but when I unwound my sarong and saw the huge gash at the end of my finger I felt faint. Determined not to lose my finger, I let the wound bleed for a few seconds to flush out the dirt from my sarong. Then, with my other hand I closed together the two sides of the cut and held it with just enough pressure for both sides to touch. A few slow breaths calmed my anxious body, and I quietly focused on the pain. The act of "being" the pain helped lessen it. Gradually the bleeding slowed. I visualized a white light, a continuous flow of energy in the wounded area. It moved back and forth across the cut, similar to the sutures Dad used in surgery. All my awareness moved to the end of my finger. Once inside the wound, a wave of anguish hit me when I felt the grief of my dying cells. The mother in me went back into the fire to give directions to her children. "It's all right. Calm down. You're still alive. Realign yourselves with each other. Let the energy flow through and seal the opening. You're gonna live."

While I soothingly talked to the wounded children in my finger, another part of me stepped outside my body, and I stood right behind myself, back to back, and watched the rainforest creep closer to form a curious and protective circle. The Tree Beings were with me. Both those parts of myself were too intent on their own purpose to be aware of each other. A third part of me observed them all. A healer, a protector, and an observer.

The Robin who stood at my back welcomed the invisible arms that reached out to cradle me. The trees loved me as if I was their most treasured child.

Why do you love me? I'm no one special, though I feel special in your presence. Is it possible you love me because I'm here, because that's what trees do, love?

"Robin, you are us. And we love because love is life."

Suddenly I heard their voices again, hundreds of voices rose in exultation. Green shadows danced in and out of my spirit while I sat on the forest floor and inhaled emerald energy. Bathed in compassion, my self-doubt couldn't withstand the love that emanated from the forest.

Seconds, or was it years, passed from the moment I cut myself to when I released the slight pressure on my finger. The whole time, I followed the progress of a minute black ant. He crawled over my slippery foot and struggled across the forest floor from leaf to twig to avoid deep water. For the ant it was a huge river of water. Rain ran so thick along the ground he could have easily drowned, but he didn't. He made it to the trunk of an enormous fig tree, climbed a few feet and disappeared under a curl of gray bark. Aaah, dry shelter. Why had he gone to that exact spot? Whatever the reasons, we each safely arrived at our destinations. My finger no longer bled.

I'd been so engrossed in my cut that I hadn't noticed the two leeches that clung to the back of my left leg. I still didn't like leeches but had grown to tolerate them. I sometimes heard the shuffle of leaves as a leech wriggled toward my blood. They even dropped off tree branches onto my head and shoulders to hitch a ride and eat a free meal. How did they know I was there? Did they see movement? Feel the vibration of my footsteps? Sense heat or maybe smell me? There weren't many about during the dry season, but during the wet, if I fell asleep in the forest, especially next to a creek, I sometimes woke with two or three leeches attached to my legs. Once fastened to my skin, they clung voraciously with a suction that wouldn't let go. I was becoming accustomed to the venomous snakes, but to pull a black, rubbery, squirmy leech off my leg made me cringe. Ugh!

I had learned to leave them alone. If pulled off prematurely, the leech's body parts could remain imbedded in my skin, which caused irritation and infection. And besides, if I let the leech finish its job and drop off when it was done, it tended to suck most of the anticoagulant back out with my stolen blood. Left to drop off in its own time, the puncture wound didn't bleed as much.

Eventually the two leeches on my leg dropped off and the storm subsided, so I gathered up my sarong, stirring stick, and knife, and wandered home. My day had *definitely* been adventurous. I felt ready to return to the truck and hang out with Ian. As I approached our beach, the rain stopped and sun rays slanted through huge billowy clouds from heaven to earth.

At camp, Ian was fixing our tent awning and was happy to see me. Had he not seen the blood on my sarong he would have found it hard to believe the seriousness of the wound. The two-hour return hike hadn't reopened my cut. When I arrived in camp I didn't need to apply sutures or dressing to the injury, nor did I clean it with disinfectant. An hour later the gash remained shut, even after Ian and I played in the creek. It healed so completely I could barely find the cut line. My fingernail remained attached and grew out all the way with only a knife split to remind me of my lesson. There were other times I cut myself in the forest and used the same loving method to heal. It always worked.

The old adage, "When it rains it pours," proved true over the next few days. That night in a dream, I heard Ian scream with desperate sobs. He sat and rocked himself, totally despaired. I knew he was hurt, and I had to find a way to help him. Then it hit me, maybe Ian really *was* crying. Maybe it wasn't a dream. But when I looked more closely at the scene in front of me, we were in our Salt Lake City apartment, not in the forest of Cape Tribulation. Suddenly an orange glow permeated my eyelids and I awoke. I was in the truck in the rainforest, and Ian sat beside me with a lit candle. He clutched his left hand to his chest. One look at his face, and I knew his agonizing pain.

"Rob. Me bloody finger is killing me, mate. Look at her. She's bloody huge and throbbing like billy-o. Can't sleep. I feel so crook."

I'd seen inflammation of the mouth before and could recognize serious infection. The ring finger on Ian's left hand was bright red and swollen fat. Ugly red lines of blood poisoning ran across his hand and up his arm. The joint throbbed with pain. He seemed fairly calm so I didn't scare him needlessly. As long as there wasn't copious blood, Ian managed quite well. I sorted through my options. If necessary, I would drive Ian back through the creeks—as long as they weren't too deep—through the mud and jungle, across the ferry to the small hospital in Mossman. That is if the ferry had come back on. I didn't know what month it was or how long it had been out of the water. Old Jake might know. If I could make it to the ferry, maybe someone could bring a boat across the river and pick him up. But even if the ferry was running, I didn't know if I could get the truck down the cliff. I knew I'd do anything if it meant saving Ian's life. In any case, we couldn't leave until morning. It would be too dangerous. I'd need light to cross the creeks and washouts, and low tide to drive along the beach. High tide might raise the water level too high where some of the creeks flowed into the sea, making it impossible to pass. Even if the water wasn't too deep along the beach, the sand beneath the water might be too soft and treacherous. I could become bogged.

"Ian, I'm going to try and get you to the hospital tomorrow."

"Screw that, Rob-o. I ain't going to no bloody hospital, bloody ratbag butchers. They'll chop me bleeding finger off. There's too much rain to get through the creeks anyway. She'll be fine."

"Listen, Ian; this is serious. If we can't get to the hospital, then I either have to lance your bloody finger or you have to use clay poultices to get the poison out."

"Okay, I hear you, Rob-o. Let's try the clay first."

Ian's temperature rose feverish and high, and he hardly touched his food and drank only water. I dug out our book on natural healing and read about the use of clay and certain foods to heal the body. Before we entered the rainforest we'd eaten raw garlic every day, but we had none with us, not even dried garlic to reconstitute. We had a huge bag of powdered clay and a large glass jar to mix it in. Daily, we applied thick clay poultices to Ian's finger to draw out infection. He had tremendous faith in his body's innate wisdom and ability to heal.

Eventually his fingers swelled to twice their normal size, so fat he couldn't bend them. We changed poultices over and over, night and day. Finally after a few days, the clay began to draw out the infection. A crack formed in the mud and great strands of pus poured from his finger. Some of the strands came several inches out of his finger and hung there, still attached. When I tugged on them and tried to gently wipe them away they didn't come loose, and I could see them pull underneath the skin on his forearm. Sometimes we waited a day or more before the strand finally pushed all the way out and broke off. At times I thought his entire insides would escape through the hole in his finger. Fortunately, with the flow of pus, Ian's fever subsided.

Each day, I hiked down the cliff to the sea for a bucket of fresh saltwater so Ian could soak his finger. Although the boil continued to drain, the saltwater took away the red streaks that ran from hand to elbow.

One morning Ian said, "Why don't you hike up the beach to Old Jake's? See if he knows anything about bloody boils. He's a smart bloke, eh?"

"Gosh, Ian, I didn't even think of that."

When I arrived at Jake's camp, he limped out to greet me with a grin and a hug. His left knee was swollen fat as a grapefruit and his big toe looked bulbous and purple.

"Twisted me bloody knee when I stubbed me toe on a piece of firewood. Bloody fool thing to do, eh? Comes with age, I guess. How youse doing, luv? Where's Ian? He's not gone and got crook on youse, has he?"

"Yeah, Jake, he has, and it's pretty serious. His finger is pouring out pus and his whole hand is swollen like a baseball mitt. He won't eat. Can't sleep cause of the pain."

"Have you slept at all, luv? Youse looking a mite knackered yourself."

"Been too worried about Ian to sleep. Gosh, what's going on lately, Jake? I damned near cut my finger off and then Ian gets this bloody boil. And look at you with your leg and toe all banged up. Maaan, what is this, injury month?"

Old Jake chuckled and said, "Things always happen in threes, luv. That's often how life works." He shook his head and grimaced, "Sounds like Ian's gone and got himself a bloody ol' whitlow. That's a boil with several heads. They's a mean bloody bastard. Too right, eh? Strewth, he could lose his finger if he's not careful. Sometimes bloody doctors cut it off. But don't you worry, luv. He's a real tough bloke, Ian is."

Jake hobbled back to his makeshift table and reached beneath it to open an old rusted tin. He passed me three shriveled onions.

"They's a bit mangy, luv, but they's still firm inside. Boil 'em up real good-like, and while they's still hot wrap the layers around Ian's finger. It'll help draw out the last of the pus, you know? Make him drink the broth too, a bit every hour or so. Helps keep the infection down. Used onions during the bloody war, we did."

Whenever Jake talked about the war, I always had the feeling that he had more depth to him than he let people know. As if some intense suffering had made life real and valuable to Jake. I too wanted that kind of depth and value in my life, more than anything else.

"Can I offer you a cuppa tea before you head back, luv?"

"I'd love to visit Jake, but I'm real worried about Ian being on his own. I'd best get back to camp. Thanks for the offer of tea and the onions. I'll let you know how Ian's doing. You take care of your leg and watch out for that firewood. We'll check in on you."

I waved to Jake and took off at a fast trot. Once out of sight, I tore off my sarong, wrapped the three onions in it, tied it around my waist and ran on fuel of fear back up the beach to the cliff.

Ian sat in his usual place in the truck with his hand over a small bucket so his finger could drain.

"Did you see Jake, Roby? What'd he say? How is he? Did he ask about me?"

Ya, I saw him. He's stubbed his toe and twisted his knee on some firewood, but other than that he was in good spirits. And yeah, he did ask about you. Said you most likely have a whitlow. That's a boil with several heads. He gave me some onions to make a hot poultice. We're supposed to boil 'em up and then you have to drink the liquid. Works a bit like garlic and will help kill the infection. Then you wrap the layers of hot onion around your finger and the heat will help draw out the rest of the pus. Jake did this during the war."

"Yeah, he's told me tons of war stories. You wouldn't believe the stuff that guy's been through. Right-o then, let's try Jake's onion treatment."

I smiled to myself at the thought of Ian doing just about anything Jake suggested. I was just happy he was willing to do the "onion treatment" because he looked pale and thin. His eyes, dark and wounded, were stricken with pain. The way Bandicoot looked when he was dying. Silent suffering. Ian had a strong spirit, but I still don't know how he stood the pain. I only knew that I loved him and that he *had* to live.

Concern made me chatter and scold.

"You oughta eat something. Even if it's just soaked fruit. You're losing a lot of weight."

"Naaah. Not interested, Roby. I'll just drink Jake's onion juice."

Scolding didn't change his mind.

"Me body knows what it's doing, Rob. Don't worry, mate, I ain't about to cark it. I'll be fine. If I start talking gibberish, then you can worry."

I tried to lift Ian's spirits by joking with him. "What do you mean *if* you start talking gibberish? Isn't that *all* you ever talk?"

Ian never missed a chance to spar. He loved it like sport, the way some men love football, but he remained silent and my shadow of worry grew. He was solid muscle without an ounce of fat to spare. Unable to get food down, his weight melted away like candle wax in the noonday sun. His arms and legs turned to knobby sticks of wood.

He seemed to take this time of sickness in stride, and actually grew calmer each day. I should have worried about his state of calmness, but I never thought that he might *really* die. I lost track of how many nights and days we stayed awake. Finally, one night I collapsed into oblivion and slept.

A second later I opened my eyes. Morning light flickered across the trees at the end of the truck. I had slept so deeply that I didn't remember falling asleep or even what we were going through. Everything sounded so intensely still I thought I lay alone in the truck. Then I remembered Ian's finger. Ian? Where was Ian?

He lay flat on his back on his side of the Toyota. His arm was propped on towels and his hand hung over the small bucket. In the peace of sleep he looked ten years old. But I couldn't hear him breathing. My heart lurched. I thought he was dead.

I put my ear gently to his mouth. Warm moist breath the size of an infant's kissed the tears on my face. With the sleeping bag pushed back I saw his diaphragm rise and fall, rise and fall. Thank God. I lightly caressed his good hand. It was huge with long fingers that stretched an inch beyond my own. In good health, Ian reminded me of a lumberjack with broad shoulders, narrow waist, and powerful arms and legs. I sat and watched him for several hours until my bladder screamed for release.

When I returned he sat propped against his pillow. He smiled weakly and said, "Strewth! I's bloody hungry. How 'bout a fig, eh?"

Color had returned to Ian's face, and his finger had shrunk almost to its normal size.

"The worst is over, Rob-o. Me finger looks a bit bloody buggered with this funny bent to her. But she still works."

"I don't care how your finger looks, Ian. I'm just glad you're alive."

"Man, I gotta take a bloody whizz. That was a long night, eh, Rob?"

"Hold on, Ian. I'll get the pee bucket."

"Won't be needing it t'day, Roby. Think I'll sit on the beach, get me some bloody sun and read. Maybe I'll soak me finger in the sea. Strewth, think I'll have a bath in the creek while I'm at it. I stink like the bloody arse end of a donkey with worms."

Unable to hold it back any longer, I laughed when Ian asked, "Where's me book? You know me Larry and Stretch?"

"Larry and Stretch?"

"You know, Rob-o, the one I was reading before me finger went crook on me? Hope I can find me bloody place again."

I doubted he'd have trouble finding his place, let alone memorizing the entire book.

We had a bucket for everything. A pus bucket, a pee bucket, a seawater "soak-your-finger-in-it" bucket. Those buckets marked Ian's return to health. First the pee bucket went, then the pus bucket, and finally the sea-water bucket. I didn't know it yet, but another phase of my own evolution started that day. Ian's return to health would once again bring movement and change into my life.

Even though it still rained some days, the wet season would soon be over. Except for the scar and slight bend in Ian's finger, it was almost healed. He appeared spindly thin, but over the weeks his energy returned to full force. He spent his days on the beach with Larry and Stretch. I spent most of my mine in the forest. But often on clear sunny days I lay beside him on the warm sand and we talked. One evening after a day spent lazing by the mouth of the creek, Ian said, "Robin, I need to leave the jungle."

Emotions collided in their need to be expressed. All I could do was cry. I sensed he was afraid to tell me that he wanted to leave. How did I feel about it? While I tried to calm myself, I studied Ian's face. He looked gaunt and yet more peaceful than I'd ever seen him. It was a miracle he hadn't lost his finger, or his life.

Ian took a quavery breath and said, "Roby, I know I'm the one who originally wanted to come to the bloody jungle, but things have changed in me. Something happened with this whole finger thing. I let go of a lot of stuff, mate."

I chuckled, not cruelly, at all the gallons of pus I buried. Ian relaxed when I laughed.

"No, seriously, mate; you know what I mean, eh? Deadset, it was like some kind of catharsis, Rob. I think I need to leave the jungle now. Been thinking 'bout me oldies. Probably give me mum and dad a call when we's out."

Since I'd met Ian, I'd ridden a strong and vital current, but I never thought so much about it until that day. Destiny has an inevitable and intensely familiar quality, like you've known it before, always known it. I'd plugged into a potent core truth. My destiny had taken me exactly where I needed to go, and Ian was my vehicle.

I'd waited a lifetime for him to arrive. Now that I'd found him, I contented myself with the unfolding adventure. I knew that in some ways it didn't matter what we did because everything lay open before me, a new and challenging experience. In connecting to my destiny, I tapped into ancient memory. I began to understand who I was as a person and who I was in relation to the rest of life. I lived each day more awake and alive than ever before. When I looked inside myself for alternatives, other desires, I found none. I no longer had another life in some other place and time, full of other people who awaited my return. There was no other life for me. There never had been.

~

As we linger in the forest
Scarred-over wounds reopen
Bleeding out residual holdings
Allowing time
This spongy earth facilitates healing
And absorbs our offerings

—RUSSELL HUME

seven

THERE IS NO SEPARATION

THE FACE THAT STARED BACK at me from the mirror had changed. No . . . it hadn't changed. I had changed. My face still had the same oval shape with fine smooth skin and delicate chin. The upper lip still curved like an archer's bow above large white teeth, and long brown hair framed deep-set hazel eyes. The eyes were filled with shock and wonder. Thin fingers reached up to touch the mirror, then the face. *That's me? No, I am more than this now.*

Almost a year had passed since I'd looked in a mirror. There was no calm water in which to see my reflection, only babbling creek and sea. Like some native who's never seen a mirror, I tipped and turned the Toyota's side mirror and touched my hair and face. I tried to match the reflection with what I felt inside. *Where's all the green? I thought I was green like the forest.* I'd seen my bare arms and legs every day for the last year, but it suddenly occurred to me that I'd stopped seeing them as flesh colored. I no longer thought of them as arms and legs. They were green and brown, and like everything else around me, part of the forest. Somewhere along the way, I became more spirit than flesh. I merged with life and lost myself in it; and in the process of losing myself, I found Robin. More Robin than I'd ever known. I no longer needed a mirror to see what I looked like or who I was. This new awareness stunned me, and I raced to find Ian.

"Iaaaaaan? Where are you?"

"Here, Roby. Down by the creek. Rinsing out sprout jars. What's up, matey?"

"Ian, you know how you asked me to untangle the vines around the truck's side mirrors? Well, I saw myself, but not in the way you might think."

"What are you talking about, Roby?"

"I haven't looked in a mirror since we got here. And when I saw my reflection, I realized how much I've changed. My features still look the same, but I've become so much more than the Robin I've always seen in a mirror. I always thought mirrors helped me see myself better, but they don't, Ian. I actually see myself better *without* looking in a mirror. I see more of myself by looking into the world around me, the trees and rocks and wildlife. They reflect back to me who I *really* am."

Ian tipped a jar to drain water off mung beans and said, "I think I understand you, Roby, but tell me more."

"Well, maybe, when we spend too much time looking in the mirror, our reflection becomes our memory or vision of who we are, even our whole reality. But I think it's limited vision. However, it's the way many of us grow up so we don't know any different. Think about it; there are mirrors everywhere we go, in our homes, stores, offices, cars, and restaurants."

"But, Roby, isn't that reflection us?"

"Yes, but that's a bit like always looking into a tiny mud puddle to see who you are and where you are. And yet, if you lift your head away from the reflection in the puddle, you will see oceans, mountains, animals, flowers, and birds. We're surrounded by a vast world of reflection. We're more than the image we see in the puddle or the mirror. We are the earth and sky, the trees and rocks . . . Nature itself. We are each other. We are the entire universe, Ian. We're enormous, like one massive organism. There is no separation."

Clear pools filled Ian's blue eyes and tears skittered down his cheeks. He held my gaze for a long time before he spoke, and all I felt was love.

"Crikey, youse so alive, Roby. Youse like the rainforest, more wild than tame. That's why I love you. What you're saying makes total bloody sense, mate. I know it's true and I feel the same. I just don't live it, not the way you do. Hell, I climb into the front of the bloody truck every now and then and use the rearview mirror to squeeze blackheads."

I laughed incredulously and asked, "You do? I didn't know that."

"Fair dinkum, mate, I see meself all the bloody time. Never really thought about it until now. We's just different, mate. Youse handling all kinds of bloody creatures. Going barefoot. Spending all your time in the forest communing with rocks and critters. You love it here. You wouldn't even remember to look in a mirror. When I hear you talk about all the bloody stuff you see and feel, it reminds me of my best drug trips."

Ian had sampled assorted drugs for a couple of years before I met him. By the time he left Australia for America, he'd given up all drugs and alcohol. He once told me the stuff would take him "too far over the edge," and he might never get back, so he quit. But in that time he'd had some "radical trips." He often compared my drug-free experiences in the forest to his best drug trips in which he experienced profound openness and insight.

I'd never been able to drink much alcohol because I was allergic to it. It usually made me sick. I tried pot three or four times before I knew Ian. The first time I felt absolutely nothing, and then I had one mildly nice experience. The last time, I had some kind of seizure. That ended my drug days forever.

Ian once said, "It's not bloody common for people to have the extraordinary experiences that you do, Rob-o."

"Well, I believe it is our nature or potential to have extraordinary experiences every day. The majority of us may not live like that, but it's what the human animal is capable of. It's who we are."

Of course, Ian understood me immediately. Semantics rarely created a problem between us. He loved to discuss philosophical and ethical issues even if, as he said, he didn't always choose to live them. I found it interesting and frustrating that someone could understand and believe in certain truths and not act upon them.

In our own way, every individual, each generation, and every nationality tends to feel their beliefs and ways are best. Pain, loss, and age have the potential to chop away imprisoning judgments and leave us humbled and filled with insight, if we're fortunate. When we're open to life, pain and loss also can create fertile soil for sprouting compassion. As I weighed my own fears and faults, I valued Ian's unique offerings. I also learned that there is nowhere to "be"; we're already there. Everything we need is right in front of us.

A true artist, musician, genius, writer, or healer doesn't create something new out of thin air, although it may appear that way. They tap into the creativity of the universe, an intelligence that's part of us all. It's just a matter of seeing what already exists and remembering who we are.

I love how life works, the things it brings me, and how it brings them. Often it's not what I *think* I want, but it's *always* what I need to grow. When I first arrived in the rainforest, I was angry. Angry about the poisonous creatures. Angry about the lack of pine trees and snow. Angry that I was so far away. Angry that Ian wanted to stay at camp and not come with me into the forest. When I hung onto my expectations of how life *should* unfold, I usually missed something far greater and more valuable. My time alone in the rainforest was exactly what I needed to heal and be more alive, help me to "be" life.

Once I let go of my expectations, I threw myself into life as if each situation was forever, and at the same time, I lived as if there was no tomorrow. I'm sure I made more mistakes than most, and lived a messier life, but I no longer gave a damn about correct and tidy living. I didn't sever one portion of myself so that another could exist. It was all life. My soul grew like the rainforest, a wild, teeming menagerie that thrust forward without a backward glance, without explanation.

Living so wild, I reentered the food chain and took many risks because I, too, yearned to grow. Claiming full responsibility for my life made it real for me. Through this time, I was blessed to have someone as supportive as Ian. Regardless of the beliefs he acted or didn't act upon, I appreciated and cherished what he gave me. He had the ability to understand me with or without words and was always hungry to hear my insights. No matter what he did or didn't do himself, he never hemmed me in. He championed my growth and exploration of the unknown and encouraged me to find my own truth.

After we finished rinsing the sprouts, I left camp and hiked through swirling fog to my circle of trees. Good-byes were never hard for me to express, but letting go was. Tomorrow at daybreak, we'd pack the truck and leave Cape Tribulation. Gray skies mourned with me in a day heavy with grief. Low clouds cried gentle tears, while sea mist crept through the forest. Its wispy arms drifted among the trees, seeking me out for one last kiss. Flat on my back on the forest floor, I flung my arms and legs wide to absorb earth and sky, as much as I could before tomorrow's dawn. Tears shimmered in my eyes and blurred the dancing green leaves high above my head. The forest reassured me of its love. "Robin, I am here with you, loving you. Let yourself cry. A proper good-bye welcomes tears."

As much as I love Mom, you are my true mother. You sustain me. I'd die without you. I'll always be drawn to earth's wild and untouched areas. That is where I find peace most easily. But you, Rainforest, are my first mother.

Your compassion and love has helped me to see the damage we've caused the earth. We've scarred and stripped her, buried her under miles of concrete and tar. Oh my dear Rainforest, I have to tell you that I have hurt the earth too, but you still love me. So does Mother Earth. No matter where I am, all I've ever felt is her love.

Before journeying into the forest, I'd heard well-known spiritual leaders and environmentalists say that Mother Earth is angry with us and will punish us for treating her poorly. A new truth formed in my mind as I lay on the forest floor.

You are not an angry God, an earth that dishes out vengeance when we pollute your air and water, gouge your skin, and kill your trees and wild creatures. You ARE Love. You . . . Just . . . ARE.

"You are learning, Robin. Do not forget what you have learned." There would be no punishment, only consequences to my irresponsible actions. I knew earth was not malicious. If I poisoned my water and air, eventually I'd ingest enough poison and become sick or die. Any so-called punishment we may experience says more about our own actions than earth's wrath. We are responsible for our lives and the choices we make. Why is it easier for us to believe that there is an all-powerful punishing earth or God who will keep us in line, than to accept the possibility that we are completely loved and there will be no punishment?

I am in love with an earth that knows *only* love. However, I believe there is a Universal Order, an Intelligent Integrity that holds the universe together, and if we are not in relationship with earth, we could throw her Universal Order too far out of balance. She does what she needs to do to maintain harmony, restore order, and heal herself. In that process we could get hurt, suffer, or become extinct, but her love never stops. She is love.

Although earth had always loved me no matter where I traveled or lived, up until now I had looked upon her wounded and polluted places as disgusting, as if it were earth that was disgusting instead of what we do to her. Not only had I contributed to her suffering, but I tended to avoid those wounded places. *Maybe I need to love her wounded places more so she isn't alone in her pain, so that she can heal.*

I spent the day with my trees. I didn't have to worry about packing. Other than my sarong I hadn't worn clothes for almost a year. I didn't miss that routine: wash your clothes, dry your clothes, mend your clothes, iron your clothes, fold your clothes, put your clothes away, get your clothes out—over and over.

Our only dishes were our own wooden bowl and spoon, one cooking pot, and our Buck knives. We each were responsible for our bowl and spoon. If it was dirty, clean it. We'd already taken the tent down, rinsed out our burlap water bags, filled our extra jerry cans with creek water, and replaced the rocks we moved when we arrived. After Ian had greased the truck and revved the engine, he hiked up the beach to visit Old Jake one more time. I let him go alone because they had a special bond. Jake and I were close in a different way. He understood my affinity with the forest, but Ian revered Old Jake.

When Ian returned I asked, "What'd Jake say when you told him we were leaving?"

"It was as if he already knew. He just said, 'After a serious illness, people tend to make changes in their lives.' He told me, 'That's often how life works.' I think he meant me bloody finger. That bloke lives on another plane, like youse do. Oh, and he also said the forest will miss you, Roby. I think he's right, it will."

I felt moved by Jake's words. I now realized without a doubt that he knew I had fallen in love with the forest. He had been aware of what was happening in me long before I saw it myself.

"Ian, do you realize we may never see Jake or this rainforest again?"

"Yeah, but that's often how life works."

Ian didn't pressure me to leave Cape Trib; it was a mutual decision. We didn't know where we'd go. He only knew that he wanted to contact his family.

I rose early the morning of our departure to walk along the beach. The new dawn held more night than day. Low on the horizon, glowing pink threads outlined thin purple clouds. I stood silent while the sun's orange ball peeked above the mercuric line of silver sea. I waited while long golden rays stretched across the water, touched my face from millions of miles away, and warmed my skin. I waited and would've waited forever to see such beauty. My God, the things we take for granted.

I accepted our leaving, but wanted to see everything one last time, again and again. Creek and sea, rock and tree, my rainforest, a lover I had to let go and couldn't.

I wandered back to camp, dragging my feet. All appeared ready, except to drive the truck off the hill. I wasn't sure it was possible, but Ian knew for certain how we'd do it.

"Oh, she's no worries, mate. We'll just put her in neutral and roll her down, eh? We's just have to watch that big bloody rock. But we can't go slow, Roby. Sorry, mate, she's too bloody steep. The truck might tip. Might even roll. We's going to have to let her have her lead. BOOM! Down she goes."

Ian slapped his hands together. One hand shot forward like a released arrow, straight for the sea. At my look of absolute horror, Ian tried desperately to retrace his steps.

"Aw, come on, Roby. With the tide out, we's got tons of room before we hit the bloody water. Once she's on the flat I'll brake and put her into gear. She'll be right. I ain't interested in getting us killed."

Killed? This could *kill* us? In my mind I saw Ian and the truck plow into the waves and vanish. In the second scenario the truck tumbled bumper over bumper down the hill and blew up.

"Ian? Do I need to be in the truck when you go down? I mean, don't you need me to direct you or something like that?"

"Strewth, Roby, there's only one way off something this steep, and that's straight down. No amount of directing is going to bloody well change that. Trust me; I won't be turning no freakin' wheel. We'll be hanging on like the bloody knackers on a 'roo jumping flat out."

"Knackers on a 'roo jumpin' flat out? Oh thanks, Ian. That REALLY set my mind at ease. Hey, what do you mean by 'we'? I'm not riding down the cliff . . . am I?"

Ian chuckled and said, "Might's well ride with me, Rob-o. Keep me company, eh?"

"Keep you company? Crikeys, what do you think this is, an epic journey? We're only going a few feet down a cliff face."

Ian talked with such bravado that I didn't at first recognize his nervousness. What finally convinced me to climb into the truck? I didn't want to live if I had to drag Ian's fried corpse out of the burning Toyota at the bottom of the slope.

Hell, we had to get the damned truck down to the beach. If he was going up in flames or into the sea then I was going with him. Someone had to do it. At least I didn't have to drive. If he died doing something for both of us, I'd never be able to live with myself.

Like a ski racer waiting tensely in the starting gate at the top of a snowy mountain, the Toyota perched at the edge of the hill awaiting our signal to lunge forward. We climbed into the truck and Ian shifted into neutral, rocked his body back and forth and yelled, "Right-o, everybody, stand back."

Everybody??? Who the hell is "everybody"? I gripped my seat and frantically looked around. A brown cuckoo-dove clung to a nearby fig tree; he was the only witness to our madness.

The truck moved, and I sucked air as we teetered at the lip of the cliff. Then, whoosh! Over we went. Ian clutched the wheel like his life depended on it. Actually, it kinda did. I wish I could have stood on the beach below and seen those two young faces behind the windshield coming at me full force. What a sight it would've been. His face—wild, tense, and determined. Mine—half crazed and hidden behind fingers spread like partially open venetian blinds. To the tune of my shrill scream, we half bounced, half careened, like a mad roller coaster car, down the slope. Ten feet short of the waves, the truck came to a stop and shuddered.

Silence.

My heart. THUD. THUD. THUD.

"Heeeeeeee haaaaaaaaaaa."

Ian's piercing whoop almost popped me through the Toyota's tiny roof vent. When he hopped out of the truck, I jumped out behind him. I needed air. Lots of it. The amazement on Ian's face followed our tracks across the sand to the bottom of the hill, proof of our miracle. He couldn't believe we actually had done it and were all still in one piece. Ian. Me. The Toyota. Laughing and whooping, we danced around the truck like painted warriors before battle. After battle was even better. I could deal with that.

If it had been years later our antics would have made a great Foster's beer commercial.

We stopped at Old Jake's for one last good-bye. As always, we found him sitting by his fire.

"So, youse 'eaded out, eh, luv? Said good-bye to the forest, eh?"

My eyes filled with tears when I said, "Yeah, Jake, but I'll still miss her."

I tried to find words to tell him how the forest had saved my life, but Jake didn't need words. His sea-green eyes looked hard into mine, then he slowly nodded his head up and down in a satisfied way and said, "It's okay, luv, I know. Youse got what you came for."

Ian put his arm around my shoulders and said, "Well, we's best choof off now, Rob-o."

"Youse two take care of each other, eh?"

"We will, Jake. You look after yourself too. Don't go stubbing your toes on that firewood of yours. And thanks for everything."

Jake shook Ian's hand and we both hugged him. I wasn't surprised when I saw tears spring into Ian's eyes. He always got emotional over good-byes, especially if it was someone he really loved. It touched me that he was an emotional man. I liked that.

"If you kids get back this way, look me up, eh? If I's not dead, I'll be sittin' right 'ere by me fire."

"Oh Jake, I think you'll live forever."

"Maybe so, luv, maybe so."

"Ta-ta, Jake."

Jake took our parting in stride, the way he handled most things. He'd seen and been through so many changes that he philosophically accepted our sudden departure as part of life. We came. We ate. We went. There was no shock, no begging us to stay. Old Jake was so at peace with himself that he wouldn't have minded being the last human alive. I have no doubt that he enjoyed our company, but he didn't need us to feel content and satisfied with himself or life. I was beginning to understand how he felt.

Compared to our trip into Cape Trib, our ride back through the rainforest to the ferry was uneventful. All the creeks were lower than usual, the road mostly dry and hard, and the washouts crudely repaired.

When we got within sight of the Daintree River we saw the old phone booth still plunked like an absurd joke by the water's edge. On its door someone had written, BEWARE OF CROCS—CLOSE THE BLOODY DOOR YOU DRONGO, with a white crayon in capital letters. While we waited for the ferry to drag itself across the river and pick us up, Ian hopped out of the truck to see if the phone still worked. I waited in the Toyota and didn't hear the conversation with his family, but I saw tears run down his face while he talked. The ferry chugged closer to the landing, so he hung up the phone, wiped his wet cheeks, and got into the truck to board. I paid Clyde the fare and prepared myself to stall for time while Ian pulled himself together. Luckily, Clyde barely noticed us. He bent over the punt's engine with grease up to his elbows and a fist full of wrenches. I doubted he remembered us anyway. Nonetheless, I was relived when an Aboriginal man drove an old red pickup onto the ferry. He had his wife and three kids with him, and was the same young man who had asked Ian for five dollars a year prior. When he spotted us, he waved happily and walked our way with a two-foot fish dangling from his fingers. He proudly held up the fish and said, "Yeah, that one a big one, eh? Der was a biiiig mob of fishes. We bin go wiiight around eberywhere." Then he looked at Ian and said, "I's seen you yesterday. You 'ave no money but you bin kind. So, I give you fish."

"I's seen you yesterday." I'd heard other Aboriginals say that, no matter how much time had passed. I liked it. He had a whole different concept of time. It wasn't something he wore on his wrist.

Ian pushed aside his pain, smiled, and shook the Aboriginal's hand. He asked the young man to follow him as he headed to the back of our loaded truck and took out some food: dried figs, dates and apples, a coconut, and freshly grown sprouts. He passed the food to our friend and his wife and said, "We're only two mouths." He held up two fingers and pointed to his mouth and then mine. Then he pointed to the three kids and the man's wife and said, "You have five mouths to feed." The children and their mother giggled as Ian pointed to each mouth in turn. "You need the fish. We have a lot of food right now. Take it." I saw understanding light the Aboriginal man's face. Uninhibited tears of gratitude sparkled in his dark brown eyes. When Ian showed him how much food we had left in the truck the young father laughed and said, "Eberybody eat good t'day. We's camped by the river. Come?"

"Thanks, mate, but unfortunately me and the missus got business in town."

We shook hands, smiled, and waved good-bye. I never saw them again. I wish I'd camped with them, if only for a while. As wild as I felt at times, their wild energy was something I was only beginning to experience. Many of them lived in another reality, one without time, and they owned almost nothing. Material possessions had little meaning to a lot of the Aboriginals I met. Their values and fulfillment lay with something seemingly intangible but nonetheless very potent and substantial. In the eyes of our Aboriginal friend, as long as we all had food to eat it didn't matter where it came from. Such a trusting worldview.

We crossed the river, bounced along the washboard track to the main road and turned south toward Mossman. On the way to town, Ian sat quiet and withdrawn. Even with both windows wide open, the air in the truck lay as still as Ian's grief. I knew he was mulling over the phone call to his folks.

When I asked him what happened, silent tears ran down his face. My heart squeezed tight and painful with sorrow. Although I sat in the truck thousands of miles from Melbourne, I saw it all in my mind. A black phone rang where it sat on a heavy mahogany desk. Lush palms and flowering plants spilled around the elegant furniture and rose all the way to the ceiling. In the corner sat a hand carved teak Buddha. A gorgeous blond woman, elegantly groomed, reached for the phone. Her long red nails were neatly manicured. Her son's name parted her lips. "Ian?" Her husband, a trim, striking man with black hair and cropped salt-and-pepper beard, strode purposefully to the phone and hovered near. Expectations on both ends of the wire rose high, then crashed unmet. The connection went through, but no contact was made that day.

I had once told Ian that no matter how many times my parents or elders told me what made the world tick, I still needed to strike out on my own and find out for myself. Most young people do. I *still* do. When we're young, we tend to think our parent's ways are old and crusty. They couldn't possibly understand us or know what we're going through. Like they've never lived. Right? Ian and I were the ones who hadn't lived and truly needed to, just like our parents before us. Although, in many cases, they didn't get to or dare to. So it can go either way or anywhere in between. A parent may want their child to do the things they weren't able to do themselves, or they might envy the youth's freedom, a freedom they never had. The possibilities are as endless and varied as the people involved.

Again I asked Ian, "What'd they say? You okay?"

He silently cried a bit more, but this time he talked while I watched the road. "Me mum answered and then put me dad on. I don't think the old man will ever understand me. He was real nice at first. Seemed glad to hear me voice. Asked how we was doing. Asked about you. Then he wanted to know if I was coming home to settle down. I told him we didn't know what we were going to do, and he got upset with me. Said it was time I pulled me bloody socks up. He'll never love me, mate."

"Oh, he loves you, Ian. I think he's like that *because* he loves you. He just doesn't always know how to show it. You're his first son, and I think he has great expectations for you. But you have to live your own life just like he did when he was young. I think that could be hard for him to accept, maybe impossible.

"My mom is a lot like that, Ian. She wasn't really happy about me leaving for Australia. At times she's angry and frustrated, but deep down she's just scared and hurt 'cause she'll worry about me and miss me. But I had to get away, or I felt like I'd die. Mom still loves me, and your dad still loves you."

"I know he does and I love *him*, but we always seem to bloody aggravate each other. Anyway, then me mum gets back on the phone. She's crying, telling me she misses me and all. Then the old man takes the phone from her and gets mad at me for upsetting Mum. I think Mum was only crying because she was glad to hear me voice."

"Ian, he's not really angry with you. I just think it may be hard for him to deal with your mom's emotions, anybody's emotions. Your dad is a deeply sensitive and emotional man. It's one of the things I love about him. But he may not know how to express his feelings, so he gets all tangled up inside. My mom is like that, but there's still so much goodness in her. It's the same with your dad."

"I guess you're right, Rob-o. I still think I need more time away so I can find out who I am. For now, do you mind if we just stay here?"

It's odd how quickly some decisions can be made, often on such apparently thin substance, but great forces guide our lives. On a soul level, whole dramas need a stage. Stories need to live and breathe. Pain needs to unravel and can look ugly in the process, but it can often be the healthiest thing that happens to us. More important, truth seeks to reveal itself. Soul is an experiential learner with little use for concept and reason.

Ian and I swam in a current deeper and more powerful than reason. Things happened fast. We were spontaneous and exceedingly independent. I'd been out of touch with my family for over a year. Unless Ian's folks knew where we were, and they sent word to my family, no one in the world knew where I was. Instead of panic over that thought, I experienced tremendous freedom. Time alone in the forest allowed me to process my feelings and my reactions to the world around me, something I'd never been able to do in the outside world. Intense emotions had always forged my life. They aroused in me great passion and shining creativity, but I was unable to fully understand my emotions or direct my life. Before I arrived in the forest, I had floated through my days light as milkweed down adrift on the wind. My path took me where the breeze blew. Fortunately, Ian crossed my aimless wanderings, and his soul spoke to me. "Jump on my back, Robin, and I'll carry you where you need to go. Don't be afraid; we know each other. You've waited all your life for me. I'm finally here, so jump on, my friend."

Ian sighed deeply, and I looked over at his sad, handsome face. I wondered if he knew the gift he gave me simply by being in my life. It felt like a once-in-a-lifetime opportunity. Maybe we had some prior soul agreement, and he came into my life to help me. Regardless, I was grateful that he was with me. I knew without a whisper of doubt that he loved me completely, without reserve. His shoulders relaxed when I held his hand and listened while he talked. By the time we reached Mossman he seemed calmer, and we had decided to stay in the Daintree area.

In town we loaded up on gas, fresh fruit, and veggies. I spotted one of the young Aboriginal women who had stood by our truck that first day I arrived in Mossman. She was probably no more than eighteen years old.

Her dark, curly hair framed a beautiful mocha-skinned face. When she smiled her huge brown eyes and white teeth sparkled. I felt pleased when she remembered me. She took my hand and led me across the street to a little curly-headed boy who sat on a patch of grass, happily waving a stick through the air. She pointed to the boy then to herself, and I knew he was her son. He saw his mom, jumped up, and flung his arms around her thin legs, hugging her. Their playfulness touched me. When the mom lifted his T-shirt and tickled his bare belly, I laughed almost as hard as he did. We romped for half an hour before the little guy began to yawn loudly. When he fell asleep in his mother's lap, she gathered him up to head home. We smiled and waved. I crossed the street and found Ian waiting for me in the hardware store.

We returned to the truck and drove north to Newell Beach campground where we spent the night. The feast we made with our fresh food tasted like a gourmet banquet. We sat on the Toyota's tailgate and talked long after the red-ball sun disappeared behind the hills. We talked until the evening turned cool and the night sky squeezed a crescent moon and silver stars from its black depth. Finally we crawled into the back of the truck and slept.

I might have returned to Cape Trib—creek crossings, washouts, cliff and all—but Ian wanted a more permanent home. And something in me needed to move on to new experiences. I wasn't sure what they might be; I only knew that my soul hungered for movement.

Earlier that day, a bloke in the hardware store told Ian about a piece of land for sale across the Daintree River. We decided to check it out in the morning. We spent the next two days looking at property until we found a parcel that we both liked and decided to buy. We cashed some traveler's checks, and within the week we owned a piece of land on the north side of the Daintree River. The first time Ian set eyes on it he winked, grinned, and said, "Why don't we call it Cloud Mountain?" I liked that name because an often cloud-topped mountain range looked down upon our new home. The acreage was partially cleared and drier than the wet rainforest at Cape Trib. To my delight, a spring and tiny creek trickled through one section of the land and wound through tall trees, palms, ferns, and vines, remnants of rainforest.

For the most part, we felt our new home would be good for us both. I had my rainforest-covered mountains to explore, and Ian had slightly easier access to town. He drove down a dirt track, then along the river to another dirt track that took him to the ferry. He waited for the ferry to cross the river and pick him up. Then he chugged back across the river, drove out to the main road—a single lane, potholed, tarred road with gravel strips on either side—and on toward town, all with no winching. In heavy rain the tracks turned to quagmires, the river flooded, and the ferry didn't run. No one went anywhere.

It was an early, muddy morning like that when Ian decided he wanted to go to Cairns to get a few supplies and of course some ice cream. He *had* to have an ice cream bar. I could tell he *really* wanted me to go with him. Although I didn't want to go, my heart softened and I went anyway. My only concern was that it had recently rained and the roads would probably be a mess. Normally, muddy roads wouldn't matter as long as the river hadn't flooded, but we were about to drive to town in our new forest-green utility truck, which had no four-wheel drive and no winch. Our old Toyota had been breaking down, so we'd recently traded it in. Ian decided that since we no longer had to ford streams and winch over washed-out roads, a Toyota utility would probably be enough, and it would be cheaper than buying a new four-wheel drive. Now I wished we had our old truck. I wasn't too eager to try the new one on muddy roads, so I attempted to talk Ian out of going.

"Maybe we should wait a day until the roads are drier. You *always* love ice cream, so it's not like you won't want one tomorrow. And besides, ice cream is really bad for you. You might lose your girlish figure."

Ian chuckled and said, "Strewth, Rob-o, try again. Youse not very convincing. You bloody lose, mate. Ice cream wins, hands down. It's not like you *have* to come with me."

When Ian said that last sentence, all innocence and pleading eyes, I couldn't help but laugh.

"Oh, Ian, not that again. I'm always making these decisions when there really isn't anything to decide. I'll only worry about you and wonder if the river is up, if the roads are flooded, if you've drifted halfway out to sea. So I might as well go with you, but if it looks bad we turn around. Okay?"

Ian's face lit like a five-year-old's, and he said, "Youse got a bloody fair dinkum deal, mate."

He grabbed a long rope and threw it into the bed of the truck. With a guilty grin he said, "Just in case, Rob-o."

I groaned, shook my head, and reminded him, "You *promised*, none of that nonsense. Remember? If it gets bad we turn around. And if you keep your promise we won't *need* a rope. Right?"

He just laughed.

When we left early that morning, it was the first sunny day we'd had in a week. Although we weren't in the midst of the wet season we'd had a lot of rain. The narrow track that led down toward the river was in good shape. I was relieved when we got to the river road and it had only a touch of surface mud. The truck handled it with ease. Then, "just around the corner," Ian slammed on the brakes. For the next forty feet mud lay plastered across the narrow track, thick as cold oatmeal. Two Land Rovers sat in it, glued to the road. One of them had slewed side-on, bogged in the middle of the track. A middle-aged man with a florid complexion and bushy black eyebrows revved the engine and cursed when his tires burrowed eagerly into the mud.

The second truck had slid to the side of the track and leaned at a dangerous angle toward the ditch. A young blond-haired woman in pink foam curlers clutched the wheel. Her lanky and pasty-looking husband tried to push their vehicle back onto the road.

Ian muttered, "Bugger me dead," and threw open his door. He jumped out of the truck, clambered onto the hood, waved his arms, and shouted,

"Right-o, everybody, stand back." The door slammed when he leapt back into the truck and jammed it into reverse.

"Ian? Iaaaannn???"

A startled kookaburra let out a maniacal cackle. I shrieked, opened my door, and half dove, half rolled out of the Toyota just before Ian shifted into drive. Once he saw I was free of the truck, he gunned the engine and raced toward the mud, laughing almost as hard as the kookaburra.

The middle-aged man leapt from his vehicle and ran for the bushes, shouting something about "no insurance" and "bloody bonkers." The young woman, still in her truck, sat stunned, her mouth opening and closing like a goldfish. Ian slipped and slid past her. Horrified, I watched as mud sprayed from his tires, flew through her open window and splattered mud freckles across her face. Her equally stunned husband stood rooted in his pushing position at the back of their truck mumbling, "Bloody strewth, he's going to make it."

Actually, from the safety of the roadside I delighted in the whole escapade. A part of me waited eagerly to see what heroics or foolishness Ian would inflict. We were much alike. He let me have all my wild antics in the rainforest, so I figured I couldn't deny him his infatuation with trucks and machinery. I knew how he felt. He loved the irresistible challenge, the test to accomplish the seemingly impossible. He usually succeeded.

At one point, Ian slid completely sideways and looked like he was floating across the mud. He slowed the engine, the tires grabbed, and the truck straightened out.

The middle-aged man crept wide-eyed from the bushes as Ian neared his truck. He stood behind his vehicle and watched dumbfounded as Ian glided smoothly past him and onto hard ground.

Silence hung suspended over the road until Ian turned off his engine and emerged from the truck. Then, like a switch turned on, we all started talking, laughing, and cheering like a bunch of rowdy school kids.

Ian grabbed the long rope from the bed of the truck and hollered, "Right-o, mates, who's first?" He hitched the rope to our truck and then to the vehicle of the middle-aged driver. The rest of us pushed while the man drove, and Ian used our truck to pull him onto dry ground. When the man climbed from his truck he laughed and said, "I'll give youse me first born, mate."

Ian beamed. "Thanks, mate, but all I want is a gallon of bloody ice cream."

The rest of us wiped mud from our faces and got behind the second truck while Ian attached the rope. We pushed while the young woman drove, and Ian pulled her vehicle out of the mud.

By the time we arrived at the ferry landing, the sun shone hot and glared off the water. It would suck the moisture from the muddy track before our return from town. The party atmosphere lasted as we all boarded the ferry.

On the way to Cairns, I secretly decided that if a doctor would see me as a walk-in patient I would have my vaginal cyst checked. I'd last had it checked in Salt Lake City when a doctor first discovered it was precancerous. The amazing thing was that I felt no intense fear at the thought of testing it. So many things inside me had healed as a result of my life in the forest that I knew I'd be okay, no matter what. But I thought it might encourage me to believe in myself if I knew the cancer was gone. While Ian drove and chatted, I realized that no matter what the doctor found, I was *still* healing. It was the only reality I would accept. Healing was a state of "being" in which I now lived.

Ian went to get supplies, and I told him I was going to do some shopping on my own and would meet him later by the beach for lunch. Then I went to a phone booth to find a directory and call some doctors. The first one I called was able to see me if I came right away. I walked over to her office and was seen within minutes. She tested my cyst, and it was all over and done with in less than an hour. I told her to send the results to the post office in Mossman and I would get them. That was that.

Ian and I had lunch on the beach, but I decided not to tell him about my doctor's visit. I wanted to keep the secret close to me just a bit longer. It helped me stay strong and clear. After lunch we picked up a few more supplies and Ian had his precious ice cream, although it wasn't a gallon. Then we headed for home. The track had dried enough for a nearly effortless return. We made it safely back without further drama. It felt good to come home to land that was ours. My beloved forest stood only 100 yards away. Though it wasn't Cape Tribulation, I felt I was still connected to it. I'd learned at Cape Trib that no matter where I traveled in the world I'd always be connected to the earth. On the edge of the rainforest, life went on. All over the breathing, sighing earth, life continued, whether I was there to see it or not. It didn't matter if it was Cape Tribulation, Daintree River, or Streaked Mountain in Maine. Earth was one living body, not the separate pieces I'd been led to believe.

I gave my new home the chance it deserved to reveal itself, just as I'd given Cape Trib a chance. My intimate connection to this new and unfamiliar piece of earth grew deeper each day. I continued to spend my days and even some nights alone in the forest. We hadn't been living on our land long when I awoke early one morning to particularly hot and humid weather. Unable to sleep, I hiked up the hill behind our tent and into the shade of the trees. Dawn's cool air clung to shadows under the canopy.

I loved to sit quietly and watch life renew itself. Birds built nests, courting commenced, and hatchlings were tended. I wondered whether sunrise infused the birds with song, or, since the birds tuned up long before sunrise, maybe their wild sonata woke the sun and inspired it to peek above the horizon.

Tiny brown skinks, speckled orange, yellow, and blue, darted among leaves and twigs at my feet. They snapped up beetles and ants faster than my eyes could follow.

Later in the day, as the sun's heat penetrated the canopy and touched the air closer to the floor, most of the insect-eating birds—robins, flycatchers, honey-eaters, and thrushes—grew quiet. Only the soft coos of pigeons remained to create a constant and soothing backdrop for all other sounds of the forest.

Even though I heard the pittas scratch among the ground litter for snails, I saw them less than I'd have liked. They were extremely alert to any movement. Sometimes I sat still for an hour before the life around me resumed its normal routine and moved in close in search of food that lay inches from my toes. When I sat patient as a rock, I became just another part of the scenery.

When we had lived at Cape Trib, I had occasionally glimpsed larger birds, like the brush turkey or orange-footed scrubfowl. They both are mound builders and lay their eggs in huge mounds of rotting vegetation that they scratch into a pile five to ten feet tall. The eggs hatch from the heat of the rotting leaves and debris, and the parents control the temperature by opening and closing the mound. At Cape Trib I had also seen a dark figure that scratched under fruit trees or crashed its way through brush. Although I hadn't always seen it clearly, I knew it was a cassowary. It's a stunning black, blue, and red flightless bird, which stands as tall as a grown man and has a rapier-sharp claw on each foot. I never went too close. Left alone, they never bothered me. It was always an exciting experience to catch even a cassowary's shadow.

I loved to imitate numerous bird calls. I collected bird songs the way a child collects marbles, feathers, frogs, worms, and other treasures. As I excelled in the art of imitation, male birds often darted at my head to warn me away from their territory. After a near eye-gouging, I learned my lesson.

Some birds are more playful than others, like the famous laughing kookaburra, a member of the kingfisher family. He's a swift, daring reptile-eater with a strong, fat bill and robust body. A few times I watched him swoop down on an unsuspecting snake and grab the reptile with his beak, give a fierce shake of his head, and fly off, all in one smooth motion. Held tight in Mr. Kookaburra's sharp bill, the limp snake trailed out on the wind behind him. Roughly a foot and a half tall from bill tip to tail tip, Mr. Kookaburra's loud cackling laughter is heard at the crack of dawn all over Australia. Kookaburra and I had many contests to see who could laugh the loudest and longest. It became one of our favorite games. He always won, of course, and when I gave up he flew to a branch above my head, just out of reach, and mocked me.

Later that morning, I crested the hill and started back down. The humidity was almost as thick as fog. At the edge of our field, I rested on a large flat rock. The instant my bare butt hit its smooth surface a slight movement caught my eye. Attached to the underside of a leaf hung a greenish colored pupa suspended by a silk thread. Gently I bent the tip of the leaf for a closer peek. The creature within lay snug in a hard case the shape of its body. Just as I leaned in for a better look, a crack formed in the pupa's surface, as if it were a timed performance and life had waited until I arrived to share this tiniest of events. Now that I had my seat, the show began. Two wire-thin legs, fine as black silk thread, poked from the opening. They hooked around the outside of the crack like two hands prying an elevator door open from the inside. Hair-thin antennae were followed by more black legs. She struggled for what seemed like an eternity to shed her metamorphic chamber. Finally her body broke free, followed by folded wings, dark blue and black. Amazing! How do such thin legs have any strength? She looked as fragile as rice paper. How does something that delicate survive?

She crawled from her protective shell and onto the branch. Her iridescent body shimmered blue. Several times I thought she'd fall to the ground because she almost trembled with weakness. I held my breath as she worked her way out of the shade to the sunny tip of the branch only a couple of inches away. Maybe she needed the sun to dry her wings or to get them working.

She safely reached her patch of sun, and I waited while she clung. I barely breathed because I didn't want her to fall and the ants get her.

At first I thought I imagined it when a long black tongue (proboscis) flicked from the butterfly's chin area, but I didn't. Her tongue flicked again, and it was at least an inch and a half long. It rewound like a carpenter's retractable tape measure. When I remembered that most butterflies eat nectar, I understood the need for length.

Who'd have thought I'd ever see a butterfly's tongue? I could live a thousand years in the Daintree Rainforest and still not see everything. I wondered; do ants have tongues? What about beetles? And what kind of eyes do all the creatures have? What do they see? Color? Black and white? Or only movement? Bees and butterflies must see colors to be drawn to flowers. Or maybe the flowers' scents attract them. I'd smelled some alluring scents in the rainforest: chocolate, vanilla, flowery, and aromatic smells often enticed me closer. But I suspected bees and butterflies were drawn to color. The few times I wore clothes to town, if they were brightly colored, bees and sometimes butterflies would flutter around me.

As curious as I was, I usually had no desire to find the answers to these questions in books. Some things, like reptiles, birds, and plants, interested me more than others, and I referred, when necessary, to my few identification books. Reading was so different from the magic I experienced through self-discovery. I learned better by watching than by reading. The more time I spent in the wild the more I preferred to observe the forest and let Nature disclose herself in her own way. She nurtured as she taught and is the best teacher I've ever had.

A slight breeze stirred heavy air as the sun climbed higher. The branch began to sway. Like a new mother, I fretted over the movement. "Rock-a-bye baby on the treetop, when the wind blows the cradle will rock." I hummed as I held my open palms beneath the swaying twig. I needn't have worried. Movement is part of a butterfly's soul. They're conceived to the tempo of gently pulsing wings. Their pupa sways to the rhythm of warm breeze. They live out the few days of their existence on wing and wind. The desire for movement was something I knew well.

A tentative stretch here, a tentative stretch there, slowly her wings unfolded, folds as intricate as an origami crane. Fully extended, she arched and stretched with slow, undulating grace, intimate and dance-like. I felt her pleasure in response to the warm sun and her anticipated flight. Black and brown patterned the underside of her five-inch wingspan. Electric blue outlined with black decorated the top surface. Each rear wing ended in a long, black spatulate tail trimmed with a thin white line.

My "she" was actually a "he" Ulysses swallowtail. The female is more subdued in color, and there was nothing subdued about Ulysses. A slight turn of wing and metallic blue scales caught the sun to create a pulsing blue hologram, from aqua-blue to royal-blue to baby-blue and back again. Shivers scampered up my back to my shoulder blades. Primal memory awoke, and I remembered how to fly. I felt the wind's pressure beneath my wings on the downward stroke. I remembered the lightness of body, the buffet of wind. I remembered. After all, we are all connected. There is no separation.

After much preening, my fragile butterfly, so like a newborn fairy, was ready to flutter into the vast world. I didn't want to miss his first flight. At what moment would he decide to go? And where would he go? In search of food and a mate? Of course, because life seeks life, and he had only a day or two to live, a short time to start the cycle over through his offspring.

My face froze immobile, inches from brilliant blue splendor, ornate black veining, detail so fine I don't believe an artist's brush or photographer's lens could capture the love in that butterfly. It was a complete and shining work of art. Aaah, the marvels we take for granted. Could you create a living butterfly? Life isn't only intelligent; it's dazzlingly creative in its self-expression.

I waited, my breath shallow. I didn't want to disturb his grand moment of departure. Any moment now. Here goes. He looks ready. A flash of movement. A darting gray shadow out of the corner of my eye. A rush of air on my cheek. The butterfly disappeared snapped up by the strong bill of a gray and white flycatcher, his first flight in the mouth of a bird. Ulysses' wings, legs, and body protruded from the flycatcher's beak as he swifted away with his meal.

In one jerk of my body I rose and raced twenty feet into the field to stop the bird and . . . do what? Resuscitate a squashed butterfly? Futility brought me to a standstill when the catcher's flight veered over the hill toward the river.

Back on my rock, I pondered the fate of the butterfly. It happened so fast that a vacuous scent still hung in the air where Ulysses once stood. Somewhere on a branch by the river, the flycatcher sat contentedly eating Ulysses. My conflicting emotions tried to settle.

If birds eat their weight in insects several times a day, then the butterfly was one tiny, but necessary, potato chip in the day of the flycatcher. Most of the insect-eating birds left the Ulysses alone. Maybe the catcher made a mistake or hadn't eaten for some time. Maybe the butterfly's wings were soft and fresh from birth and the bird knew it. Did the flycatcher watch and wait for the exact moment to snatch his breakfast? I'm sure he did. I'd seen too many creatures watching and waiting for a meal to believe otherwise.

Usually I found the remains of large butterflies in orb-weaving spiderwebs. Their bodies were wrapped in the spider's silken threads, injected with enzymes to dissolve their insides and then sucked empty. Often I spotted the butterflies tougher, scaly wings rejected on the ground beneath an enormous web. Some of the orb-weaving spiders (web-building spiders) are huge. The golden orb weaver with her bulbous gray body and long, thin black legs with yellow dots at the joints, weaves a gold-colored web. Spread wide, she spans a good seven inches. She's magnificent. Her web is so strong even small birds can become tangled in it. They, too, are sometimes eaten. I often saw golden orb weavers' huge nets stretched between trees and shrubs, and even when my head accidentally hit their woven homes, they never bothered me. After I had my face plastered with web a few times, I watched more carefully where I walked. Without a web, they couldn't eat. Their webs were objects of art—thin, symmetrical, and fine. I called them beauty, but the flies that landed on the sticky web knew it only as death. I respected the spiders and was glad they weren't big enough to catch humans.

I was reminded of the swift flycatcher that ate Ulysses. His strong bill would bring a quicker death than the spider's enzymes. At least I hoped death hit quickly and painlessly for the butterfly. Maybe it didn't? Regardless, the flycatcher still has to eat. Maybe that's part of the "deal" of life; we eat, but at some point we must become the eaten.

I could hardly believe that Ulysses once stood on the now empty branch next to my leg. His short life was a miracle. Of all the eggs his mother laid only two percent of the caterpillars live long enough to become adult butterflies.

Ulysses must have felt such joy when he stretched his wings in the sun. He had shimmered with excitement over his new freedom. The more I thought about Ulysses' death, I realized I'd witnessed only one small scene. That number was magnified a billion times throughout the rainforest, a trillion-times-a-trillion throughout the world.

The enormity of the rainforest left me feeling small and humbled. I was only one tiny beetle snore in the wake of millions of years of existence. It made me cherish the time I'd been given. I felt a sense of awe and peace because I also realized that even if I died, even if the rainforest didn't survive another hundred million years, life itself would go on in ecstatic frenzy with or without me. It would flourish in some unique form, forever. My destiny was to merge with this infinite love.

Feeling my smallness within such grandness made me feel safe. Someone or something was watching over me, like the night Ian and I made love and I had floated in the Milky Way galaxy, safely watched over and loved. The Universal Intelligence was, after all, larger than man and could include us and our mistakes. For me, that didn't mean that our ill-mannered and harmful actions were okay or that we each shouldn't do our part to live in harmony with other life forms. It simply meant that there was something so vast that it would never end, that it was so large and boundless it could experience and encompass all things . . . and continue to live. It had existed long before I arrived and would go on long after my passing. And so would I, because I was part of it.

I left Ulysses' branch with the empty pupa still attached and hiked once more up the hill into the trees and cool shade. I wasn't ready to go back to camp. I looped around and ran into the trail of the creek where I sat with my feet in a pool of rapidly churning water. When sharp teeth bit the end of my big toe, I yanked my feet into the air with a yelp and moved to a calmer spot where I could see bottom. I wasn't sure what nipped me: a fish, a turtle, or an eel, something after its dinner. It's a good thing there was a 115-pound body attached to my toe or I'd have gone the way of my butterfly that day. Always something eating something.

The longer I lived in the rainforest the more I reflected on my feelings about life and death. I thought about my own brush with cancer and even the shutting down or near death of my spirit in society. If I hadn't gone to the rainforest at the age of twenty-five, I wouldn't have lived beyond thirty. Luckily I found my way home and was able to heal. The rainforest is one of the most exquisitely beautiful places in the entire universe. It is heaven. Do we realize that we are the custodians of heaven?

With all these thoughts washing over me, I left the creek and hiked back to camp. When I approached the edge of our property, I tapped the ground with my stick as I walked. Unlike the forest, part of our land was cleared. The trees had been cut down long before our arrival. I waded through an ocean of six-foot-high, razor-sharp grass, an introduced species that made a great hiding place for snakes. I didn't balk at the snakes, but I did want to warn them that I was coming and give them time to slip away.

I always listened and watched, alert to sounds and movement around me. A high-pitched whine of a bee abruptly drew my attention. I cautiously tracked the sound in front of me and went to investigate.

There in the long grass beside a melastoma bush, I found them. A three-inch praying mantis was gripping a screaming bee, vise-like and was eating it alive. Tipped upside down on his back, the bee kicked and struggled violently for his vanishing life. His dagger-sharp stinger thrust repeatedly at the mantis but struck only air. The lime-green mantis tightened his grip on the bee and warily watched me for signs of danger. His triangular head tipped left then right. With big eyes he studied my face and movements like some alien being. When I didn't interfere, he settled down to enjoy his meal.

Fascinated. Horrified. Amazed. I squatted on my heels to watch. My gut tightened as the bee's screams grew higher pitched and more desperate. My stomach ripped and tore open along with his. I tried to relax my fingers when they clutched in revulsion and self-defense at my own warm abdomen. The mantis chewed the exoskeleton from the bee's belly, tossed it aside and dipped his head into the exposed cavity. The bee continued to scream even with half his body eaten. With three legs ripped off and flung aside, stomach organs almost completely consumed, he screamed all the way down the mantis's gullet.

Even though I stared at the little scene in horror, I *still* felt the contentment of the praying mantis. He occasionally looked up at me with just a glance and continued to eat. I felt his enjoyment over such a fine catch. Each glance he said, "See what *I've* got?"

The mantis wasn't cruel or evil, merely hungry. He had the right to relish a hard-earned meal, one he risked his life to catch. He cleaned his face and "hands" in such a human way, I couldn't help but smile.

The bee was gone. His life force coursed through the body of the mantis. I made myself watch as, once again, life and death flowed together with violence, passion, and necessity, until I couldn't tell them apart. I walked away changed. Another small incident in a chain of a thousand that became my life. Simple as they seemed, they left a lasting impression.

I left the mantis and continued toward camp. As I looked down at our land, I realized that although the rainforest loomed green and cool 100 yards from my tent flap, I felt exposed on our land and didn't like it. I would grow native trees and plants, but that took awhile. Just like it took awhile to fall in love with my new home. I had to plant fruit trees and muddy my hands and feet in the earth.

Down in our spring I found a little depression in the ground, almost big enough for two people to sit in. I noticed that tan clay lined the bottom. Water bubbled from the ground and filled the hole with a slurry of mud. It was silky smooth and splendidly cool. I made the pit deeper by stirring more clay until I could sink my whole body into a thick mud bath. This was my secret place of healing.

Healing abilities of clay are often underestimated and overlooked. I had read that it can heal the body in many ways: balance energy, remove toxins and radiation, and heal wounds. In some countries small clay balls are sucked to stave off hunger.[1]

I often found animal tracks around my pit where wildlife had come to stand in the hole to keep cool or to heal. When I scooped clay out, fresh spring water bubbled up, which I mixed with new clay to refill my bath. Over time the bath grew and could have held three people. I enjoyed sharing the pit with my wild friends. Maybe *they* were sharing it with *me*. No matter, we all used it weekly, even Ian had a few fun-filled mud soaks with me.

Although we supposedly "owned" the land, it wasn't ours. All manner of life, generations of flora and fauna had lived there for millions of years. I needed to learn who else occupied this small piece of earth. What were their habits? Where were their territories? Whose home had I invaded?

I was especially interested in some of the plants. After a few weeks, I collected and dried a few samples of flora with intriguing scents and unusual growth patterns. On his trips to town Ian posted them to the CSIRO (Commonwealth Scientific and Industrial Research Organization) for identification. Often the CSIRO could give me no information about the plants. That was okay. They were living beings with no less value for lack of proper Latin names. They were already complete in themselves whether I identified them or not. I knew enough about plant identification and harvesting to pick a plant and not cause it long-term damage. Nonetheless, I didn't want to disturb the rainforest anymore, so I stopped sending greenery to the CSIRO and went back to the smell, taste, and feel method. I survived.

On one of his trips to town, Ian came home with some mail. We hardly ever received mail because we never wrote anyone. Occasionally Ian received a letter from his mom or I received mail from the CSIRO. This time the letter was for me. I knew what it was when Ian asked, but I told him I wanted to open it by myself. He didn't seem to mind at all and said he was going to do some work on the truck. Before I even opened the envelope I knew the answer, I felt it as I held the letter in my hand. Slowly I slit the seal, unfolded the paper, quickly scanned it until I found the word *negative*. I no longer had a precancerous cyst, what remained of it was very small and benign. Life instills life. Like the bee's life force that flowed into the mantis, the life of the rainforest had flowed into me, healing my body.

Ian had only known that I had a cyst. I had never mentioned that it had been precancerous. As I told him the whole story he was extremely moved and said how much he respected the trust I placed in my body and its ability to heal. He hugged me close and told me that I could do anything.

Months passed as we settled into that land. I lost track of how many and was swallowed in the seasons' gentle cadences. Months blurred into colors, shades of green trees with new pink and red leaves, scents of salty sea, steamy nights and wallaby droppings, songs of pheasant coucal, kookaburra, and sulfur-crested cockatoo. Grand and intimate events and wonderfully tumultuous emotions shaped my days and nights. It didn't matter what month it was; my life flourished, too rich to care.

I remember three hot nights in a row. The air hung dense and muggy. Moisture from the coast sniffed out the base of our mountain and sat there. Unfortunately, it forgot to bring along the sea breeze, which was unusual. Ian was hot and frustrated because he'd already run out of the tent once to chase away feral pigs that rooted around our cassava and taro. Feral pigs are fascinating creatures. They have cast-iron constitutions. A Parks and Wildlife Service ranger told us, "They can bloody eat almost anything and it doesn't kill 'em, including poisoned bait. They can even get bitten by the deadliest of Australian snakes and often keep right on goin'. Those bloody buggers will eat stuff that'd kill us in two minutes flat, like your cassavas that contain hydrocyanic acid. The only way to get rid of 'em is to build a big pen with one-way access and fill it with rotten fruit. Then get a high-powered rifle and shoot the bloody buggers. Otherwise they'll tear up the whole place and foul your bloody spring water."

Later that night after four sleepless hours of listening to the pigs' squealing racket, Ian snapped. He sat up, crawled out of the tent, grabbed a two-foot log, and hissed through clenched teeth, "That's it."

At the sight of a stark-naked man with a log club trying to sneak up on "the three little pigs," I started to giggle.

"You look like a primitive caveman, Ian, a real Neanderthal. You go, dude."

"Shhhhush, Rob. You'll scare the bloody bastards away."

"Isn't that the idea?"

"No! I want to kill those blasted pigs."

At Ian's this-is-serious-business tone, I couldn't help but giggle. I knew he'd never get near them. They were too alert and fast. I tried to muffle my laughter with my hand, but I could hardly contain myself as he snuck up on one of the pigs and swung like crazy. I chuckled harder when it occurred to me that Ian was so distraught over his sleepless night that he hadn't even thought to get the rifle from the truck. After Ian's first *attempted* smack with the log, the pigs took off for the hills and left him swinging the air with his club. He raced after them, and I yelled, "Watch out for snakes, Ian. You're barefoot." In his half-crazed state he forgot his snake phobia and charged wildly into the night, chasing the squealing pigs, his club raised in angry frustration as he yelled obscenities at the retreating porkers.

"You bloody fat bastards. I'll get you. You stinking rotten bloody rat-bags. Hang around here and I'll feed your carcasses to the bloody freakin' crocs. You lard buckets. Lousy bloody bastards tearing up me taro."

I finally rolled around on the ground in a fit of hysterical laughter.

Ian returned awhile later and, if nothing else, appeared satisfied to have vented his frustration. We climbed back into the tent and tried to sleep. At least it was quiet for the time being. Ian went straight to sleep. Hot and restless, I continued to toss and turn. That's the only reason I heard the rapid thump, thump, thump a couple of hours after the pigs' departure. I lay in the tent with the flaps wide open, my head exposed to thick warm air, my nostrils full of dark musky night. The familiar sound of wallabies filled me with excitement. They bounced back and forth across our field like a dozen rubber balls thrown onto a hard wood floor. There must have been a whole mob. I wished I had night-vision goggles.

In the morning I woke to discover that the hungry pigs had returned while we slept, and I was stunned at what I saw. I shook Ian awake.

"Hey, mate, wake up. Ian, waaake uuuup. The pigs destroyed everything."

"What do you mean *everything*, Roby?"

"Come take a look, you won't believe it. It's all gone. They've dug up everything."

Ian climbed from the tent and stood speechless at the sight in front of him. "Bloody strewth. They've destroyed everything. Our garden looks like someone rototilled it. Where's the bloody taros? The yams and cassavas? They're all gone. I can't believe it."

"Yeah, that's what I meant by *everything*. Check out the fruit trees. They're gone too."

Our young fruit trees: avocados, pawpaws, rambutans, breadfruit, and custard apples had all been dug up and the roots eaten. Discouragement overwhelmed me until I was distracted by the sight of flattened patches of grass and three-toed prints where kangaroos had rested in the night. I felt comforted by their presence and forgot the damage left by the pigs. I could hardly wait to hear the 'roos again.

That day came sooner than I expected, and I got more than a listen. Two days later, I rose at first light and splashed water from our white bucket onto my face and arms. When I stood, I heard a rustle and slow shuffle in the grass next to me. Just beyond the tent, a brown pear-shaped body revealed a black-tailed wallaby, also called a swamp wallaby. Dainty coal black "fingers" parted the tall grass, and although I couldn't see her face I knew she peered intently at me. Laughter almost escaped from my throat. She reminded me of a kid who thinks if their face is hidden the rest of their body can't be seen. I averted my eyes and spoke low and gently so I wouldn't startle her.

"Hi. How are you? You've come to visit, eh? Yes, it's safe here. We don't have any dogs or cats. And I won't touch you. Won't even move. We'll just talk. Okay?"

She finally stuck her head from the grass and tipped it to the side. Dark doelike eyes with long black lashes searched my face with keen interest. Large ears twitched forward and backward at each rise and fall of my voice as she divined my intention from the sounds I made. Tender protectiveness rose in my chest and spilled over in tears. She pretended to ignore me. I pretended to ignore her. Although she was cautious and tested me, her curiosity was as alive as my own. She appeared to love the sound of my voice. It probably was the first human voice she'd ever heard.

As I talked in breathy singsong tones, she slowly closed her eyes and relaxed onto her haunches using her long tail for support like the third leg of a stool. Remiss in her alertness she startled, jerked her head up, and sniffed the breeze for danger. Like a bird on a branch, she darted quick looks in every direction. I waited.

I never tried to feed or tame my wild friends. Wildlife survives far better fearing man. What does it really mean to tame? To substitute free food and shelter in place of the hunt? A possible fence or structure to keep others out and keep me safe? Or is it to keep me in, separate and controlled by fear? What does it mean to tame? To inhibit freedom of thought and organic impulse? To crush one's will to live? To merely exist? To survive, but not thrive? A slow deadening of the senses? Removal of all instinct? A loss of freedom? A loss of wildness?

I wouldn't tame my wild friends. Not when I desperately sought freedom through my own wildness. I had to be very aware of how I behaved, and careful not to teach the wallabies to trust my kind. Sometimes we humans can be extremely crass and out of control. We're a species that can destroy wildlife without shedding a single tear. We truly are something to fear in this world. What's more, not all wildlife is interested in humans. In any case, I couldn't risk endangering them in any way. If I harmed one, I harmed them all. Life in the forest is connected to itself. Massive trees and damp spongy earth, colorful birds and scented orchids all live inside the wallaby. And the wallaby lives inside them.

I suppose I should have shooed her away, but at the time I figured if I didn't feed or pet her I wouldn't intrude too far into her life. Nowadays I'd be tempted to chase her away, although it would be extremely hard to do, maybe impossible. It's heartbreaking when the need to connect and communicate with other species sometimes is a very real one, but not a safe prospect for the last remaining wildlife. The next person might have a rifle hidden behind his soft-spoken words, perhaps a dog with sharp, biting teeth or tempting smells that lead to poisoned bait. Rarely did I touch wildlife, unless it was dead or actively sought out physical contact with me, and even then I tried not to let it get too close. Its trusting and beguiling ways were hard to resist. I grieved when I couldn't freely invite these friends into my life, but unless I could protect them I had to leave them alone.

I sensed that my wallaby, like me, wanted to make contact for no other reason than to communicate. She never came close to our tent like one who has a taste for human food and searches it out. I never ate in her presence, except the new growth that sprouted where I'd cut the tall grass around our tent. I plucked the sweet, tender shoots with my fingers and ate alongside her. After that morning, she came to visit every day before sunrise.

One cloud-filled morning she hopped tentatively into the clearing and stood twenty feet in front of me. Grass protruded from the sides of her teeth like green whiskers. She reminded me of a kid sucking up strands of spaghetti as she pulled the succulent blades into her mouth with her lips. She never ate much grass, only a bite or two. Maybe it was more pretense for being there than anything else.

She stood upright on muscular legs and strong tail. Her long, flat feet left three-toed prints in the soft earth around our camp. Wallabies are marsupials, members of the kangaroo family, and like all marsupials they have pouches in which they carry their young. They also are macropods, which means "big foot." One of the three toes on each of her hind feet was actually two toes in one. It had two nails that could be used the same way we use tweezers, or as a grooming tool.

Like all kangaroos, the wallaby's arms or forelimbs were particularly petite compared to her stout legs and body. Very little fur covered her arms. This allowed her to lick the blood vessels just beneath the skin to remain cool. Her tiny hands looked startlingly human, and often were used in human ways. Or maybe we use our hands in wallaby fashion. In any case, our arms and hands were very much alike.

Without touching her, I knew her fur would be velvet soft and forest clean under my hand. Coal-black striped her tail and gloved her delicate hands and large feet. Two light yellowish patches streaked the sides of her face from lip to ear. There was nothing dingy or drab about her.

In the month that followed, we sat and browsed together every dawn. Eventually she became used to Ian puttering around camp and no longer startled. Most visits she stayed only fifteen minutes or so, but it was more than enough. She was my female companion, my closest wild friend. I found her very feminine and thought I'd like to call her Wanna Be Wallaby. You wanna be in my presence. I wanna be in yours. As we relaxed in each other's company, I didn't know whether to rush out and wrap my arms around Wanna Be's endearing ways or laugh my head off at her comical behavior. In the end, all I did was sit, watch, and heal. I loved her.

Eventually Wanna Be's brown belly grew full and fat. She carried a joey, not more than twelve inches tall, a replica of his mother—minus some of the black markings on tail and hands. One day he hopped from her pouch and bounced around like a kid on a pogo stick, back and forth in front of the tent. Wanna Be and I sat and watched junior play the way two mothers sit on a park bench and watch their children play. Each of us plucked grass and nibbled contentedly.

I burst out laughing at the joey's buoyancy and uninhibited freedom. My mother friend didn't even flinch from the sharp and foreign sound. However the joey startled, shot straight into the air, turned, and dove head-first into his mother's pouch. His hind legs scrambled air to get inside. His tail and one foot didn't quite make it, and they protruded like some grotesque growth from Mom's belly. Wanna Be's head bent and followed the tiny wallaby into the pouch to offer comfort.

After about eight months in the pouch, a joey is too big to ride in his mom's fur-lined pocket. But he will remain at her side as a "young at heel." Even after the mother gives birth to a new joey, the young at heel can put his head in his mom's pouch and nurse. Since she's able to produce milk of different strengths from different size nipples she can nurse both the tiny newborn and the larger joey at the same time.

The last day I saw Wanna Be, she took three hops in my direction and stared intently into my eyes for at least five minutes. Then she was gone. I missed her terribly and always looked for her, but in some ways I was glad she was gone. Her contact with me caused me to worry about her safety. Then it hit me that she might be dead, her joey also. I prayed not, but there were feral dogs and probably dingo-dog crosses, pythons, crocodiles, and humans, all dangerous to wallabies. After knowing Wanna Be, I became far more cautious about making friends with animals in the wild. It was hard, though, because wildlife can be keenly curious, naturally trusting, and very bright.

Wild animals are capable of making their own choices and decisions. Even the choice to love. Some might think we have to bribe them with food and other enticements for them to befriend us, love us, and be part of our world. When animals don't respond to us in a desired manner, they often are perceived as base and unintelligent. Maybe the lack of intelligence lies not with other species but more possibly with us and our inability to perceive and understand other forms of intelligence. Maybe other species have their own desires and needs, their own equally as important thread to weave in the web of life.

Are we humans misplaced and out of rhythm? Have we stepped away from life, separate from the rest? A lonely species?

My wild friends taught me that they have individual souls as real as my own. Sure, we might be able to get them to do as we wish by bribing them with food, but they may not reveal their souls to us. That must be given freely. They're no different from you and me. When we truly love, we don't have to be bribed; we love because we're compelled.

Wanna Be taught me something else about wildlife. Although they live in a world where they must continually be aware of predators, they still play. Many animals have a sense of humor. We aren't the only species blessed with playfulness. I watched other species play and express affection, concern, irritability, grief, contentment, and more.

Some of my wild friends came to visit me daily. At first I could hardly fathom that they came to visit *just* because they wanted to see me, talk with me, possibly play a game, and share their wisdom. The presence of wild creatures filled my life with joy. My untamed friends taught me how to be human again by helping me to find the benevolent or humane part of myself. They also showed me how to be an animal again and how to listen to my heart's wild hunger. They were my community. I was safe with them all: snake, bird, wallaby, and insect. With the earth wrapped around me, I was alive instead of isolated, sterile, and dead. As I woke to full consciousness I began to grasp my place in the scheme of things, and my realization of the equality of all life was born.

This ruptured cultural carapace
Cannot sustain me
My hunger not arrested
I chant the song of my beloved
I dance the longing of my heart
And I am melded into the womb of life

—RUSSELL HUME

eight

CROCODILES, FERAL PIGS, AND PITCH BLACK

WE HAD DECIDED TO BUILD A HOME ON OUR LAND, and Ian danced around anxious to leave for Cairns. He wanted to price building materials and pick up supplies. I chose to stay at camp to tend our fruit trees and garden. The day's trip back and forth to Cairns was longer than I cared to make.

We sat in the late afternoon sun and wrote our supply list. Ian usually detested organization of any kind and would have happily driven off to town without a list. Once he arrived in Cairns, he would have bought everything we *didn't* need and more. Ian loved to buy "stuff" in bulk, especially on sale. Fortunately, Far North Queensland had few stores that sold things in bulk. At a small produce store in Mossman we occasionally purchased a whole crate of fruit or veggies, things that we didn't grow: grapes, mushrooms, apricots, and other delicacies. By the time we consumed it all, we didn't want to eat that fruit or vegetable for another year.

Ian's impatience increased, so I helped him find his wallet and finish his list. Wallets weren't needed in the rainforest. They could lay hidden wherever we dumped them after the last trip to town, three or four months earlier. Ian ferreted around in the tent and found his slightly moldy leather billfold, which I placed next to his clothes for town.

A trip to Cairns, or even Mossman, was a big event. It seemed more important to Ian than to me, maybe because he grew up in the city. Although he loved the bush in his own way, he still didn't share my yearning to be among the trees. I nonetheless spent every spare moment in the rainforest. Ian rarely went into the forest's shadowed depths and when he did it was usually because I wanted to show him something remarkable, such as a huge tree, a particular rock pool, or a dead animal.

I found it increasingly difficult to understand the unfamiliar world of town. The rainforest had become my home. I loved and understood the ancient green world better than any other.

Ian decided to leave right after supper and spend the night at the ferry landing down by the river. The punt only ran between 6:00 AM and 6:00 PM. We had no watches, so he needed to be there in time for Clyde to pick him up. If he missed the first early morning run, he'd have less time to spend in town. As he threw his clothes into the Toyota, he gave me last minute instructions.

"Keep the tent flaps done up tight and you'll be right. I think the bloody batteries are still good in the black torch. I put it under the platform in the tent."

I loved how Ian called a flashlight a torch. It had a nice old-fashioned sound to it and made me dream of a time when humans had only fire to light their way in the dark. Our tent *wasn't* old-fashioned, but it looked like something out of the 1930s. It was a funny affair because it had no floor, and the front and rear door flaps tied instead of zipped. Rainforest critters could have ambled right through the tent and out the other side if they had wanted to, but it still sounded good to hear Ian say, "Do up the tent flaps and you'll be right." He reminded me of the husband who says, "Lock the door while I'm gone and you'll be okay, honey."

I usually went with Ian on the rare trips to town. We hadn't been apart much except for my hikes alone into the forest, but I always knew I'd return to find him in camp. As he continued to tell me his plans I sensed we needed to reassure each other.

"I'm driving down to the river in a bit, and I'll sleep there tonight on the front seat. That way I can catch the first ferry run in the morning. If I don't, I might not get across till bloody seven. I want an early start. I'll catch the last ferry tomorrow evening and be back a bit after six. Well, best nick off and get some bloody sleep. Love you, matey. You'll be right, eh? Ta-ta."

I always felt such a wrenching when Ian and I parted, as if I might never see him again. Tears filled my eyes when he hugged me really hard. I stood at the top of the hill and waved until he disappeared down the track.

Dusk crept up the valley so I hustled through my chores before dark. Our new fruit trees were still very young. They replaced the trees the feral pigs had destroyed. Some of them wouldn't produce fruit for years, but I watered them lovingly as if they already supplied us with food. I'd also replanted amaranth, cassavas, yams, and taro on the gentle slope that led down to the spring. I grabbed my long, sturdy pole and two five-gallon buckets and slogged down the hill to get water. I'd become so strong I could easily carry two full buckets. They hung at either end of the pole that rested like a yoke across my shoulders. The spring bubbled a quarter of a mile from our tent. Some days, depending on whether we did laundry, bathed, or watered the fruit trees and garden, I might haul twenty buckets of water up the hill. My thin frame turned to solid sinewy muscle. I grew strong enough to carry Ian on my shoulders for half a mile without stopping. If he'd been bitten by a snake while hiking with me, I could have carried him out of the forest.

The hiking I did each day added muscle to my thin legs for the first time in my life. I usually hiked miles in my wanderings and never grew tired of exploring. Ian rarely knew how far I ranged. No one did. He still wanted me to carry a whistle in case a snake bit me, and hoped he'd find one on his trip to town. Most days I hiked naked and barefoot, but occasionally I wore my faded red sarong and a pair of handmade leather moccasins. Sometimes I still strapped my mildewed belt around my waist with Dad's hunting knife and my blue fanny pack looped over it. The fanny pack contained six ACE bandages I'd purchased in Mossman. A wide stretchy bandage is the best way to stop the systemic flow of venom from Australian snakebites.

As I watered the avocado and breadfruit trees, my thoughts drifted to a snakebite treatment workshop given by a bush guide in Cairns. Matt, our presenter, was a fair dinkum Aussie. At least he played the part, well dressed in his greasy, dust-covered, brown stockman's hat and white T-shirt with "Castlemaine XXXX Bitter" stamped across the front. Along with handling snakes, Matt must have sat on many a pub stool handling tinnies. His bulbous, heavily veined nose and pillow-shaped gut betrayed a lifelong affinity with "piss," and his tanned, leathery skin showed his love of the outdoors. His brown Stubbies (a brand of shorts) appeared like he'd slept in them on the bare ground, swam in the sea, and then rolled in the sand while he was still wet. The elastic sides of his Aussie work boots were so frayed they looked like they'd exploded. His crusty nondescript socks made me hope his boots stayed on his feet. Yup, as far as fair dinkum Aussies go, he looked mighty convincing to me. Except for the brand-new Castlemaine T-shirt, Matt was a study in grunge. And yet, for some reason he didn't smell. Maybe it was clean grunge. He appeared about sixty-five, and most of his life must have been lived in the bush handling dirt, eating dirt, and breathing dirt. Fascinated, I listened while he talked.

"G'day, mates. So, youse 'ere to learn about bloody snakes, eh? First off, me name is Mad Matt. I guess 'cause me mates reckon I's a bit of a larrikin. Guess I am at that, handling bloody snakes and all. Grew up in the bush running wild. Well, enough about me. Good to see we's got a few Sheilas 'ere t's arvo. You bloody blokes aren't going to like this one bit, but it seems to me youse the ones who's more scared of snakes than the Sheilas. Well, we'll see what we can do about that t'day. At least youse all 'ere, that's a start."

At the end of nearly every sentence, Matt tugged shyly at the brim of his battered hat. After several sentences, only the point of his chin remained visible. I never knew the color of the hair hidden beneath his grimy hat-band. He could have been bald.

Posters, books, flyers, and slides of snakes from all over Australia, along with a ton of bandages and an assortment of splints, lay on tables around the room. He gave a quick introduction, and true to Aussie form, he got right to the heart of it. I tried to keep up, because even if I didn't learn about snakes, I'd learn *something* from a character like Matt.

"Aussies have one of the most advanced methods of snakebite treatment in the world. And remember, this information is for Australian snakes, *not* 'merican snakes or snakes in other areas of the world where treatment might be quite different."

Matt wiped his palms down the front of his brown shorts and took a deep breath. It occurred to me that as much as he loved to talk about snakes, he might be unaccustomed to being around people. I could relate.

"First off, never, and I mean NEVER, wash the area of an Australian snakebite. One of the problems is people get bitten and then real tidy-like go and carefully clean the wound. That's a complete no-no. Antivenom kits rely on stray venom near the bite site for immunological identification of the snake. In other words, bloody doctors need the venom to find out who bloody well bit whom. If the snake can't be identified then polyvalent antivenom, which is antivenom that neutralizes the venom of all dangerous Australian species, must be used. And believe me, it can be rather nasty. Monovalent antivenom, which is antivenom for a specific snake species, is always preferable."

I couldn't decide if Mad Matt was quite educated, quite mad, or quite both. One minute he spouted mouthfuls of Aussie slang and the next he sounded like a scientist with a Ph.D. Regardless, he had our attention.

"Another no-no is NEVER CUT. Do you hear me, mates? NEVER cut the bite area. And strewth, don't go using yer bloody mouth to suck the venom out, eh? Youse not a bloody leech, and believe me, it's not effective anyway. Could even be 'armful."

Before Matt could catch his breath and continue, a young, impudent, red-haired, freckle-faced Canadian interrupted, "Then what the hell are we supposed to do?"

Heads snapped around at his rude tone, and the tension in the room rose like a swarm of provoked bees. I admired the way Matt refused to rise to the challenge in the young man's voice. Instead he said, "Youse a bloody Canadian," in one lazy breath and, "Youse just sit nice and quiet, Red, and youse might learn something, eh?" in the next. *Then* he replied to the impudent young backpacker's question.

"Mostly 'ere in Oz we use the compression or bandage method 'cause our poisonous snakes are front-fanged elapids. Believe me, there's different types of bloody poisoning. With most of our snakes the bloody damage is widespread to the nervous system or cardiovascular system, although we do have a few that cause serious necrosis."

Freckle-faced Red rolled his eyes and muttered, "What's this necrosis stuff anyway? Sounds obscene to me."

"That's localized tissue and sometimes bone damage in the immediate area of the bite. And believe me, if it happens to you, Red, youse going to think it's bloody obscene all right. Take yer pit vipers, for example, like the 'merican rattlesnake, water moccasin, and copperhead; they cause tissue damage in the area of the bite. So, with these guys, a compression bandage that holds the bloody venom in the area might increase local tissue and bone damage and cause some awful nasty pain. Sure, those things might not be completely life threatening, but you'd most likely end up in the bloody body shop needing all kinds of skin grafts and intense repair to the area."

"Yeah, man, but what if you get bit by more than one snake at the same time? Bet you never thought of that, huh?"

"You aren't scared are you, Red? Youse calm down now and we'll just take this one snake at a time, mate. You might learn more if you listened instead of jabbering away like a madcap galah."

Freckle Face looked around to see if we were all looking at him. Of course, we were. He quickly looked forward as if he were contriving his next challenge. Moments later it came, cocky voice and all. "See if you can answer this question. Which snake is the world's deadliest?"

The energy in the room shifted from tension to total disgust at the young man's tone of voice and continued interruptions. Matt's attitude shifted to one of amused tolerance.

"Right-o, Carrot Top. Youse the expert on snakes, so I'll just take a seat and you can run the lecture. Just make sure to drop me a note next time youse bit by a snake and let me know if youse still alive."

Everyone laughed but Carrot Top. When he didn't get the joke and looked questioningly around the room, we all laughed even harder and Matt said, "That's all right, Carrot Top. We's not laughing with you, mate. We's laughing at you."

While Carrot Top muddled through his confusion, Matt forgot the youth and said it was time for a quick break.

Once we were all seated again Matt continued with a slide show of various snakes. He knew a lot about their habits and how toxic their venom could be to humans. Even though I'd already seen several of the snakes and handled a few of them, the lecture and slide show fascinated me. He showed us how to bind a snake-bitten limb while we all asked questions.

"Okay, first off, you immediately place a folded pad over the puncture area, whatever youse got with you, even if it's a piece of clothing folded into a pad. Then bind the entire bitten limb from hand to armpit, or foot to groin with a bandage, like so, eh? Remember, the bandage isn't a bloody tourniquet. Youse not trying to castrate a bloody ram. So don't go applying the bloody bandage too tight. Ya hear me? We don't want yer bloody leg dropping off. Do it up about as firm as you would a sprained ankle."

"If we don't do it up tight, what good is it?" The housewife asked.

"Most venom spreads through the lymphatic system. All the bandage does is slow down the bloody spread of venom until you reach professional help, like a hospital or such. After youse done wrapping the bloody arm or leg you bind a splint to the limb with another bandage, like so."

I imagined some fool like Carrot Top ignorantly crawling head first into a tiny cave full of snakes, and I blurted, "What If someone's bit on the head or the neck or even the torso? What do we do then?"

Mad Matt grinned and said, "Youse a bloody Yank, eh?" and then continued in one uninterrupted breath. "Believe me, if youse bit on the head, neck, or torso area, youse going to have to bind as much as you can with yer bloody bandage. If you can't bind it, hold a compress against the bite with firm pressure. And DON'T release it. And then youse going to have to pray like billy-o."

A shy middle-aged businessman who wore black glasses and a gray business suit raised a meaty hand to the side of his thick neck and began to press. The white-haired gentleman in front of him cupped his thin neck with long bony fingers. Imaginations worked double overtime. Carrot Top rolled impatient eyes, let out an exaggerated sigh of disgust and said, "Well, that's never going to happen to me." To which Matt replied, "Of course not, Red, youse the expert so you can leave anytime, mate." Score ten points for Matt.

During my years in Australia, people told me all kinds of snake stories and gave just about every kind of bite information anyone could receive: "Always keep a snakebite victim as still as possible" and "Always carry them out on a stretcher to prevent the spread of venom." I sometimes heard the opposite: "Once the pressure dressing is in place, a bite victim can walk out." Since I hiked alone all the time, I practiced continual awareness, a bit like defensive driving. I also went prepared with walking stick that could be used as a splint.

The middle-aged businessman must have read my mind when he politely raised his hand and asked, "Should you carry someone out of the bush who's been bitten or can they walk?"

Carrot Top looked at the businessman's raised hand, snickered, and said, "This isn't grade school, man."

The businessman quickly withdrew his hand and shifted uncomfortably in his seat. We all ignored Carrots-for-Brains.

"Believe me" and "Bloody" were Matt's all-time favorite phrases. "Believe me, if youse able to carry a bloody snakebite victim out of the bush, it's always best. But if youse alone, youse going to have to hike out or you might bloody well die, depending on what kind of snake bit you and how much venom it injected, if any. The main thing to remember is, ALWAYS wait until the snakebite victim is under full medical attention before you remove the bandage or compress. Believe me, once you remove that band-age the venom can spread though yer entire system like the devil's fire through dry bush. Believe me."

Believe me, we bloody believe you. At that thought I couldn't stop the laughter that erupted from my throat until Mad flashed me a wounded and indignant glare. My attention returned to the group when a pretty young blond with a thick-as-golden-syrup Australian accent asked, "Does anyone ever live if they get bit and can't get to help? I mean, what if youse to go into the bush unprepared?"

"Well missy, youse a bloody stupid fool if you go into the bush unprepared." I love the way most Australians say "stupid." Broken up, it's pronounced ssshhh-tee-you-pid. They say the word the way it's meant to be said. "Youse a bloody sshhh-tee-you-pid drongo, eh?"

As the word "sshhh-tee-you-pid" played over and over in my head, I couldn't help but laugh over this dichotomy of a man so professional, almost medical in one sentence, and bloody brash the next. I managed to contain my laughter and let Matt continue.

"Now, as far as living through a snake bite without professional help, this is the deal. If youse to use the bandage or pressure dressing you usually have several hours before youse seriously crook or end up bloody dead."

Matt tugged at the edge of his shorts as if suddenly embarrassed at how short they were. Irritated by his own vulnerability, he flicked his hat back from his face and revealed his eyes, two pieces of crisp-blue sky in a sun-browned face.

"Even without any bloody antivenom there are cases of people who survived a deadly bite to bloody well tell about it. It depends on the type of snake involved, how much venom is injected, and the condition of the person bitten."

I ventured one last question of Mad Matt, a man whose character I'd grown to admire. "Say, Matt. I've heard a lot of talk over the issue of which snake is the world's deadliest. Over the years I've heard or read all kinds of things like, 'Twenty-two of the world's top twenty-five deadliest snakes are in Australia,' and 'Australia has the top ten most deadly snakes in the world.' Etc., etc. What's your opinion on that?"

Matt eyed me warily, deemed my intent worthy of a serious response, and said, "Strewth. There's all kinds of bloody things that determine what makes a snake poisonous to humans. One snake may have less potent venom than another but is capable of injecting huge amounts of venom in a single bite, or he might be a bloody multiple striker."

"Excuse me, sir, but what's a multiple striker?"

Matt almost choked when the businessman called him "sir." But he stifled his reaction, although he seemed secretly pleased at getting his due respect.

"Yes, well, a multiple striker is a bloody snake that strikes you more than once. He may zap you several times, even grip on and chew, injecting an overall massive amount of venom."

"Are all bites deadly?"

Matt sighed in exasperation and said, "Like I mentioned before, a bite may or may not be lethal depending on when youse bitten, whether the snake has recently killed to eat, how much venom is injected, whether the snake has been surprised or flat out harassed. Snakes that bite because you've startled them often don't envenomate—they can decide whether to release or withhold venom. But if a snake is wound tight as a bedspring because some bloody fool bastard has harassed it, it might be more likely to envenomate."[1] Mad Matt ended the talk, and as Carrot Top stormed out someone muttered that it wasn't soon enough. We all laughed knowingly. A few of us hung around to ask Matt more questions until he said he was "jack o' the city" and had to get back to the bush. I chuckled to myself as he walked out the door still tugging at his shorts.

With so much information crowding my brain, I decided that dead is dead. What really mattered was my relationship with the forest and all of her creatures. The more I understood my world, the better equipped I'd be to protect myself and the lives of the animals and plants I lived with. Once I stopped thinking that poisonous snakes were evil beings seeking out innocent victims, I began to see them through clear eyes and calm presence. Australian snakes rarely strike unless seriously provoked. Most are shy and retiring and will kill only to eat.

Panic is our worst enemy in an encounter with a snake. Someone once related to me a story by the famous snake handler, Eric Worrell, that told of a guy bitten by a snake. The victim's fellow hikers caught and killed the reptile and took it to the hospital for identification along with their dead friend. The supposed culprit, a common tree snake, is nonpoisonous to humans and was killed due to human ignorance. The man panicked and died of a heart attack, not toxic venom. Neither snake nor human needed to die. Maybe that's what we're doing as a society. Are we reacting so violently out of fear that we're killing ourselves and other species?

I frequently encountered snakes on my walks, and their curiosity astounded me. At times we sat side by side in a patch of morning sun, neither one threatened by the other. Some snakes, particularly those I ran into every day on the same path, would tentatively slither toward me for a better look. I always remained calm as we stood a few feet apart and studied each other. Life is curious about itself.

I reminded myself daily to be aware of where I put my hands and feet, where I sat, and under what tree I rested. After awhile awareness became a natural part of who I was in the rainforest. A few times a snake dropped from a tree and onto my body while I sat beneath the tree's branches. I had to remain calm so that I wouldn't frighten the snake and possibly become bitten. After several years, I learned to freeze until the snake slithered down my shoulders or across my legs and moved on its way. I was always keen to see what type of snake had landed on me. It usually was a scrub python. They can be huge, heavy, and daunting, but harmless. Another snake that occasionally dropped out of trees was the whip-thin common tree snake. He can grow to about six feet long and has no fangs. When threatened he sometimes inflates his neck to appear larger. He also can produce a rank odor from his anal glands to protect himself.

I always felt more alive after these encounters. They stretched the boundaries of my courage and strengthened my friendship with the rainforest. I became a more integral part of the forest and the creatures I lived with. My respect for their survival skills grew daily. It's impossible to harm something that you venerate. I was proud to be a part of their world. I don't think I've experienced a greater honor.

The few times Ian hiked with me, I had to remind him to freeze when he spotted a snake. He usually responded with a hysterical gyrating jig that panicked me and every snake in the vicinity. I could always tell when he'd seen a snake or a spider. I learned the difference between his two cries. One I named his spider call, "iiiiiiiiieeeeeeeiiiiiiiii." His snake wail rang out much longer and louder and rose to a high-pitched finale, "hhhhaaaaaaaabababababahhhhaaaaaaaaalalalalalala." When Ian joined me in the forest, I tried to keep a tad of distance between us because I didn't want to be near a snake tangled in his dance of fear.

I thought of Ian spending the night at the river. I hoped he'd remember that there were crocs down there and that he shouldn't hop out of the truck and pee on the bank. There was a plastic container in the Toyota for that purpose. I smiled to myself when I realized his dread of snakes would keep him safely *in* the truck after dark.

Some nights we slept in the tray of the truck, but Ian had the Toyota, so once I finished watering the fruit trees I stretched my sleeping bag across the wooden platform inside the tent. When it rained hard and water ran across the ground and through the tent, the platform kept us and our gear relatively high and dry. As I climbed into my bag I decided that Ian probably was fast asleep. As long as he slept in the truck, I didn't mind that he spent the night on the riverbank. Occasionally when we'd crossed the Daintree River, I'd seen a croc resting on the shore with his mouth open to keep cool. A thrilling primordial memory surfaced every time I saw his impressive jaws full of long peg-like teeth and his tough scaly hide with dinosaur ridges down his back. Within my own body I felt the latent power of his legs and tail. He fascinated me . . . from a distance.

While my thoughts wandered, it quickly grew dark. Familiar night sounds whispered around the tent on dainty mice feet and silent owl wings. Horatio Bandicoot scratched at something beyond the front flap. Although I'd seen other bandicoots in the forest, Horatio was the only one who ever came into camp. Ian and I went to the spring to get water one evening after cooking an early supper of breadfruit and tomatoes. When we returned, we heard a loud scratch and a grunt and discovered a bandicoot had crawled into the huge cooking pot. His eyes bugged out and he frantically licked the remaining tomato sauce from the pot as is if he hadn't eaten in months. If he could have spoken he might have yelled, "Whoa! What is this?"

When I picked up the pot to gently tip him out, he spread his legs wide and braced against the sides. He wouldn't let go and he kept licking the whole time, making this weird snuffling sound. I jiggled the pot a bit and he braced even harder. But wet tomato made the pot sides slippery and he slowly slid from the pot, leaving a trail of claw marks through the sauce. He stood at my feet looking at me beseechingly, still licking his chops.

Ian laughed through the whole thing and said, "Anyone with that much determination deserves a name like Horatio."

I was again reminded that I should not leave a dirty pot unattended. I didn't want the wild creatures to develop a taste for human food. I loved Horatio and never fed him, but he still came nightly to visit. He just strode into camp as if he owned the place. He did. We had intruded onto his territory. His home.

How could I have been so insensitive all my life to assume that humans are the only ones who need the land, the only ones who make homes and raise families they love and care for, the only ones who need food, water, and shelter to survive? What about the wallabies? The bandicoots? The birds? The trees? The reptiles and insects? What about their families?

Horatio Bandicoot helped me to see the world differently when I realized he was forced to share his home. His curiosity and desire to make contact made me feel shame. I had colossal respect for his ability to adapt to our intrusion, but it also saddened me. I didn't yet know if it was a good thing or not. Sure it kept him alive, but at what price? Is there a line between healthy adaptation and unhealthy but necessary adaptation? Or are they the same?

The thing I loved most about Horatio's personality was that he didn't just cruise around camp. He sauntered along his path in a contented, bebop fashion, like a teenager listening to a radio. If I was anywhere near camp he'd veer casually closer until he purposefully walked right over the tops of my bare feet. He never looked up. Or at least not until he was ten feet away when he'd look back over his shoulder, slightly lift his head, and drop it with a definite nod as if to say, "Carry on." Then he moseyed on. Ian started to call him the Inspector or the Night Watchman. As Horatio marked his territory, he let me know that I was part of his clan. He came at dusk every evening to check on me. Of all my rainforest friends, Horatio had the most flamboyant character. Independent and confident, he always made me laugh.

As I lay in the tent I felt comforted by Horatio's presence. He knew I was in the tent, but he never entered. I could hear him breathing on the other side of the canvas wall. I also heard Mr. Whoop Whoop Bird, the pheasant coucal that lived nearby, let out one last descending "whoop, whoop, whoop, whoop whoop," as he sat in his favorite melastoma bush in the field.

With Ian gone, I had plenty of room on the wooden platform to stretch out. I didn't mind hard surfaces. I preferred them. I slept, sat, and lay on bare earth almost every day. Flat on my back, I flung my arms above my head and my fingertips brushed against something cool and unfamiliar. I froze. Was there a snake in the tent? It didn't feel like a snake. My fingers had only brushed it briefly, but it didn't feel smooth enough. It had felt almost like suede. I searched the list of possibilities while my heart raced. Halfway through the usual list, I came to a screeching halt. It didn't just *feel* like suede; it *was* suede. I sat up with a jolt.

"Oh nooooooo! Ian's wallet." I wailed.

At the sound of my sudden outburst, Horatio dramatically leapt away from his scratchings at the front of the tent. Right where I'd left Ian's town clothes sat his wallet and supply list. He didn't even have travelers' checks with him. I'd put them in his wallet the night before to remind him to open a bank account, something we *still* hadn't done. Suddenly I remembered the flashlight. We hadn't used it or the candles in months. We both went to bed with the sun and woke with the sun. I hoped the batteries still worked like Ian said. Although I didn't sense a snake lay under the platform, I slooowly reached, keeping my face well back and my fingers off the ground, until I touched the hard plastic flashlight. I knew Ian had left his wallet, but I had to see it for myself. Sure enough, there sat the brown billfold.

Ian carried only a little cash in his pocket, which he'd spend on the ferry run and ice cream in Mossman. He normally put his wallet and our traveler's checks in the glove box when we went to town and wouldn't realize they were missing until he reached Cairns. Frustration ate at me and sent my thoughts haywire as I flung open my sleeping bag and crawled from the tent. Now what? It was pitch black and Ian was at the ferry. He'd go all the way to Cairns tomorrow with no money and no list. Holy moly, he wouldn't notice the missing wallet until he went to buy something. *Damn it, Ian!*

The dark forest didn't scare me, but to reach him I'd have to walk toward the Daintree River at night. I'd had to watch for crocs in the sea at Cape Tribulation, but it was always daylight. And the Daintree River was their real stomping ground. I knew how to behave around snakes and wild pigs, but crocodiles worried me. Crocs have a keen sense of smell, sharp hearing, and acute eyesight, even at night. I no longer thought of them as vicious monsters. In fact, I thought they were fascinating creatures.

On one of our forays to town, we met a bloke at the ferry landing with a life-size fiberglass casting of an eighteen-foot crocodile. He'd killed it before the ban on crocodile hunting had been enacted, and, with the crocodile still intact, he made a fiberglass casting that appeared completely real in color and size. Had I seen it on the riverbank I wouldn't have been able to distinguish it from a live croc. The thing was inconceivably huge. I'd seen crocs at the water's edge before, but never this close. The teeth on the casting were so long they would have pierced clean through my upper arm and out the other side. They were longer and bigger than my fingers. His thick cavernous belly looked like it could have easily accommodated four adults, two stacked on top of two. No worries.

The lifelike fiberglass croc dwarfed Ian's six-foot-plus frame when he lay on the ground beside it. Eighteen feet of crocodile is a lot of reptile.

The owner of the casting said, "The truly big crocs aren't always the real danger. They can be deadly, no doubt, but most problem crocs tend to be in the five-foot to just over eight-foot range. At that size they're mobile and *very* fast."

All these thoughts raced through my head as I tried to decide what to do about Ian's wallet. One part of me wanted to let him go all the way to Cairns and back without worrying about him. Then I remembered that the truck had just enough gas to get to Cairns. He'd have to fill up for the return trip. Without his wallet he couldn't get home. He'd probably have to stay in the city and wash dishes for a few days just to get back to the Daintree. I knew he'd worry about me when he couldn't get home for a day or two. He might think he'd lost his billfold in town and not know I'd found it. Since we never locked the truck, he might think someone in town had stolen it.

The situation wouldn't have been a big deal for people who live with phones or credit cards. But if I wanted to reach Ian I'd have to walk to the river, and I didn't know how far crocs strayed from the water. I'd heard rumors of people who had sighted them in the middle of the dirt track quite a ways from the water. I also had no idea how close the river ran to the track. It wasn't an area I normally hiked; I usually hiked up into the hills, away from the river. It wouldn't be much of a problem, as most of the walk wasn't near water. But I had to be prepared, just in case. A slim chance of a croc grabbing me at night was still a chance, and I had only one life.

I remembered how trappers in Maine disguised the human scent on their traps by boiling them in pine needles or sometimes dunking them in mud.

I decided to use the same "mud strategy" to hide my human scent from the crocs. I didn't know if it would make a difference, but I knew it wouldn't do any harm. In the starlight I found the white container of rich mud I'd brought from the spring to help fertilize the garden. It still sat by the yam patch. The plastic lid protested loudly as I pried it open, an oddly artificial sound that spoke rudely to the sleeping rainforest. I unwound my red sarong, let it slip to the ground, and plunged my arms into sticky brown ooze. Smooth mud slid onto my torso and legs. I smeared every inch of my body, even my groin, armpits, face, and tied-back hair. Covering myself with mud didn't bother me at all; I was used to clay baths.

When I was done I dunked my fanny pack, which contained Ian's wallet and shopping list, into the mud and strapped it around my waist. The smell of damp earth, dank and familiar, rose from my body and blended with the night air. But I needed more than mud. If I walked down by the river, I had to be in the right frame of mind, aware that crocs or possibly feral pigs might have a go at me. The pigs didn't worry me much. I'd crossed paths with them several times, and they usually ran away. But the crocs? Could I slink by unnoticed? Could I fight for my life? What was the best way to go about it? My best defense was to be odorless, soundless, and invisible. No, that's not true. My best defense was to stay home, but I couldn't. Or wouldn't.

Something wild and elemental raced through my veins and drew me into the dark night. Some primal force drove me to test myself until I understood the laws of Mother Nature, even if it meant risking my life. I couldn't allow myself to be limited by fear. I had an insatiable appetite for living. I wanted to explore other realities and possibilities. How brainwashed was I? And did it reduce my life experience to mediocrity? What lay beyond social taming and the known world?

Prior to arriving in the rainforest I had never been through any initiations, no tests of courage or rites of passage—none that mattered anyway. The forest offered me a way to challenge myself that I'd not found in society. I was able to uncover a compelling sense of self, based on firsthand experience, which would last a lifetime. I sought out adventure because it set me free and showed me who I am and what I'm capable of. We're often unaware that we have great courage until we're forced

Crocodiles, Feral Pigs, and Pitch Black   263

to draw on unused resources hidden deep inside us. I had to find out. I needed to know.

Things that were maybe commonplace to some Australians were larger than life for me. It reminded me of how Ian once said, "Bloody strewth! Living in Maine in the winter is scary. It's like living inside a bloody icebox. How do youse all do it? People must die, eh?" He had never lived with snow. The closest thing he'd experienced to a Maine winter was reaching into the freezer for an ice cream bar. Because I grew up in Maine I thought nothing of sub-zero temperatures and two-to three-foot snowstorms, even though there were many winters that people died from severe cold.

As my thoughts returned to Ian, I realized he hadn't left the rifle. We hadn't used it in so long that neither of us remembered it. I might have felt safer with the gun because I was a fairly accurate shot, though it was only a .22 repeater. It was all a moot point since the rifle rested behind the seat of the truck. I scanned our gear for something else to defend myself with if I needed it. The large curved brush hook (scythe) we'd bought in Mossman when we moved onto Cloud Mountain rested against the tent. I'd sharpened it the day before, and it easily could have shaved hair from my arm. When I first bought the hook my swing was awkward and clumsy, and I damned near cut off my legs a few times. But after months of using it around camp, I developed a strong accurate swing. Although I was thin, for the first time in my life, cords of muscle ran up and down my arms. The brush hook seemed the best choice. It was all I had.

No matter how sharp, I seriously doubted my ability to scratch a croc's hide—not with all those scales and the bony plate running down its back. I'd have to reach his side, belly, or throat. In the remote chance that a croc charged, he'd have to open his mouth at some point to grab me. Maybe I could ram the brush hook down his throat if I saw him, if I could react in time. The hook was wide, heavy, and thick, and would probably jam in his mouth. Although he might snap the long handle clean off, the metal blade would still be an awkward mouthful. It might slow him down long enough for me to run. If he were able to uneventfully swallow the blade, his stomach acid would happily dissolve the metal. I could barely imagine stomach acid so strong it could dissolve bone, metal, hair, hoof, and tusk. Think of the things you could eat. On your next camping trip, you wouldn't need a can opener. You could eat your beans, can and all.

After I covered the brush hook and flashlight with mud, I set off to find Ian. The first part of the track led down a hill that ran perpendicular to the river. There was no danger of crocs that far from water. I wished I had a high-powered beam that I could have used once I reached the river, but all I had was my puny flashlight. I flicked it on to make sure it still worked. It was almost dead, so I shut it off.

Since I couldn't see snakes on the track, I lightly tapped the ground with the handle of the brush hook. The farther I went, the closer I came to the water. After awhile I quit tapping the ground because I didn't know how close I was to the river, and sooner or later a hungry croc might be attracted to the sound. Instead I sent the snakes my thoughts. *Any snakes on the road, listen to me. I'm headed your way and I mean you no harm. So please warn me if I get too close. I don't want to step on you. Okay?*

The track felt slightly muddy under my bare feet. I'd have to be careful not to slip if I moved quickly. When I snuck up on wallabies and other creatures, I'd learned to walk in a slight crouch and roll each foot from outside edge to inside edge. This allowed me to feel a dry leaf or branch under my arch *before* I placed my full weight on the earth. I could always retract my foot to avoid making noise. My feet were so calloused and tough that I could step on a thumb-tack and not feel it. But when I first started to go barefoot, rolling my feet allowed me to gradually ease each foot onto anything sharp that lay on my path.

The road was fairly smooth, but silence and slow movement were still essential. The dark night quivered with watching eyes.

Suddenly to my right, "Tssssst." A loud hiss snapped at me, roughly two feet away. I froze but remained calm. I thought about the flashlight but didn't want to make any movements that could be interpreted as a threat. Moreover, I didn't want to waste the batteries. Given time, the snake would pass.

It's okay. I won't harm you. Go on your way.

I waited.

Listened.

Wonder what kind it is? Wish I could see him.

With a soft rustle of grass, the snake moved on. So did I. Relief and confidence flooded through me until an inner voice warned, "Don't get *too* confident, mate."

"Arrrr, arrrrssssstt, arrrrrooooon." Croc sounds suddenly rose loud and wild between the river and me. I knew they weren't as close as they sounded. They were probably several hundred yards or more away. At least I hoped they were. I still wasn't sure how close I was to the river. Their rumbling growls evoked primitive fear, wild and haunting.

I was shocked when I heard the swish and crawl of big bodies, probably two crocs. Although I suspected they weren't close, my thumb flicked on the flashlight to check the road ahead for huge loglike reptiles. The dim yellow circle vibrated on the dirt track. My hand trembled. The light flickered off and on, and blinked out. The batteries were dead. Darkness devoured me and left me alone with the growls of crocs. I shoved the flashlight into my fanny pack and frantically strained to define lurking shapes and stealthy movement in the cloying blackness. Sweat ran down my cheeks beneath the thick mud that covered my face and naked body. My bare feet padded soundlessly on the dirt track. Knees slightly bent, I placed each foot carefully.

Gradually, I adjusted to the varied shades of black. The track appeared slightly lighter than the ebony jungle that grew along the road and blotted out most of the sky. The moonless night arched high with a galaxy of stars. They winked at me through the opening in the canopy made by the track. My muddy hands clung to the long, curved brush hook I held out in front of me. I was forced to confront fears that had crippled me all my life.

I didn't send the crocs my thoughts. They were preoccupied and unaware of me. I wanted to keep it that way. Excitement and terror clung to me and dripped off with the mud. Animals can smell and taste fear. Some are repulsed and threatened by the acrid odor. Others, sensing a helpless or vulnerable animal, a meal, are irresistibly drawn to it. The rainforest taught me that if I wanted to survive, I had to get a grip on my panic and react consciously. I couldn't afford to panic. I decided to visualize myself as completely invisible, and if need be, extremely forceful and huge. Every single muscle in my body was acutely aware and ready. To stay focused and deal with my terror, I tried to remember everything I knew about crocs. I knew they ate rocks to aid digestion and stay submerged. An average croc has ten to fifteen pounds of stones in its stomach. I wondered what size rocks they ate. Or was it just gravel they swallowed?

Even though I feared the crocs, I was even more disturbed that we could drive them into extinction. At least they were fairly common in Australia, and if protected, had some chance of survival. Australians banned crocodile hunting in the early 1970s, but in the 1960s over half of the twenty-six species of crocodilians in the world were near extinction. Australia has two species of crocodile: the estuarine or saltwater crocodile and the freshwater crocodile. The latter is found only in Australia and seldom is a threat to humans. Both species have salt glands, so if they swallow too much salt they can excrete it through the glands in their tongue. Saltwater crocs actually swim in the sea. People have sighted them 800 miles (1285 km) off the coast.

Clyde had once warned, "If youse ever to fall in the bloody river stay real still-like. Don't go bloody thrashin' 'bout in the water. You might lure crocs. Salties got these little bloody pressure gauges—or sometimes they's called sensory pits—along the sides of their jaws and all over their bodies on each scale. They register bloody movement of potential prey in the water."

No wonder saltwater crocodiles haven't changed much in 65 million years. What's to change? Their every feature is geared for long-term survival. These extraordinary creatures are the largest reptile in the world and have amazing maternal instincts. When baby crocs are ready to hatch, they squeak so that their mother will dig them out of the nest and gently carry them in her mouth to the water. Only about one out of ten hatchlings survives to adulthood. That's about five hatchlings of the fifty eggs laid in a nest. Their nests, made of dirt and debris, are washed away by floods. The eggs are eaten by goannas and feral pigs, and the hatchlings are often eaten by other crocs. Crocodilians have the ability to work as a community or members of a group and usually have nurseries where one mother watches the young of several mothers.

I decided that I'd be all right. I was probably too far away from the river. And it wasn't like I walked to the river every night. Crocs, like many other species, often learn by watching. If I showed up at the river's edge every day at the same time and location I'd probably be in more danger... one day they might be waiting for me.

When I thought about my fear, I realized I needed to learn more about crocodiles. Why was I so afraid of them? Was it because we humans aren't always at the top of the food chain? Sometimes fear seems so irrational. Some might stay out of the rainforest because they're afraid of crocodiles or poisonous snakes, but rarely does fear of predators keep us out of cities, nor does fear of an accident stop us from driving automobiles or using kitchen knives. So why do we fear things that walk on four legs or move with no legs? When was the last crocodile world war or the last croc final solution?

I silently chuckled at my thoughts and felt a bit calmer. My eyes had adjusted to the dim light of the stars, but my ears offered the best defense. A croc might not attack from the front. He might sneak up from the side or from behind. However, just as I'd heard the snake in the grass I'd probably hear a croc, unless it suddenly burst out of nowhere. In spite of a very small brain and sluggish appearance, salties didn't fool me into believing they were slow moving or slow-witted. Some crocs are able to jump from a dead standstill, their full length out of water. Some smaller crocs can actually gallop for a very short distance in pursuit of their prey on land. Humans can run at least three times as fast as a croc, so I could outrun one if I heard it coming. In the water, it would be a different matter. I'd never outswim a croc, not at fifteen miles per hour, which a croc can do in short bursts. They prefer catching their meals along the water's edge using a stealthy silent approach with a lightning-quick lunge.

I walked slowly and deliberately. Blood barely flowed through my fingers as I gripped the brush hook. Once more a snake hissed a warning at my feet.

"Tssssst!"

Once more I waited and then crept on. Compared to crocs, snakes seemed as benign as earthworms.

Suddenly something crashed through the bushes and bolted straight toward me. I braced my feet, gripped the brush hook with both hands, and faced the direction of the sound.

"Oooeeeeeeeeeee. Oooeeeeeeee."

A feral pig's loud squeal tore through the night. I relaxed, but remained ready because feral pigs, while not anywhere near as dangerous as crocodiles, could be a potential threat. Usually when pigs saw or smelled me they tore off squealing all the way, unless they felt cornered or had young ones with them. An ample sow, the mother of two chunky piglets, once charged me and chased me up a tree. She was huge. Two hundred and fifty pounds of gyrating flab and angry muscle thundered toward me. I raced for the nearest tree, a *very* small acacia. With my hands around the trunk, I crashed my way through its puny branches. Mama pig treed me while agitated green tree ants swarmed en masse from their leafy nest to attack me, the monster intruder. The air stank of formic acid and my bare arms and legs itched, stung, and crawled with lime green ants. I wanted to reach the nest, break it off, and throw it to the ground or maybe onto the sow. But I clung to the tree's puny trunk and didn't dare move for fear the branch would snap and I'd crash to the ground. At least the nest was very small. I'd seen larger trees that held several nests, some the size of footballs.

I was grateful that the acacia bent at an angle over the edge of an embankment and put me out of reach of snapping teeth. Sows don't have tusks, but they can deliver a painful and dangerous bite.

After the green ants calmed down, they took pleasure in exploring my entire body. As long as I didn't panic and brush at them, they didn't bite as much. I was still worried that so many bites might make me ill.

When the piglets grew restless and started to stray, mama pig finally followed them and left me to lick my wounds. While I'd heard the phrase "teach tolerance," I never thought pigs and ants would be my teachers.

"Oooeeeeeeeee."

Another piercing squeal jolted me back to my predicament by the river. Most likely the pigs would leave me alone, but I braced myself and raised my razor-sharp brush hook toward the sound. It would inflict serious damage to a pig's hide.

Three blacker-than-night blobs burst through the scrub and onto the track. Two medium-sized pigs ran past me. The last one, a large male, stopped six feet in front of me. Hot odorous breath rose to my face, stung my nostrils, and made me want to gag. I couldn't see his eyes, but I felt him pierce the darkness to try and size me up. I waited motionless as a tree trunk and breathed inaudibly through my nose so he couldn't catch the scent of my breath. He reeked of raw, male animal, a scent that instinctively tightened my fingers on the brush hook, ready to swing. In the darkness I made out two vague pale points. His tusks.

Male feral pigs can completely disembowel a dog or human with their tusks. I once saw a dog's belly that had been splayed open by a boar. The poor mutt limped along howling while his intestines trailed behind him.

The boar couldn't get a clear scent on me. He knew something was there, but didn't know what. I felt his confusion. He didn't know whether or not to charge. Impulse urged me to lash out wildly, catch him off guard, and chase him with fearless rage. However that impulse was motivated by fear. In my heart I couldn't deny my affinity for his unmolested power. I respected his ability to survive in the wild and would not harm him just because I was afraid. I'd only use the brush hook if my life depended on it. I also couldn't afford to attract attention to myself. I needed to get away from him as quickly as possible. Any commotion might alert the crocs, and I still had to walk closer to the river to reach Ian.

In the blackness of night I could scarcely make out the boar's darker bulk against the road. I stood ready for him. At six feet, I had plenty of room to sink the brush hook into his side.

Seconds passed.

I waited.

With a loud snort he tore off toward the river.

I lowered the brush hook, silently let out my pent-up breath, and listened to his noisy retreat fade into the night. The soft backdrop of frogs, insects, and night birds helped calm my nerves. But when I again heard the sounds of crocs my ears tuned like radar. I strained to hear the close movement of gravel or bush. All of a sudden a loud, high-pitched whistle, like a bomb falling, ripped through the blackness, maybe a lesser sooty owl. When his whistle ended I reoriented myself to the night and continued down the track, which now led straight for the river. The crocs sounded like they were 100 feet away, but were probably more. I debated whether to run as fast as I could to Ian and the truck, but I barely could see ten feet in front of me. Any snakes on the path needed time to feel my approach and retreat into the brush along the road.

Another couple of minutes passed, and I began to wonder how far I was from the ferry landing. As I got closer to the river, apprehension crept across my shoulder blades like cold, skeletal fingers.

Suddenly out of nowhere, SPLASH!

Then, "Oeeeeeeee. Oe . . . "

Silence.

Although I had never hiked to the river, I still knew all too well what a sudden splash and a cut-off pig squeal meant. At least *that* croc wouldn't be interested in me. My imagination mated with my fear and bred like rats. Only it wasn't some wild concoction of my own or even about the pig. I remembered a horrible incident that occurred along the river a few months before, which outweighed anything I could've imagined.

After four straight months in the bush, Ian and I ventured to town. As our truck approached the ferry landing to cross the river, we noticed a new sign. Ian got out and hollered it back to me.

"WARNING. *ESTUARINE CROCODILES INHABIT MOST RIVERS, SWAMPS AND LAGOONS THROUGHOUT THE CAPE YORK PENINSULA.* Bloody strewth! We's all know that. Must be for the tourists."

There was always time to visit while crossing the river, so we asked Clyde about the new sign.

"You two never come out of the bloody bush," he said. "If youse did, you might know what goes on 'round 'ere, eh? Bloody locals, a few of 'em got together for a Christmas party and a lady got taken by a croc. They musta been swimming in the river or one of the creeks."

Clyde didn't know all the details. Ian and I figured we'd ask someone about the incident in Mossman. We hadn't expected to hear about it so readily, but when we strolled into the little produce store we immediately overheard a tiny middle-aged woman telling a white-haired gentleman about the lady taken by a croc.

"My friend told me they had a barbie at the Daintree just before Christmas. I guess someone suggested they go for a swim. It was brutal hot that night, and it's not like anyone has ever been eaten. They probably figured it'd be safe. Me friend said they were having a good ol' time. Several people splashing 'bout and all that, but they weren't the ones attacked. The woman who got taken was standing in 'bout a foot and half of water, no more. She was bent over trailing her hands across the top of the bloody water, and next thing she was gone. Just like that!"

The tiny woman snapped her hands together like a croc's jaws. Her eyes were as black as her long hair and grew huge with horror as she went on with her story. She told the tale well, as if she had told it and retold it many times. It seemed she couldn't comprehend what had happened, and if she recounted the story enough the events might make sense. I knew how she felt. I wondered how I'd sleep that night. When she continued, I didn't know whether to cling to her words or flee the shop.

"My friend said there was no bloody warning. No sound. Nothing. Happened so fast she hardly saw it. They say the croc must have grabbed the woman's ankles and yanked her in. Crikeys. It could've been any of them, even my friend."

The woman abruptly turned away and left the shop. It looked like she was crying. I'd heard more than I wanted. In a state of numbness, Ian and I purchased a huge tin of raw peanuts, a jug of olive oil, and an assortment of other staples, then left the shop's heavy atmosphere. I knew that we both remembered the first night we arrived at the Daintree ferry and slept twenty feet from the river. A croc could have grabbed either one of us and dragged us into the water. I shuddered at the memory and refused to think about it.

Ian went in search of some tools while I went to buy him some hot chips. I felt like a zombie who shopped in automated silence. A woman was taken by a croc . . . I tried to erase all images from my mind. When I found Ian by the truck he said he'd heard the same story in the hardware store.

We purchased the rest of our supplies and drove back to the ferry. Clyde and another man who had boarded before us were curious to know if we'd heard any news about the lady taken by a croc. When Ian told them what we'd heard in town Clyde said, "Crikeys, I's swum in the river to fix me ferry and never had any trouble. Generally the crocs leave people bloody well alone. But strewth, they's fast. They can jump out of water and grab a bird sitting on a branch faster than you can bloody blink."

The other man seemed to quiver over the conversation and moved closer. His face was flushed like he'd been heavily drinking and his small piggish eyes were a little too eager when he said, "He most likely grabbed 'er leg, pulled 'er into deep water to drown 'er and done a bloody 'death roll.' It breaks the victim's back, you know. After that he mighta lodged 'er somewhere to rot. He'll eat 'er later."

"Okay. I think we get the picture." I wanted to scream at him, "Bloody strewth, shut up!"

The part about a crocodile lodging its freshly killed prey under a log or rock wasn't necessarily true. A few months before on a trip to town I'd read an article that questioned whether crocs lodge their food to rot or not. It concluded that usually crocodiles like fresh food and only scavenge when nothing else is available.

Even though Ian was stunned over the incident, I knew he wasn't too fazed by Piggish Man's graphic description of the event. I shook my head over his practical response.

"Aaahh, sometimes us humans get so upset when other animals kill. We don't kill our own food anymore. Where do we think the meat in the market comes from? We think it's bloody murder when a croc kills to eat, especially when a human's taken. Of course it's tragic, but strewth, if I don't want to get eaten I better stay out of their way."

I knew Ian was right, and I admired him for his blunt truth, but it was several months before I could get the image of that poor woman out of my mind. As I walked in the pitch black toward the river with Ian's wallet, I tried to think of other things, but imagination and fear make a potent brew. Piggish Man's words echoed through my head. "He most likely grabbed 'er bloody leg, pulled 'er into deep water to drown 'er." Occasionally I disliked my overactive imagination. At times I had no control over it. I drowned in images as large as a movie screen and became the lady taken by a croc. In my mind, bone-crushing jaws grab my ankle and drag me horrified and helpless into the river. I desperately claw for air. My arms flail frantically. No one can help me. I'm going to die. My body is tossed like a rag doll, wrenched and torn. I suck water into my lungs.

Pass out. Dead. Would Ian search for me in the river? Why bother? He wouldn't know I came down here. What would he tell my family in America? The croc took me for only one reason . . . food. Would my family sleep unknowingly as I lay under the cold, dark water, ashen skin, mouth agape, and hair waving like river grass? My imagination boiled out of control and a scream almost tore from my lips until I remembered I was near the river. Fear ripped through my body like splintered glass. My ears thudded so loudly I couldn't hear. Suddenly I looked up. Through the darkness I saw a vague, boxlike shape. Ian! Our Toyota wasn't more than twenty feet away. Leaving my imagination by the river and forgetting the possibility of snakes on the track, I raced for the truck and safety. My legs pumped like pistons and my feet pounded bare earth, fueled by relief. I reached the Toyota, grabbed the side mirror, pulled myself onto the hood of the truck, and stared through the windshield straight into Ian's wide, horrified eyes.

"Ian. It's me, Roby. Open up."

While I scrambled down off the hood, Ian wrenched open the door, lashed out a long arm, and pulled me into the truck, mud and all.

"What? Crikeys! What the bloody hell youse doing here this time of night? Are you mad? You bloody drongo. What's that muck on your skin? What's that smell? Youse covered with mud. Oh yuck, Rob. Bloody oath! Why'd you come down to the river like this?"

I held up his wallet and list and watched his jaw dropped open. I laughed as he pretended to bang his head on the steering wheel.

"Wow, and I'd have gone all the way to bloody Cairns with no money. Crikey, I'm a fair dinkum drongo. Still, you should *not* have walked to the river at night. Deadset, youse a wanker."

Ian's words fell away like rain. I was safe. He could rant and rave all he wanted. My reaction would have been the same if he'd walked to the river at night. I slid off his lap and into the passenger seat. He started the engine and turned the Toyota back toward camp. I talked ninety miles an hour about my night and why I wore a mud suit, but soon the safety of the truck relaxed my tense nerves and made me drowsy.

"Strewth, Rob-o. Is there anything you won't do? Damn it, Rob, we slept on the bloody riverbank. Remember? That first night on the Daintree. That was enough. Do you hear me? Crikey, I can't even think about that. Let's not."

He stopped right in the middle of his rant and said, "That was a pretty cool idea with the mud," and then went right back to scolding me.

"Crikeys, Rob, I get scared 'cause I don't know what you'll do next. Youse got to promise me you'll never do *that* again. Never."

"Only if your life is at stake, Ian. Okay?"

"Bloody fair dinkum, mate! If I's being ripped apart by twenty crocs and a dozen wild boars let me bloody well die before you do that again. I don't want you ending up like croc bait."

Ian took a deep breath, looked over at me, and smiled adoringly. He picked up my muddy hand where it lay on the seat and squeezed it really hard. In the dim light of the truck I saw pride and hungry love light his eyes. I knew how he felt.

The Toyota's headlights lit the tent as we pulled into camp. The two buckets of water I'd left by the tent were still there. I needed an immediate bath. The passenger seat had to be wiped off, and Ian needed a clean shirt and pants.

Despite the scolding, I knew he wasn't *really* angry. He was always proud of me and never hid it. Ian encouraged my free spirit and adventurous ways because he understood my need to test myself. I was particularly moved when he once told me that he'd seen the true Australia through my eyes. Sometimes I felt like a part of him lived through me, and a part of me lived because of the life he made available to me. He knew me and what I needed as if he *was* me. I loved him for many reasons, but I loved him most because he understood the deepest part of me, sometimes better than I did. Ian had both a depth and innocence to him that I'd never known in another human being. He was tremendously insightful. What's more, I never knew him to be jealous. I don't think it ever occurred to him to compare himself to other people.

When I finished bathing and we'd wiped down the front seat, Ian and his wallet left for the ferry landing and I went to bed. After the walk along the river, my night alone in the tent was a night at the Ritz. Secure and luxurious. I'd gone from imagined death at the bottom of the river to a safe warm sleeping bag and tent.

I lay in the dark and thought about fear. As a kid I'd expended enormous amounts of energy shutting out my fears. Fear of water, fear of heights, fear of riding in cars, fear of people, fear of being alone, fear of death, fear of fear. Escaping my fears required constant vigilance. I couldn't *ever* let my guard down. In many ways I was exhausted from continual awareness, but awareness of the wrong kind, or with the wrong focus. I was *only* aware of my fear. I'd lived too many years in the dark and known nothing about the world around me and the lives of my fellow beings. The more I knew the less I would fear.

I think understanding is the key to overcoming our fears of potentially deadly life forms. We can grow not only to understand the superb creatures around us, but also we can grow to *love* them. We must marvel at their evolutionary tenacity. Their ingenuity for survival. Their creativity at interacting with other life. Their struggle to endure in a world that we humans are rapidly changing. If we stop and listen, they are eager to teach. We have much to learn. Instead of dreading the crocs, I needed to learn from them. What could they teach me? What do they need to survive? What makes them unique? How do they feel toward their young? Toward humans? And why do they feel that way? How do they mate? Do they feel love? Yes, love. We are not the only species capable of love. With this new insight into fear, I experienced an eagerness to learn as much from life as I could. I suddenly saw my remaining years on earth as an explosively powerful gift. I had so little time and so much to learn. One lifetime to know Mother Earth.

That night something changed. The brace I'd worn on my crippled spirit began to fall away, and I understood how to walk with my eyes and heart fully open. Although I still had fears, I recognized them as part of myself that I needed to fill with insight and wisdom. And without that, my fear-fueled imagination ran rampant. I remembered how the trees once told me, "Fear thrives where there is little understanding and no true wisdom." I now knew what they meant.

This new awareness brought heart-wrenching gratitude; I was alive. I gave thanks for the lessons I learned and for my safekeeping during those lessons. Tears ran down the sides of my face. I sent a prayer into the night for the woman who died from something we all make: mistakes. I, too, made mistakes when I slept on the bank of the Daintree River and walked to the river's edge in darkness. I just happened to be blessedly lucky. That's all. Exhaustion brought deep peaceful sleep.

Barefoot walks
through the crucible
of dark hidden dangers.

I must know
I must burn
my doubts away.

Fists full of soil
raised to the sky
in tactile bliss.

I must know
I must experience,
LIFE

—RUSSELL HUM

nine

Do Not Intervene

I NEVER AGAIN NIGHT-WALKED TO THE DAINTREE RIVER. Once was all I needed. I could safely view crocs from the ferry while crossing the river. Besides, the forest-covered mountain held more than enough excitement and adventure. Even on our land there were things to see and learn every day. One morning as I trudged down to the spring for a bucket of water, I heard the desperate call and agitated flutter of a bushlark. Her cry shattered the morning air and startled me. My footsteps slowed, cautioned by another sound, "shhhwisssshhh, shhhwisssshhhh, shhhwisssshhh." It was one I knew all too well—the rhythmic swish of slow moving grass. A snake, a very large one by the sound of it, was after the bird.

I tracked the lark to a patch of tall, coarse grass just above our spring and stopped short at the impressive sight of a twelve-foot scrub python, five feet away from me. Usually the scrub python is nocturnal so I was delighted to see one so close during the day. Sun gleamed off his iridescent, olive brown skin with its distinct black and brown zigzag markings. His head was large and broad, and each fat curve of his body bulged as he propelled himself in a hypnotic fashion, inch by inch, in one fluid motion toward the lark's nest.

The petite grayish brown bird ignored me, her focus glued to the python's threatening approach. Terror protruded her tiny black eyes and made the feathers on top of her head fluff up. I thought she might use her finchlike beak to peck the snake, but she didn't. I looked around for her mate, hoping he'd rescue her, but I didn't see him. Maybe the python ate him. The little lark hopped up and down and flapped her rust-colored wings. The snake ignored her and indulged a look in my direction. As long as the bird guarded her three babies in the nest, his breakfast remained secure. Even if she abandoned the nest, he could snack on the young.

He turned toward me, now only two feet away. I stood motionless while he raised his upper body and flicked his long tongue. When he tasted no potential danger, hunger returned him to the lark.

The bird darted and dove at the snake's diamond-shaped head. Her wings flapped wildly. The long, elegant snake slid closer. Undaunted. Unhurried.

The entire rainforest seemed to hold its breath and listen for the outcome of this life-and-death confrontation. Every blade of grass, every tiny insect and bird, every bit of breathing life froze. Silence hung nearly undisturbed in the early morning air as the forest watched and waited to absorb the lark's inevitable death. Fear bulged her eyes. Her cries grew more anxious as she sought to lead the scrub python away from her young. As if they instinctively knew of the danger, the three babies huddled together, silent in the cup-shaped grass nest.

The python slithered closer.

Closer.

I assumed she'd let the snake have her young. At least then she could live to raise another brood. She must have known they couldn't survive without her. Not that young. Even if no predator found them they'd die when hunger grew larger than their paper-thin bodies.

Closer.

I gasped in surprise when the dainty bushlark flew into the face of death. With seconds left to live, the lark abruptly ceased her frantic dance and positioned herself between her babies and approaching death. She stood perfectly still, tipped back her head and sang the most beautiful song I've ever heard. A rich melodious tinkling, clear and sweet, floated on the air and echoed off the trees down in the spring. The death song. Or perhaps the sweet song of life. I heard her voice as if she spoke directly to me.

"If I must die then I shall live my last seconds to the fullest. I'll die bursting with life, my song upon the wind. The world shall know of my beauty."

There was no resistance from the lark, no need for the python to suffocate and subdue his prey. Less than an inch away, the snake opened his jaws and swallowed the lark whole and alive—song, head, wings, feet, tail . . . silence. Life flowed into life and the ancient rainforest released a collective sigh.

Everywhere I turned, life devoured itself. While the python swallowed the lark, two feet away three red and black ants dragged a fluttering tan moth to their nest. I observed them as I watched the snake yawn his jaw back into place. While the ants struggled with the flopping moth, two small birds chased a larger bird out of the east sky. He carried one of their eggs in his beak. Stolen. I followed the birds' progress, watched the snake finish the lark, and the ants battle the moth. I plucked a blade of grass and ate it. I swatted a mosquito on my leg as she sucked my blood. Billions of life-and-death struggles took place around me. I tried to understand the immense organism called the rainforest, an organism I knew only as love.

I left the baby larks to Mother Nature and walked back up the hill, my face damp with tears. It wasn't the loss of the lark and her babies that upset me; that was just part of the forest's cycles. I cried because I was profoundly moved by the courage of all life, in many ways so fragile and yet in every way, highly intelligent and relentlessly tenacious.

I thought about something Dad told me when I was in high school. It was fall and he'd just come home from a deer-hunting trip on an island off the coast of Maine.

"Gosh, Robsy, each year it gets harder to kill. I've got so good at stalkin', I can creep up really close to a deer. This time I drew my bow and crept until I was just a few feet away. Suddenly the doe stopped in her tracks and turned to face me."

Dad raised his hands as if he held an imaginary bow and sighted down the arrow's length. His body went still.

"She stared at me with huge brown eyes. I stood so close I could see her long lashes. She *knew* I'd been followin' her, and she looked at me as if to say, 'You don't get it, I'm not just some dumb deer.' In that moment I realized she wasn't. I could see the intelligence in her eyes, and I felt like I was stalkin' another human bein'. She wasn't *just* a deer. She was intelligent life like me, Robsy. In certain ways maybe more intelligent."

Dad's face glowed with excitement as he looked inward remembering the deer. His eyes flickered with awe over his new discovery. The scent of fresh air still clung to his green and black wool shirt. His hands smelled of the leather wrist and finger guards he used with his bow. He searched my face to make sure I listened.

"After that, all I could think of was, she's got a rough winter ahead of her. Probably with little food. When I first lifted my bow she didn't even run. Just stood lookin' directly into my soul. She knew I couldn't kill her. It was the weirdest thing 'cause she spoke to me without words, but I heard them in my heart. 'You won't kill me. It's not who you are anymore. You don't need the meat, but you do need to be in the woods. That's what you seek.' And you know, Robsy, she's right."

Tears glistened at the corners of Dad's eyes, but never gathered into droplets and fell.

"As I get older, Robsy, it gets harder to justify killin' another creature. I know there's a large number of 'em some years. They often starve if there's too many and not enough food. Some people say we're doin' the deer a favor by keepin' their numbers down. Maybe we are, but I'm not so sure that's how *they* feel about it. And who knows, maybe we're killin' the wrong ones, the strong ones that woulda lived through a long winter instead of the sick or weak ones."

Uncertainty flitted across Dad's face. His palms ran over the top of his bristly crew cut.

"I just don't know anymore, Robsy. We've messed with nature so much everything's out of whack. Somehow there's a balance out there that we're tamperin' with. We think we're so smart, but sometimes I think the wild creatures are heaps smarter than us. They all seem to function together. Everything kinda balances out. And then we humans come along."

Dad never shot another deer. I was too young to realize the depth of insight he was after, but it didn't matter since it still affected my life in a tremendous way.

Remembering that conversation with Dad made me think about the balance the rainforest maintains. A laser-bright intelligence exists in a life force able to sustain harmony while continually chomping its way through itself, driven by insatiable appetite, like a newborn baby greedily suckling its mother's breast or a lover moved by passion to eat its mate. I watched that same life force replenish more than it took. It poured out life, multiplied life in infinite form, and always in a process of finding balance. I found peace and safety in such a wise being.

As I began to accept the ways of Nature I learned not to intervene. That's why I didn't take the lark babies back to camp and try to keep them alive, or kill them like I'd killed Bandicoot. After his death, I renewed my promise never to interfere with the workings of the forest. You might still wonder why I didn't at least save the mother lark from the python by shooing her away from the nest in hopes the python would eat the young instead. Or I could have easily chased the snake away from the lark and her babies, but he probably would have come back after I left. He'd have found something else to eat. Sooner or later the python had to eat or die. So did I. So did millions of other living beings. I could have done half a dozen things. There were times I was tempted, but I kept my promise to the forest and did not intervene.

Living with such intense life, I realized my human outlook had limited my perception of the natural world. I learned that my ignorance made me deadly to other species and sometimes myself. I'd been taught nothing about survival in the natural world, but in the rainforest I recognized my own need to survive, and with that awareness I grew to respect the survival instincts of other life forms. The concept of good and evil, of deadly killer and innocent victim, doesn't exist in the forest. It wasn't my place to choose who should or shouldn't be allowed to eat, who should live and who should die.

Everything lived gloriously on the edge and single-mindedly fought to survive and, when possible, thrive. Sometimes life only lived for mere seconds, long enough to ensure the survival of another species. There are no rules. In the forest, life clambers over, climbs up, stretches across, and clings to itself, wherever and whenever it can.

I was intensely grateful to witness life at its most organic and fundamental level. I often reflected on why I was given this opportunity, something beyond the normal range of life experiences. If Ian hadn't led me to the rainforest I might never have gone, let alone thought of it. I must have been blessed by a thousand angels of heaven to be led to such a place. It's an almost inconceivable miracle.

Once I understood, deep in my body, that I dwelled in the arms of a highly intelligent, creative, and harmonious being—the rainforest—I learned to listen more and judge less. As a result of my new openness, the forest taught me not to interfere in the life-and-death struggles I witnessed everyday. I was forced to discard my social conditioning in which I had perceived these occurrences as disgusting, evil, and unfair.

"Robin, when the python eats the bushlark or the flycatcher eats the butterfly, it is no different from when you eat. Everything must eat; even fungus is a predator. Also, remember that being held prisoner in the viselike bill of a flycatcher is no less horrifying than being held in the jaws of a snake. You have been taught to perceive the snake as evil and the bird as beauty. Both are death. Both are life. And both will kill with ruthless speed when they need to eat. They are only trying to stay alive. They are not evil killers, no more than you are. Evil does not exist in this forest."

As I reflected on these words, my thoughts returned to my night walk to the ferry landing and the lady taken by the croc. I began to glimpse the food chain through new eyes. I better understood why I wanted to know the creatures of the forest, especially the potentially deadly creatures. Like the python that ate the bushlark alive, and the flycatcher that ate the butterfly alive, I too wanted to eat life whole and alive. I salivated for the wild raw energy of the rainforest. A primordial memory of a life once lived in the food chain had awakened in me and lured me into the night. I wanted to know this long-forgotten and unused part of myself still stored in my cells. I hungered on the most basic level to experience it, if only for a time. Instinctively I knew it would help me to heal. To know my ancient self would help me be more fully present in this current time. I would know my place with the rest of life on planet Earth. I would know myself as both human and animal. I would *know* my origins.

Although being taken by a crocodile is a horribly gruesome death, the crocodile isn't evil. Death by wildlife in the rainforest—whether it's by crocodile, snake, or ants—would only return me to the Mother Organism to nourish its existence, and therefore maybe my own existence because I am birthed from the mother. I think I will always reemerge in some form as part of the vast and endless cycle of life, of love. A cycle with no beginning and no end, where all things are part of the "whole."

Not only did I start to understand that crocodiles aren't evil, but after my walk to the ferry landing I started to learn more about crocs. They not only eat very little food, but they don't eat very often. Australian saltwater crocodiles eat crabs, turtles, fish, wallabies, flying foxes, feral pigs, birds, and dogs, and they *sometimes* will attack and eat a human if the human invades croc territory or a female croc is defending her nest. However, most crocodiles won't go out of their way to hunt humans. In many cases when a human is attacked, the crocodile has mistaken it for its usual prey. The crocodile doesn't think, "Oh man, there's another of those rotten people. If I can eat this one there will be one less human to destroy my habitat. Ha, ha, ha." The croc isn't diabolical; that's an image from a bad Hollywood movie. He's just another hungry animal like you and me.

When I chose not to accept the myth of the evil killer, whether it was a potentially deadly snake, jellyfish, shark, insect, or other creature, I took responsibility for my actions. I was forced to respect the territory and needs of other species. I could no longer bungle along unconscious, inconsiderate, and disconnected from other life forms.

The forest had lived in connection with itself longer than me. I'd only begun to connect to myself and Mother Earth after years of adolescent conditioning. The rainforest had been in existence so long that I willfully drowned in millions of years of wisdom and love. That must have been how my father felt when he camped deep in the Maine North Woods and canoed the Allagash River. He was happiest and most alive while hiking and canoeing. When he arrived home he exuded calm contentment and seemed satisfied with the world. It was like he brought a piece of the wilderness into our home. A vibrant energy clung to his broad shoulders and shone from his eyes. I think I loved him most then. He sparkled with life and smelled of sweet pine and green moss on wet stone. Without words and without me consciously knowing it, that wildness burst through my deadness and spoke to my heart.

In the rainforest, I understood Dad's burning desire to be in the woods. Something larger than me, a fundamental wisdom that *knew* me, continually lured me around one more bend in the creek and up one more hill until I'd wandered miles through the forest. I was like Dad trying to find that one last tree on Streaked Mountain in Maine. Sometimes I felt as if the forest owned me. She did, and I didn't mind. Her love, like an enzyme, broke down my defenses and made me digestible, more easily absorbed into "the whole," the Mother Organism.

Earth patiently awaits our return. In our memories we have stored a kinship with all life. Can you feel it in your bones? I felt like the forest had been awaiting my arrival.

I'd been shut down all my life. As I started to awaken I saw the rainforest through new eyes everything appeared fresh and exciting, as if the forest could hardly wait to show me everything she is. She called out, "Come, Robin. Come and see me. Come and see before I am gone." I hated to hear her say, " . . . before I am gone."

When I complained that I didn't want to hear such dismal thoughts her reply was stern but honest. "If you do not like to hear me *say* it, you will like it less when your kind comes to destroy the rainforest with their machines. Do not cover your eyes to what already exists. Let your fear be a potent motivator and guide. If what I tell you frightens or wounds you, then do something about it. I will help you."

What do you mean "do something about it?" What can I do? I'm only ordinary ol' Robin Easton. Nobody knows me. I don't even have a college degree.

"No excuses, Robin. Forget the college degree. That is not your path. You have a different path. The day will come when you will return to the world of man. It is then that you will be asked to share what you have experienced here, but that time is not yet. You are now here with us, so learn all you can."

Oh no! Please don't tell me I'm gonna have to leave. You're the one who always says I can do whatever I want. That I can create my own reality, anything is possible and all that stuff. Well, I don't think I'll ever wanna live in the outside world.

"Robin, I tell you nothing that you do not already know in your heart. You can take in only so much love and wisdom, and then you must eventually pass it on if you are to receive more, if you are to keep your soul and spirit alive.

"There is enormous beauty in this world, but there also is a great deal of suffering. For as long as one is lost, part of yourself is lost. We are all one, Robin. When the time is right, you will go. In due course, you will know what you must do. Remember what your father taught you. 'Listen to your inner voice, your heart voice, in all things.'"

I couldn't imagine leaving the forest, nor could I fathom it vanishing forever. On the other hand I knew the havoc my species could create. I remembered life on the outside. It, too, consumed—but in a different way. It gave little back.

I perceived the forest as a living, feeling being with needs and desires no different from my own. The more aware I became of her, the quicker she communicated with me. She expressed her own moods and emotions. Her reflective and still days drew me inward to contemplation and rest. Her tumultuous and stormy days unsettled me and scoured my spirit of decay. Her brilliantly clear days roused me to celebrate being alive. Her moods became part of mine, and mine part of hers.

With absorption into the Mother Organism, my isolation ended. Such a huge being communicates inexhaustible amounts of love. Only a will of steel could keep someone separate. We often have wills of steel encased in cities of steel.

The Kuku Yalanji, the rainforest's original people, had been driven out of the forest by European invaders long before my arrival. As much as I rejoiced over my solitary time in the forest, I felt appalled and upset that I experienced something that some of the Kuku Yalanji had lost—their home, their best friend, their living connection to the rainforest. I don't think I would have survived without her. How do any of us survive without her? I'd never been drawn to something with such starving desire. In another lifetime, had I once lived in that very forest? Perhaps as a giant tree? Who knows? One thing I know for certain, the forest awoke primal memory stored in my cells, unchanged for *billions* of years. The history of the universe was imprinted on my soul, passed down through the genes of my ancestors. From microbe to amoeba. From algae to tree. From reptile to bird. From mammal to primate. From one human to another. From clouds of dust and rock, planet Earth is formed, and over 4.5 billion years later I am born.

In the rainforest, I felt like the first human to stand in sprinkled sunlight beneath the green canopy of one of the world's oldest tropical rainforests. The first person to discover a new and unexplored world and inhale sweet air that had never touched another human's lips. But I wasn't. Sometimes I felt the shadows of the forest's early people cross my path and hide behind rocks to watch my passing. I thought I heard their soft laughter echo off the trees. Their souls left imprints that still linger.

If I ever have to leave this place, part of my soul will remain here clinging to the giant trees. It can't be any other way.

Once I stopped fighting the forest and accepted her on her terms, I turned effortlessly wild and could barely understand how I'd been able to live any other way. Since Mom and I had clashed most of my youth, the rainforest was my first experience of a feminine, nurturing Mother. Absolute love. In her care my soul grew vast and vibrant, too boundless for taming. I shed my restraints as easily as my snake friends shed their skins. Never again would I lose my connection to the wildness of Nature. Nor the wildness of my own soul.

Although my relationship with the forest remained strong, I was nevertheless jarred into the world of man. Ian finally connected with his family and his father wanted to financially help us build our house. It seemed like an extremely generous offer, but every time Ian returned from talking with his father at the phone booth by the river, he appeared upset and more stressed. I loved them both, but was concerned where it was all headed. I sympathized with John Barkworth's desire to have Ian settle down and be in his life, but I understood even more and related to Ian's need to be free. The contention was caused by the same old story of the parent who wants their child to live the life they've planned for them and the child who wants to find his own path and live his own life.

Their phone discussions continued, plans progressed, and our land was eventually dozed open to create a level building site. Construction of our house was no longer a thought; it was happening. I felt frightened and tossed between two worlds. The whole stressful process reminded me how quickly the outside world could invade the beloved forest. I was shocked that a bulldozer could make it all the way out to the rainforest, and how rapidly and effortlessly it changed the face of the earth. Such permanent and unnecessary change appalled me. I felt stricken with bilious grief and began to see the bulldozer through the eyes of my forest friends. I saw only a huge terrifying monster, belching noise and smoke, slaughtering everything in its path. Now I knew what the forest meant when she said "when man comes with his machines to destroy the rainforest." Humans can change the face of the earth overnight with mind-boggling speed. We act without thinking of the consequences. What would happen if our intent were different, if our intent were to heal the earth?

That afternoon after the dozer operator left and part of our land lay exposed by the bulldozer's blade, I hiked up through the trees to the top of a ridge behind our camp. I sat beneath the canopy and sobbed with despair over what I'd done to the earth. I knew some people might consider my grieved reaction extreme, but the forest taught me that my reaction was healthy and real. Her calm, weighty presence accepted me without judgment. She taught me to never let anyone invade or desecrate my emotions, no matter what I felt. She was so loving that she didn't even judge me when I tore open her flesh. Nature doesn't work that way. Still, there are inescapable laws; if I cut too deeply and too often into Mother Earth, I'll eventually destroy myself in the process.

Is Nature real to us? Does she flourish in our awareness, in our minds and hearts, and breathing cells, everyday? Flourish to the extent that we are Nature and are in love with ourselves? Or have we, without realizing it, slipped into an anesthetized state of being and Nature is only a vague concept that's out there somewhere? Are we manifesting this detached reality?

Things that have no meaning often slip away into the gutter, like an old piece of paper, crumpled and dirty. That piece of paper once was the flesh of a living tree.

Does Nature need our awareness of her so that she can remain healthy and strong? Do we need an awareness of her so that we remain healthy and strong?

Both my tears and laughter were safe in the grace of the forest. I could express anything I felt without ridicule. I could ask any and all questions, and did. It allowed for abyssal exploration. I often felt like a spelunker traveling into the dark and silent caverns of earth. Through the expression of my tears I became aware of my priorities, my sensitivities, and my connection to the wild. Something I once took for granted, the dozing or tearing of the earth, now tore me to pieces, as if my own flesh had been gouged open. It made me realize how little I'd previously thought of such things and what I'd accepted as normal.

Exhausted from crying I fell into a heavy sleep on the forest floor.

Suddenly I heard human voices and dogs barking. Something I rarely heard. I sat up with a start and searched the valley below. I was shocked when I saw our house completely finished. The whole valley spread out stripped and dotted with houses like the bedroom communities I'd seen in the States. I couldn't find our spring. It was gone. All the trees, palms, and ferns had vanished. Paved parking lots, driveways, and roads replaced trees. Fields of sugarcane grew on the lower slopes of the mountainsides. Harvesters lumbered back and forth, spewing cut sugarcane. Cars and trucks scuttled along the roads like industrious ants. Crazed with panic, my heart raced until my head swam, and I started to suffocate. In a profuse sweat I raced down the hillside as fast as I could until I tripped over a root and fell . . . and fell . . . and fell. Over and over I tumbled through space until I woke to the feeling of cool damp ground beneath my face. It smelled fresh and pungent of decomposing leaves. Tears and dirt clung to my face. I sat up and leaned against the slender trunk of a fig tree. Dusk crept into the forest as I contemplated my dream. I imagined thirty or forty years down the road: houses all through the rainforest, people who arrive with dogs and cats, generators and toxic cleaning products, herbicides and pesticides, cars, trucks, and bulldozers. What if they run tours through the forest and build strip malls, restaurants, and resorts? Will they bring cement and tar to cover all signs of living earth? Where would Wanna Be Wallaby and Horatio Bandicoot live? Would anyone remember the forest?

My feelings about our gouged land brought back the memory of a road the Douglas Shire Council had dozed through Cape Tribulation National Park, through nineteen-and-a-half miles (thirty-two kilometers) of virgin rainforest. A courageous group of individuals created a blockade at Cape Tribulation to stop bulldozers from going through the forest. Despite the protesters' persistent and valiant efforts, the road was ripped through untouched rainforest to Bloomfield, opening a deep bleeding gash. The rains that followed were intense as the sky wept for the wounded forest. The exposed and helpless earth bled mud into the creeks, down the mountainsides to the sea, and out to sea where some believed it may have injured the onshore reefs.

As I sat on the hill and wiped away my tears, I tried to let go of my memory of the road and the pain of my dream. That was hard to do when I thought about returning to our dozed land. I wanted to hike miles into the rainforest, disappear and never look back, but then there was Ian. I loved him. I thought about my deep connection to him as I hiked back to camp.

The sun had set by the time I arrived home. While I sat and told Ian about my dream hundreds of flying foxes flew over our camp. I told him how scared and hurt I felt about dozing the land. He was quiet for a long time, then he simply pulled me into his arms and said, "Roby, somehow it will all work out. You know . . . we could always plant more native trees on our land. I'll help you." He held me while I cried, and together we watched the flying foxes overhead. They left the mangroves two miles away on the coast where they roosted through the day, then, at dusk, flew into the forest to feed on fruit.

These little people of the forest conjured prehistoric memories within me. Their leathery wings spanned at least three feet, and rose and fell with slow rhythmic grace. More than any bird I'd seen, I envied their lazy and effortless flight, an almost silent phuf, phuf, phuf. Multiplied hundreds of times, it was a breathtaking experience. Setting sun shone through the thin skin of their wings and made them glow transparent. Some of them flew so low the wind of their flapping brushed my face and hair.

"Wow, Rob. Look at them. They look like little humans with wings."

"That's funny you say that, Ian, 'cause I read in one of my books that they're not foxes or bats. They're primates like us. Amazing, isn't it? These guys are related to the lemurs, which are primates in Madagascar. My book said that flying foxes navigate by eyesight and smell and don't use echolocation. That's what bats use. These little blokes, along with the cassowary, are the most important seed dispersers in the rainforest. I don't think the forest could survive without either of 'em."

Ian tossed away the blade of grass he chewed and grinned at my enthusiasm. I loved to talk with him. His face glowed whenever I told him of the things I'd seen in the forest and what I'd learned about her creatures. It reminded me of when he talked about the stars and how I could listen forever. We talked until all the flying foxes had reached the forest. Fog rolled up the valley and left the night starless and pitch black.

I knew Ian wouldn't give up construction of our house. So I helped him build our home, but I never forgot the dream I had that day on the ridge.

Like all construction sites, ours had piles of lumber and roofing tin spread everywhere. One morning Ian and I took a break from lugging timber. We sat on a pile of rocks that would become the steps to our house. A few days earlier he had laid a large piece of tin on top of the pile to make a flat sitting area. As we sat there a thought flittered through my mind. *There's a snake coiled in the rocks under this tin.*

When I told Ian what I sensed he jumped up, ran a few feet away, and said, "No bloody way." He eyed the pile of rocks with horror and said, "Crikey! Youse telling me there's a bloody snake inches under me bleeding arse?"

"Yup. I can feel it, right under your bleedin' arse. Wanna bet on it? You fix dinner every night for a week if there's a snake under the tin."

Ian scoffed and rolled his eyes at my absurdity. We never ate regular meals, but it was all I could think of to wager.

"You got a deal, mate. But if youse so sure there's a snake, then how the bloody hell can you sit there so calmly? And what kind is it?"

"I think it's a taipan."

"Rob, are you pulling me leg?"

"No. I'm serious. I can feel it."

"Strewth, Rob-o! How the hell do you *feel* a taipan?"

"I can feel that he's aware of us. Kinda like when you know someone across a room is watching you or listening to you. Know what I mean?"

"Yeah, sure . . . but a taipan? Strewth! How do you know it's a taipan?"

"That's what I saw in my mind."

"But we's never seen one before, except at the reptile park. You never ran across them at Trib. So why here?"

"It's a bit drier here, Ian."

He chuckled, shook his head, and said, "I don't even know why I question you. I should know better by now since you're always right about stuff like this. Okay, so who's going to lift the bloody tin off? Not me, mate."

I hopped off the rock pile and said, "Let's both do it. Real slowly, Ian. One of us at each end. Ready?"

I was surprised when Ian agreed. Then he muttered under his breath, "No freakin' snake is going to hide where we've been parking our bloody arses for days. Every time we sit the tin rattles up a storm."

As we began to lift I laughed when he gingerly held his end of the tin with one finger. Once the roofing was away from the rocks he dropped his end with a clatter, and ran. Before I let go of my end I caught sight of a foot-and-a-half-long baby taipan. He sat just as I'd seen him in my mind's eye, coiled in a small hollow in the rock pile, completely unfazed by the clattering metal and his sudden exposure to sunlight. I slowly snuck closer for a better look.

"Yup, my guess was right. At least it looks like a taipan, Ian. Notice how his head is distinct from his body. See? His jawbones extend beyond his thin neck area. You can't always identify a snake by color. I'd have to do a scale count to know for sure, but this is one set of scales I won't be counting. It's best we just leave him alone."

"Is a baby taipan deadly, Rob?"

"Sure, he's born fully equipped and as poisonous to us as an adult taipan. He might not be able to inject as much venom, but what he injects is equally as potent and deadly enough to kill. If we go away and leave the tin off he won't hang around. He's not interested in us."

Later, I wished I hadn't told Ian what lay beneath the tin. Before I could blink he said, "We can't have him around camp." He grabbed a six-foot metal pipe and began to chop the snake into sections.

I yelled, "Stop, Ian. Stop!" But it was too late. Ian was so fast that the baby taipan never knew what hit him. After it was all over I saw pain on Ian's face, tears in his eyes, and I realized he hurt from what he'd done. He'd reacted out of panic. I'd done it before, not with snakes, but with people. Sure, I didn't go around chopping people into little sections, but I avoided them. We're all afraid of something.

Ian threw the metal pipe onto the ground and looked at me with shock in his eyes.

"Roby, I just get so scared of snakes, I don't think clearly around them. Now I feel awful about what I did. Poor bloody bastard. He was just an innocent little creature minding his own business. It wasn't right what I did. Wish you'd never told me he was there."

"Me too, Ian. You know, they aren't seeking us out to harm us. You could actually get bitten trying to kill a snake that's not even interested in you. Listen, how 'bout we agree to never kill another snake unless we're being attacked, which just won't happen if we respect their space. Let's move all our building supplies a tad farther from camp. We'll stack 'em in a way that leaves no space for snakes, or else we can leave so much space it'll discourage hiding. Okay?"

Ian got right into the spirit of it and went in search of his gloves to start moving timber, rocks, and tin. Snakes no longer hid in our building materials.

A couple of hours later, Ian left for Mossman to get supplies. I gently picked up the three severed sections of the baby taipan and carried him into the shade of the tent. Since taipans were rare I wanted to count his scales and verify his identity. But before I could do that, I had to accurately piece him back together with sewing pins.

I understood Ian's depressed mood when he'd left for town. I felt the same. Holding that limp fragile body in my hands, I felt dishonorable.

When Ian arrived home that night and discovered me bent over his chopped snake full of sewing pins he couldn't hide his interest. I lit an extra candle and showed him the different types of scales and how to count them. His earnest fascination moved me. So did his tears, because I knew he still hurt from what he'd done to the snake.

My snake identification book helped me recognize the snakes in my area. It not only contained pictures of Australian snakes but showed a simple method of scale counting. This required that the reader know how to handle snakes (which I do not recommend) and that they also be *comfortable* handling snakes if they want to count their scales. A snake will sense if you are frightened, and it could panic.

Visual cues are helpful, but a snake's color can vary somewhat according to the territory it inhabits. The color, size, shape of the head, tail, body, and whether the scales are keeled (a slight ridge down the length of each scale) or not, help to identify a snake. It's good to know a snake's habitat and area of the country in which it's found. Since I felt comfortable handling snakes, I loved the accuracy of the scale-counting procedure. I counted his mid-body scales diagonally across his dorsal (top) surface. Then after I counted the ventral (belly) scales that ran from his neck to his anal covering, I asked Ian if he wanted to help. That night he handled a snake, albeit a dead one, for the first time.

Finally, I counted the snake's subcaudals (the scales that run from his anal covering to the tip of his tail), which were divided. When I found a single anal plate I knew he was an eastern taipan

"Wow! He's so bloody smooth. He's not slimy at all, Rob-o."

"Snakes aren't slimy, Ian, eels are. This little guy is stunning, isn't he? This'll probably be the only time in our lives that we'll touch a taipan. They're a very shy and elusive snake. You hardly ever see 'em. I don't think they were sighted by Europeans until the early fifties. Though I'm sure the Aboriginals knew about 'em all along."

As my fascination with the wild creatures increased, so did Ian's, but he was more intrigued by ants, frogs, and toads than by snakes. It didn't matter what interested each of us as long as we could share what we'd seen, heard, and felt. There was always something new.

A few days after the taipan incident, I'd just come from the spring with a load of water when I heard a thud followed by a squeaky high-pitched "Eeek, eeeeehk." I waited and listened. There it was again. "Thud, eeek. Thud, eeeehhk. Thud, eeeeehk." Whatever it was, it sounded distressed. The thuds sounded kind of scratchy, a bit like someone throwing a softball into a cardboard box. I remembered the empty box by the tent and ran to look. A huge fat cane toad sat trapped inside. He repeatedly hurled himself at the sides of the box. When he couldn't get out, he screamed. I never heard a toad scream. The frustration and despair in his voice sounded human.

I hollered to Ian out at the back of the Toyota. "Hey, mate, come have a look at this." He came running after my first call, probably figured I'd found another snake. I loved him for his eagerness.

"What the bloody hell is that, Rob?" he asked as he got closer to the box. "Snakes can't make sound can they?"

"Come see for yourself."

Ian strode toward me and stopped abruptly at the sight of the eeeekking toad.

"Bloody Strewth, Rob-o. Look at that, will ya? Poor bastard. Didn't know toads could cry like a baby."

Ian gently lifted the bulging toad from the box. I'd seen plenty of cane toads, but this one was the size of three or four cane toads lumped together. He squatted plump and content in Ian's large palm. His greenish brown skin made great camouflage with its bumps and ridges.

"Youse the bloody fattest toad I's ever seen. Must be the granddaddy of all toads, eh? Fair dinkum, Rob-o, youse left the poor bugger in the box the whole time I was walking up the hill? He's 'bout as happy as a bastard on Father's Day."

When Ian laid his hand on the ground Granddaddy Toad sat in his palm for a full two minutes before he hopped off. Either he felt too exhausted to move or he found Ian's warm hand soothing. Maybe both. He obviously knew we weren't going to eat him, or else he was too tired to care.

The cane toad, a native to Central and South America, was the first toad to inhabit the Australian continent. Oz didn't have any real toad species before 1934. They had tree frogs, ground-burrowing frogs and nursery frogs. Nursery frogs don't have tadpoles. They lay clumps of eggs in the soil under damp rainforest leaf litter. Regardless, Australia had none of the world's hundreds of toad species. After hearing stories about the Hawaiian and Caribbean success with the cane toad eating up pesky beetles in sugarcane plantations, the Australians decided to give them a try. A box of about 100 toads was shipped from Hawaii to Gordonvale, just south of Cairns. Mr. Cane Toad wasn't much good at getting rid of sugarcane pests, but he did well in his new homeland. He did so well that he also moved into New South Wales, Queensland's gulf country and the remote northeastern Northern Territory. There went the neighborhood. Most native snakes and frogs that attempt to dine on "Citizen Cane" usually die the moment the cane toad enters their mouths due to highly poisonous glands on the toad's shoulders. The only snake able to eat young cane toads without ill effects is the keelback snake.

I once found a dead small-eyed snake—considered to be one of Australia's dangerous species—with a dead cane toad in its mouth. When I first showed it to Ian, he said, "Crikey, Rob, looks like the snake's got two tongues, mate. Maybe he's retarded, eh?"

I chuckled and said, "It's frog legs, you boofhead."

"Fair dinkum. The bloody thing's croaked on a cane toad. Bugger me dead, Rob. We's *really* seen it all now, mate."

The moment the snake's jaws latched onto the cane toad, Mr. Toad secreted poison from the glands on his shoulders. He killed the snake on contact, but it did him no good. The potent venom from the fangs of the small-eyed snake killed the toad simultaneously. No one ate that night except the ants.

In captivity cane toads will eat almost anything from dog food to mice, and probably Pop Tarts, and can grow to almost nine inches and weigh more than four pounds. That's huge! There are a few bird species, when in captivity, that have figured out how to eat the toad without getting poisoned. They kill the toad and carefully turn him on his back, pull away the soft belly skin, and eat the internal organs. They've learned not to eat the skin and the deadly parotid glands.

How did they learn that? Through observation? They must have watched other birds eat the cane toad and then die. Maybe they lost their mate or found another bird lying dead beside the toad. So how did they work out which parts are deadly? Did they actually see birds die when they ate the shoulder glands? Think about it. Wouldn't that take some pretty careful and continual observation?

At first I felt angry that there were feral toads, pigs, cats, and dogs that disrupted the balance of the native wildlife, but Ian shared with me a less judgmental and more kindly perspective.

"Rob, they can't help it. It's not their fault. They didn't book a bloody flight to Australia. It's our fault, human's fault. People bitch about feral animals and we's the worst feral animal on the planet. The little blokes are just trying to survive in a world humans are changing. I'm not saying we shouldn't have certain protective measures or even eradication programs at times, but it should be done thoughtfully and humane-like."

Ian and I learned from each other in different ways, both equally as valuable.

After a few days in camp I needed some time alone so I hiked into the forest along one of the creeks. In the past I'd followed it a good distance up the mountainside, but I always turned back every time I came to a wall of black boulders that tumbled down the steep hill. Slippery green algae covered the shale cliff that rose forty feet. The creek flowed like liquid glass and fell in a mini waterfall over the rocky surface. Ian had gone with me the last time I hiked along the creek. When we reached the wall, he said, "Maybe if you had wool socks on you could scale it. The socks might give you traction on the bloody algae." When he used the word *you*, I don't think he literally meant me, but with the seed planted the idea took root just the same.

At the base of the cliff, I stripped off my red sarong, stuffed it into my fanny pack and pulled on my thick wool socks. It felt odd to have something covering my feet. I hadn't worn socks in a long time. Once they were wet, I could feel the rock a bit better and was able to grip with my toes. I tested one sock-covered foot on the algae and the sock didn't slip.

Ian didn't know I'd decided to tackle the cliff that morning. I hadn't told him because I didn't know whether I could do it. I don't know if it's all people or just me, but I find I lose my power if I tell someone what I'm going to do. Especially if it's something that is very challenging or is something I'm not sure I can do. If I keep it to myself, I feel stronger and more confident.

I knew Ian wouldn't doubt my ability to climb the cliff. It was my own self-doubt I wrestled with. He never doubted my abilities. No matter what he thought he could or couldn't do, for some reason he thought I was capable of anything. He believed in me and trusted me completely. He once told me that I lived life from a foundation of solid common sense and a willingness to face my fear. It was time to face my fear of heights.

I thought of all these things as I stood at the bottom of that rock face. Some of the rocks were so big and so far apart there were very few nooks or crannies for foot or hand holds. While I listened to the creek tumble down the mountainside behind me and the waterfall splash in front of me, I knew I had to be extremely cautious. If I fell, it would either kill me or cripple me for life.

Why did I always need to confront my fears? Maybe in doing so I felt as if I took back my life. Maybe even my right to be fully alive, to be a whole human being. I wanted to know my own strength and maybe my own worth, both physically and spiritually. Some people seem truly content to skim across the surface of life, like the rocks they skimmed across water in their youth. Why couldn't I have been like that? My life might have been easier, but I wanted to test myself, to find out just how far I could go. And then I wanted to go beyond.

Fear stung my hands as they reached above my head for purchase in the shale. My brain warned, "Don't look down." My spirit argued, "But I gotta look down. I wanna be aware of how far off the ground I am." My heart won out as it reminded me of Ian's unwavering belief in my courage. It silently urged me to be brave and to let my feet seek solid toeholds. Thin fingers tested jagged edges before they bore my full weight. Water rushed down the mountain, sprayed my face, and blurred my vision. Sock-covered feet tested their grip through long strands of algae. My fingers ached as they clung to cracks in the rock. Arms and legs spread eagle, I ascended the cliff face the way I'd seen a giant green tree frog, with long legs and disked toes, stretch, cling, and walk vertically up a huge rainforest leaf.

I remembered reading that frogs don't drink water through their mouths, but instead absorb it through the skin on their lower abdomen. This is great if the water is clean, but if polluted with pesticides, herbicides, or other man-made pollutants the poisons pass directly through the skin and into the frog's body without being filtered through its stomach. All over the globe, frogs are dying. They're warning us. Are we listening?

My thoughts returned to the cliff as the muscles in my left hand started to cramp. Forty feet off the ground may not sound like much, but if you have never climbed before even twenty feet can be daunting, particularly when the surface is wet and algae covered. It didn't matter how much exercise I did, some part of my body was always weak. My legs and toes were strong from constant use, but my fingers ached brutally and started a tremble that ran all the way up to my shoulders. To compensate for my strained fingers and to keep my balance thrown forward I imitated the tree frog. I pressed my bare belly against the black stone. Most of the rock was smooth and wet, but halfway up I realized my belly was scraped raw and red. I'd lived so long without clothing that the rainforest had imprinted itself upon my body with scars from rock scrapings, branch gougings, leech suckings, and tick bites—Mother Nature's tattoos. I hardly felt my scraped belly, but the trembling in my fingers grew worse and there was no quick way up or down, not at twenty feet off the ground. Silently, I pleaded for help.

I managed to turn my face side on. With my cheek pressed to the rock, I hugged the wet stone and cried. It's fascinating how a painful experience or emotion in our present can trigger similar memories and pain from our past. Present pain, allowed expression, can be used as a vehicle to travel into our past to better understand ourselves.

As I clung to the rock, naked except for my wool socks, leather belt, fanny pack, and Dad's hunting knife, I thought about my father and heard his voice.

"Robsy, take a slow deep breath. You're okay. I'm with you. Just stop for a few minutes, lean into the rock, and relax your whole body. Don't think about gettin' to the top or goin' back down. Just breathe."

Tears rolled down my face and washed away with the creek. I felt like a small child again. It was not the first time Dad had talked me through my fear. As a child I had been terrified of everything: water, heights, canoeing, skiing, change. Given the chance I refused to be part of family outings, but Dad wouldn't have it. He could have hired a babysitter and left me at home, and probably had a more peaceful day. I remember him prying my clinging fingers, one by one, from the stair railing as I tried to escape upstairs. He loaded me kicking and screaming into the car with the rest of the kids.

When we arrived at our destination, as much as I wanted him to, Dad didn't abandon me to my mother or leave me by myself. He tucked me under his wing and spent hours with me as he took me beyond my prison of fear. Even though I threw up every time we went somewhere in the car my parents always included me.

I remember skiing down the slope between my father's legs, my tiny skis snow-plowed inside his. I also remember my first summer on Lake Pennesseewassee. While I knelt at the shore's edge Dad gently coaxed me to close my eyes, then he placed some treasure on the sand beneath the water. "You can't open your eyes, Robsy, until your face is underwater. If you can find the treasure you can keep it." I closed my eyes, pinched my nose, gulped air and bravely lowered my seven-year-old face into the lake. When I opened my eyes for the first time in the liquid world, I found treasures: a coin, a freshwater clam with a pearl attached to its iridescent side, a large red garnet that lay in my father's palm.

Through Dad's patience, new worlds opened up for me, and over the years I came out of myself. Things I'd feared grew to be my greatest source of comfort. Dad once told me he remembered one winter day on the mountain. He stood at the bottom of the ski slope and waited for me to catch up. I was about thirteen years old. When he looked up the hill he saw a skier swoosh around a bend in the slope, graceful as a bird in flight. He looked beyond the skier in search of me, and then realized it was me who swooshed down the mountain with my skis together, body in perfect rhythm, and a huge smile on my face. I'd finally learned to ski.

Dad cried when he told me that story and he said, "From that day on I couldn't keep you off the slope, Robsy. You lived on the mountain durin' the winter. The lift operator once told me that he had to keep the lift runnin' through blizzards, freezin' rain, and sub-zero temperatures for one young girl."

Although I was in the tropics, the skiing still hadn't stopped. Night after night I swooshed down snowy mountains in my dreams. Over and over, I swayed to a rhythm my body would never forget. Freedom in movement.

My father eventually got me into the canoe and its silent motion became an extension of my spirit. It opened up a whole world to explore. I became an excellent canoeist and craved to be on the water. I paddled Lake Pennesseewassee for miles, sunny day, stormy weather, or starry night. It didn't matter.

Dad instinctively sensed what I was like inside, how trapped I felt, and he set about to face my fear with me. He gave all he knew how to give: his time, his patience, and the things he most loved to do in life. I think he believed without a doubt that if he could get me past my fear I'd love the outdoors as much as he did. He was right.

Clinging to the rocks in the rainforest I realized that when I was a child Dad laid a strong foundation in regard to facing my fear. The groundwork had already been set in place by the time I arrived in the rainforest. When confronted with fear, I eventually knew I had to face it because I could not live a fear-restricted life. I also knew the sense of accomplishment I felt when I faced fear. Maybe that was one of the many reasons I loved Ian. He respected and understood my courage. Ian once told me, "Roby, you're very brave, and you know yourself well. Always trust what you feel. Don't turn on yourself with doubts and feelings of inadequacy. They's a bloody waste of time. It takes guts to believe in yourself. And remember, it's okay if other people *don't* understand you or believe in you. It's not their job to do that, but it is your job to be true to yourself. If you don't, you ain't got bloody nothing, mate."

I thought of something my father once told me. He said, "Robin, remember that sometimes people can't see in someone else what they don't have in themselves. They can't confirm what they might have forgotten or have never known. When you're unsure and alone in your convictions turn to Nature for truth."

I rejoiced as a new me—who *knew* me—emerged. I understood why it had been important for my father to share with me what he enjoyed doing. He not only loved the outdoors, but he loved *me*. He sensed the clean untouched truth in Nature and it made his life real. The capital D for *dumb* that I'd been branded with in school began to fade. The scar healed. For years it sat in the middle of my forehead for all to see, but Nature told me the truth. Nature *always* tells the truth.

A warm breeze blew across my back. I didn't know how long I'd clung to the rock, but when I continued upward the voice of the trees encouraged my progress. "Robin, forget about your fingers and draw strength from the living rock. It will support you whether you are horizontal or vertical. It does not matter. Your fear of falling is in your mind. Do not focus on the empty space behind you; focus on the magnetic force of the rock in front of you."

Arms and legs spread wide, I steadily moved up through the waterfall. I felt the power and mass of the rock pull me inward as if I'd become part of it, atoms of flesh merged with atoms of stone. Once I was secure in my movement my thoughts wandered. I didn't yet know why, but I felt an almost painful urgency to thank Dad for what he gave me. The more conscious I became, the more important life grew. Even though my family was thousands of miles away, I felt *closer* to them than I had my whole life.

Only a few feet from the top of the cliff, slow movement caught my eye. A snake hung six inches of his olive green body over the edge of the cliff. From what I could see of him, he resembled a snake I'd identified a week earlier. A woman who lived several miles up the road had heard that I knew how to identify snakes and had dropped off a specimen for me to look at. She had smacked the poor thing with a flat board, scooped it into a wooden box and left it at the end of our drive with Ian. When I arrived home, I gently pinned the snake down with a forked stick and lifted him out of the box. His tail curled slowly around my arm. I talked Ian into helping me, which meant that he had to turn the snake's body while I held it and counted its scales. I was immensely proud of him and honored that he trusted me, but more important, he was proud of himself. It was a major step toward facing his fear of snakes.

Once I'd identified the reptile as the first rough-scaled snake I'd ever seen, Ian and I walked our friend a mile down the track and set him free. I didn't know if he'd stay there or travel all the way back to his home. Snakes are very territorial so I suspected he'd return, although the memory of the savage board might discourage him. I set the box on its side and walked ten feet away. After about a minute the snake slithered rapidly from the wooden container and disappeared into the bush. He seemed unharmed, but snakes are very fragile creatures. I hoped the blow to his body hadn't caused permanent damage.

The rough-scaled snake that hung over the cliff's edge just above my head appeared to be an adult specimen, a bit longer than the one I'd seen a few days before. He had the same olive-green coloring with dark-brown cross bands. His heavily keeled dorsal scales gave him a matte appearance.

I couldn't cling to the cliff much longer. I wanted to yell at the snake, but yelling could unbalance my precarious hold on the rock. Besides, sound was useless since he couldn't hear me. Waving my hand would have been too risky; he might strike and I might fall. The snake slid another couple of inches over the edge. Most Australian snakes usually don't move closer to humans, but retreat long before we see them. I figured the vibration of the creek diminished all other vibrations, and he had happened upon me unexpectedly. If he went too far over the edge of the cliff he wouldn't have enough leverage to retreat. Three feet of snake isn't very long, but it was enough for him to hang some of himself over the lip. He couldn't go too far because there was nothing for him to grip, except me. At that thought I stayed *extremely* calm. He wouldn't bite unless I freaked or he felt threatened.

He was a bit to my right, a few inches from the running water, but still in my path if I was to climb onto flat ground. Since my head was only about a foot away from his I didn't dare look down or move. Movement might startle him. I didn't blink. I was just glad I'd looked up when I had. The feel of snakes didn't bother me, not even one slithering over me, but the rough-scaled snake is listed as one of Australia's extremely dangerous species. I hoped that when he realized I didn't smell like a frog, a bird, or little delectable snack he'd go away. He lifted his head and the ten inches of his body that hung over the cliff until it stretched out straight, horizontal to me and the rock wall. He hovered with a slight sway above my head. We were so close I could see each overlapping scale. His underside reminded me of soft, creamy yellow butter covered with dark blotches. His tongue darted in and out, tasting my approach. He knew I was too large to eat so it was just a matter of whether he felt threatened by my closeness. Mr. Rough-Scale wasn't capable of swallowing anything even one-fourth my size. Had he been an anaconda I think I'd have been the first woman in history to flap her arms and fly away. But Australia doesn't have anacondas.

I'd read that rough-scaled snakes prefer to retreat, as do most Australian snakes. Mr. Rough-Scale is normally harmless, which appeared to be the case with this guy. Although if provoked, they're very aggressive and will usually bite. Their venom is neurotoxic, but it also affects the blood and causes severe muscle damage. It can be fatal.

Just as humans use nonverbal communication, so do snakes. It helps if one is able to understand their body language. His neck and forebody weren't raised in an "S" shape, which was a good sign. When a rough-scaled snake is about to strike, it raises its neck and forebody and curves it into an "S" shape, with its head pointed directly at the offender, sometimes with its mouth slightly open. It may snap out several quick hisses before striking. His body was relaxed and his head *wasn't* pointed directly at me. We watched each other side on.

I tried turning my eyes away from him like I'd done with other snakes, but he didn't seem to want to leave. He sat there looking at me as if he couldn't understand why I was having trouble getting up over the cliff. He was incredibly calm, but I still didn't dare move forward with him so close. I knew I'd have to get to the top of the rock soon because my fingers continued to tremble and my inner thighs ached intolerably. One of my socks was coming off. It slid down my ankle and hung off my toes like a little balloon half full of water, which of course made it harder to feel toeholds. I absolutely needed to get to the top and sit.

As my frustration mounted I decided to have a thought-to-thought conversation with him. It wasn't like I could spit on him and he'd go away. Most likely he'd bite me on the nose in self-defense. What's more, I didn't want to dishonor his curiosity and fearlessness. I very slowly turned my whole face away from him, not just my eyes. I would no longer show interest in him nor be in his space. It took a certain amount of trust to do that, but I let him know what I was doing as I did it. I sent him my thoughts.

Okay, I realize you're curious and unafraid of me, but my legs ache like hell. If I don't get off this cliff I'm gonna fall. I'll die. Could you please move back a bit so I can get up there too?

I felt a keen, almost playful curiosity from the snake. If my legs hadn't ached so much I'd have been delighted at the snake's inquisitiveness.

Seeing another rough-scaled snake so close was a thrilling experience. He wasn't afraid at all. He was like a kid that knows you're saying "no more," but lingers to see if you might continue to play with him. I wasn't scared, so he wasn't scared, but I needed to get off this cliff immediately. With a jolt, the snake's head shot into an alert stance. I caught the abrupt movement out of the corner of my eye and had all I could do to remain still.

I waited.

Waited.

Finally Mr. Rough-Scale responded to my thoughts, retracted his head and disappeared. I couldn't tell how far he went because I couldn't see over the lip of the cliff. At least I could cautiously continue upward. When I unbent my cramped fingers, pain tortured them back into knotted talons. They'd been too long in one position. After two more toeholds, my head and shoulders peeked above the lip of the rock. The snake was gone.

I figured the last stretch would be the easiest. I was dead wrong. I found nothing at the top to grab. No branch. No rock. Nothing. I had no idea how to climb over the edge. If it had been dirt or dry rock I could've dug my nails in, raised my right knee onto flat ground, and hauled myself to a sitting position. But I couldn't move my leg on the slippery rock without falling. There was too much algae. My frustration started to mount. One slip and I'd splatter onto the rocks below like bug guts on a windshield.[1] Blood painfully pounded through my throat and head, slammed through my veins and tried to jar me off the cliff. I whined like a trapped animal. Suddenly, an impatient and direct voice, one I'd not heard before, entered my thoughts.

"Inch by inch, slide your arms over the edge of the cliff. Keep your weight forward at all times. Then slowly slide them way out in front of you onto level ground and never take them off the rock. Lean into it as far as you can, and also keep your head thrown forward. Imagine your upper body is very heavy. It will hold you to the cliff. Find two more toeholds, then with your elbows and belly, inch yourself slowly over the lip like a snake."

Like a snake! Inwardly I chuckled and imagined that the snake had come to meet me and help me over the edge. In the slowest slither of my life, I inched myself over the rim of the cliff. It took almost as long to go over the top as it had to scale the rocks, but I made it to level ground with the help of Mr. Rough Scale.

After that nerve-tingling slither I really appreciated a snake's ability to move forward using only its muscles and scales. Snakes are fascinating creatures. Some of them, like pythons, have tiny spurs at the base of their tails, remnants of the days when their ancestors (possibly monitor lizards) had legs. Sometimes I think they were put on this earth to keep us humble and to bring us into awareness. They sure have brought about my awareness.

Scraped and bruised, I rested flat on my back next to the creek. I sensed my need to test myself was over, at least for the time being. Bit by bit, the trembling left my fingers and inner thighs to be replaced with blissful calm warmth. I remember little after that. My mind grew completely empty of thought as I rose to the canopy above me and became lazy patterns of rearranging green leaves.

Later in the day, I hiked down the mountain along a different, easier route. One that took me into new territory, through a small gurgling spring lush with rustling palms, bright green ferns, and needley lawyer vines. I descended with mindless ease.

When I arrived at camp, Ian had not yet returned from Mossman. It was still a bit early for bed, and normally I would have waited up for him, but after my day on the rocks I couldn't even keep my eyes open. I crawled into the tent, lay down, and immediately drifted off. Sometime later, Ian arrived home because I vaguely heard him say something about a letter from Mom, but my body was far too heavy with sleep to fully awaken. Tomorrow. . . .

Sequestered to our cell
Quarantined from wildness
We move awkwardly, out of step
Left with the distress of the unfulfilled
We spread our pain over the land

—RUSSELL HUME

ten

I Am an Animal

WHEN I AWOKE, I WAS EAGER TO READ Mom's letter because my family and I had been out of touch for years. The envelope felt thick; it also contained a photograph that I saved for last, like dessert. I anxiously read Mom's neat handwriting and turned the picture over and saw it was Thanksgiving Day. Dad sat at the food-laden table with Mom, all four of my brothers and their wives, and a family friend. My father's smile was as handsome and disarming as it had always been, but the photo slipped from my fingers and fluttered to the ground. I instantly knew Dad was dying. He had cancer. My thoughts wailed, "No! Not Dad."

My fingers felt like stubs of wood as I picked up the photo and brief note.

"Ian, where are you? Iaaaaan?"

"Out here, Roby. By the truck. I's unloading the rest of the bloody supplies. What's up, mate?"

"Dad's dying of cancer, Ian."

"Strewth! No way. Why? What's your mum say?"

"Nothing about that. They don't even know yet. She only mentions the family, cold weather, stuff like that."

"So what makes you think your dad's dying?"

"I don't know how I know; I just do. The moment my hand touched the photo I saw a darkness in him. Oh, Ian, I feel so sad. He's all alone and probably scared, but doesn't know why, not yet anyway. But I can see the fear in his eyes. His body already knows."

"Let's have a look, Rob-o."

I passed the photo to Ian. "Strewth. Looks normal enough to me. But then, like I've said before, I ain't like you, mate. You see things I don't. If you bloody well see it, then it's real."

The truck and supplies were forgotten while Ian and I looked at the photo of Dad.

"I really liked your old man, Rob-o. I could talk with him. He was a funny bloke. I mean he *is* a funny bloke. Didn't care what other people thought of him. Always did his own thing. I mean *does* his own thing. He was bloody different in a cool way, a real free thinker. Real creative about living and how he raised you kids and all."

Even though Ian kept correcting himself when he talked about Dad in the past tense, I realized he knew that Dad was dying.

He sat with me while I cried. I told him about my day on the cliff and how I'd felt Dad there with me. Tears rolled down Ian's face while I reminisced about my father. I told him how Dad loved to sing in the car with us kids, and I remembered this old song, "If you'll be M-I-N-E mine, I'll be T-H-I-N-E thine and I'll L-O-V-E love you all the T-I-M-E time. Rack 'em up, any ol' way."

"Ian, isn't it funny the things we hate as kids that we end up treasuring as we get older? Did I ever tell you about air sauce and wind pie?"

"I don't think so."

"We'd say, 'Daddy, we're hungry. What can we eat?' And Dad always said, 'Air sauce and wind pie.'"

"Air sauce and wind pie? What's that?" Ian asked.

"That's what Dad told us to eat when we had no food in the car. He'd smack his lips and say, 'Yum. Yum. Here have a piece of my delicious apple pie with ice cream on top. Can't you taste it?' Then he'd laugh and hold out his hand like it had a wedge of pie in it."

Ian chuckled over the story and asked, "What did you kids do?"

"Oh maaaan, when he said that we'd get so angry and frustrated. He acted like he was offering us something really great, when it was just 'air sauce and wind pie,' in other words, nothing. I think he loved our reaction the most. The whole time we squawked, Dad acted oblivious to it and just kept describing his pie in detail."

Ian and I laughed when I imitated my childhood reaction. "That's not funny, Daddy. I mean this time I'm REALLY hungry. I think I might be starving maybe. Daaaadyyyy, it's not funny. I could die back here," I said in a then-you'd-regret-it tone of voice from the farthest back section of the old blue station wagon. "Can't you drive any faster, Daddy?"

Dad chuckled and slowed the car to a crawl. "If you'll be M-I-N-E mine . . ."

In the rainforest there was time to share our stories and feelings. Time to be human. But the day grew cloudy. We were moving into the wet season, and the tarp over the truck wouldn't keep our perishables completely dry if it rained, not with the wind picking up.

It had become almost impossible to cut off my emotions. Luckily, Ian was comfortable with my crying while I helped unload building materials. In his eyes, nothing was amiss. Crying was as much a part of our lives as laughter. Dad was dying and the loss would be incomprehensible.

Although Ian cried with me he couldn't experience my grief for me. Later that day a deep and essential need drove me to the one place where I could freely feel my pain, the forest. The rainforest had opened me up so much that the only way I knew how to grieve Dad's illness was with every cell of my body. I had to grieve in the wildest, most untamed part of my being. To reach a natural resolution, I had to fully experience this change in my life. I couldn't and didn't want to stuff it down, think it away, rationalize it, and smooth things over. This was another door into the mysteries of life and death, and it beckoned me to explore. Dad deserved more than a mere smoothing over of my emotions. I wanted his soul to know how much I'd miss him, how much I loved him. Although I believed he'd always be with me, I couldn't live that reality immediately, not when I was full of grief. I refused to do the grown-up thing and act as if nothing had changed. Everything had changed, and I knew it.

Ian needed no explanation when I grabbed my red sarong and retreated into the forest. I splashed through the creek and headed for the trees: they would understand my sorrow. Anguish over Dad's illness loomed so huge and heavy it threatened to crush my heart. I lay on the forest floor and sobbed convulsively. At first I cried over my own loss, but then I found myself grieving for Dad and marveling over the exceptional gifts he'd given me.

The more intensely I sobbed, the more I became part of everything around me. I felt closer to the earth than ever before. The rainforest absorbed my pain and cradled me in merciful arms while I cried. It always was that way in the forest. I never cried alone. Through grief I connected to all things.

I rose from the forest floor and continued to walk uphill. As I wandered through the trees, I was suddenly overcome with weightiness and could barely move. My arms and legs felt thick and dense. It was a familiar experience to exchange bodies with a tree. I stood still and waited while my arms felt as if they morphed into branches. My legs and feet fused and sprouted roots that hungrily sought anchorage in the rocky soil. Fluid pumped up my trunk and surged to branch and leaf, filling me with enormous energy and strength. I always knew which tree I'd become. I could feel it. I never really knew if the tree chose me or I chose it. It didn't matter *why* it happened; it just did, and it felt so astounding I didn't fight it. I knew what it was like to be a tree, and I more fully understood their timeless wisdom. I often asked, "If I am you right now, are you me? Can you feel me?"

After sharing with the tree, I wound my way through some lawyer vines and found a creek filled with large boulders. My spirit drifted through the dense rock and sat inside its solid strength and stable energy. I sat motionless by the stream for hours until I became the water that flowed and rippled. Like liquid velvet, I slid downward and curved over stones with ease. My fluid body came upon a waterfall. I slipped over the edge and with weighty pressure displaced the water that lay in the pool below.

By literally entering into the life of the rainforest and becoming tree, rock, water, and wallaby, I was safely held while I poured out my anguish. I wasn't alone with my pain. The whole forest felt my sorrow and responded with love for my father and me.

As I wandered through time, in an instant I existed where everything happens at once. I flew into dark, silent space and found light, a place where all things are one, and I knew the hearts of everyone dear to me. I felt my father's presence all around me. I was awed that Dad had six kids and he still took the time to love me. I had become the best part of him, wild and strong.

My father grew up in an era when sons were expected to follow in their father's footsteps whether they wanted to or not. He was my grandfather's only son. And even though he yearned for distant lands, more creative and daring adventures, he was expected to carry on family tradition and pressured to become a dentist. I felt deeply grateful that Dad had not pressured me to "become" something. Only myself.

With no one around for miles, I cried out to my father. "Daaaaad, can you hear me? I don't want you to die. I'm not ready." Years of grief poured from my eyes as I cried with Dad. At least it felt as if we cried together. Once I started I couldn't stop. I cried for my father who rarely cried. I cried for my dear and courageous mother, for my brothers and sister whom I shall always love. I cried for my dead grandmother, and how she used to gather pinecones with me and pick gill-over-the-ground flowers each spring. I cried for my mother's mother, a woman I never knew. She died of leukemia and left my mother, who was twenty years old, to fend for herself. I cried for generations of human suffering and brave human joy. My father's fading life opened a door that allowed me to enter the soft world of compassion. In that searing moment of grief I found my connection to all of humanity. I wanted to take the people of the world, all the wounded and suffering, into my arms and tell them, "You are loved. I know you don't know me, but I cannot help but love you. I, too, have experienced suffering as well as the desire of dreams. It takes courage to be alive, doesn't it?"

One of the most healing experiences I know is grief given full expression. Yet we seldom allow this purging emotional beauty to touch our lives. The sounds that came from my body returned me to ancient animal knowing, a "remembering" of self. My mind grew clear, clean, and razor sharp with awareness. All the lost and fragmented parts of myself drew together to create wholeness. I felt compassion for Robin and began to like the human I uncovered. I forgave myself my fears and shortcomings. Through sound, I grew more *sound* in body and soul. As I began to forgive and understand myself, I was better able to understand my mother and father, their failings, losses, and joys. The sound of my grief, along with my tears, led me down a path toward love. I felt less afraid of my feelings . . . less afraid of life.

The rainforest supported my grief with companionship. I stopped in the midst of intense sobbing to imitate a nearby cockatoo. A small skink darted through dead leaves and stopped on top of my toes. I scooped him up and marveled over his tiny feet as he sat in my warm palm. He seemed to know I wasn't going to eat him, and when I lightly stroked his back he fell asleep. After a bit, I gently woke him and set him on the ground. He disappeared among the leaves. Something rustled through the brush along the creek. I knew it was a wallaby from the way it moved. When they walk slowly they place their front paws on the ground, and using their tail for support they swing their large hind feet forward. Wallabies are exceptionally sensitive and inquisitive creatures. The little guy hiding in the bushes snuck closer while I told him about my father and cried. I couldn't see him, but I knew he was less than twenty feet away. I could have lured him closer, but didn't. His comforting presence was enough. I was more than content with that. I had no expectations because I already had all I needed just "being" in the forest. I was living.

I thought of Dad halfway around the globe, sitting in his dental office. Did he know I thought of him? I believed so. I had learned that death wasn't what I thought it was when my grandmother died. It wasn't being forever cut off from the people I loved. Dad would always be with me. Nothing could change that. Thousands of miles away, my love pierced the core of my father's heart and returned to me with his words. "It's okay, Robsy. You're still my girl. Things are what they are and we're both safe. We always will be." The earth absorbed my father's and my pain, and on the tail of his voice I heard the trees.

"You are loved, Robin. So is your father. You love him as yourself. Remember that when you are feeling unworthy. You could not love another so deeply without being worthy of that same love. When you lose someone you love and you grieve your loss, it is a form of praise. If you don't express your grief, it can lead to depression. You were not taught to feel your own pain, let alone another's pain. You are all one. When you grieve for yourself, you also grieve the unshed tears of your ancestors. You heal not only yourself but you heal all the generations who came before you and all the generations to come."

Organic and consuming emotions compelled me to lay naked upon the damp earth.

Such intimate contact with my Mother. Living flesh against living flesh. My bare breasts against the living breathing earth. What is this? What am I? I'm not what I thought I was. I'm so much simpler and far more complex.

Primitive memory forced itself up through the earth and into my gut. Like a cold diurnal snake responding to morning's warm sun, my insides uncoiled.

For the first time in my life, I know compassion. What's happened to us? We're so lost. Frightened. Disconnected. How did we get this way? So far away.

Tear-filled eyes watched fascinated as the hands in front of me, my hands, clawed desperately at the earth.

I must touch the truth, feel it in my hands. It is here on this rainforest floor. Here in earth's moist womb.

A force of their own, my hands grasped for leaf and twig. With life clenched between my fingers I remembered who I am. My ears pricked at the sound of a primitive wail.

"Oooouuuaaaaahhhhhh!"

Is that animal cry mine? Is that me who cries out thirsting for life?

Once the female animal remembers who she is, she won't willingly forget. She'll fight ruthlessly to protect her acute animal intelligence. A wild, sensuous longing drove me to scoop up handfuls of earth and rub it onto my arms and legs. Brown dirt smeared my tear-stained face. My hair hung wild and full of leaves and debris. My entire body sobbed and laughed as I awoke to pain and joy, more life than I imagined possible.

Your love decomposes all that is not me. You leave me with wild prehistoric eyes. In our mating I forget myself and separation vanishes as if it has never been.

I lay spent on the forest floor, and yet my body was filled with enough love to heal an entire universe.

I've fallen desperately in love with the earth. If we don't desperately love a thing, we can't care for it.

I wasn't alone anymore. Mother Earth loved me as her own child. She is a life force able to love so many and yet love each one intimately. I hadn't known that I could let go into such sweet release. Maybe a day would come when I had nothing left to hang onto. That would not be so bad. Much of what I'd held had been an illusion. That being the case, I would rather lose it all and have nothing, be nothing. At least I'd know where I stood.

The day wore on. Crickets and other insects sang their early evening songs. Dappled light slowly vanished from the rainforest floor as shadows settled into hallowed places. Mist drifted between the trees. Its damp fingers lingered on my face and back. Soon dusk would creep through the forest, but I wasn't worried. The forest was my home; however, I needed Ian's comforting arms that night. I gathered myself from the jungle floor and drifted out of the rainforest, a lone and naked figure.

I feel so alive, as if the entire world is mine. I like how my bare feet tread softly. Oh, dear Mother Earth, you are so ingrained into my flesh that I don't know where I stop and you begin.

Walking quietly along the creek, I listened to the melody of water over rock and the dove's soft, haunting echoes off trees.

When I arrived at the edge of the field and looked down on Ian and our camp, I thought about the choices I'd have to make concerning my father's cancer. Neither Ian nor I had talked about leaving the rainforest, not yet. Ian was good at letting things sit until I was ready to face them. He understood that I had a way of coming to them on my own. I knew that he knew I'd return to see Dad. In doing so I'd return to a world I feared, a world I no longer related to. I wasn't quite ready to open that box of tangled disorder. I needed a bit more time.

I didn't have to call or write home to confirm my father was dying. I already knew, and it might only frighten my parents because they didn't yet know. There was time to make decisions, but they still seemed huge and impossible. The world I'd left behind held another lifetime light years away. I'd changed so much I didn't know how to be part of it. I had no desire to return to that world. I was still worried about leaving the safe integrity of the rainforest, the place that was healing me.

I must take your love with me. I will have to stand strong in the world and hold onto myself and my truth. What if I don't know how to interact with other people? Do I even want to?

The trees heard my anguish and responded to my cry.

"Robin, be open to new experiences. Live and love as abundantly as you possibly can, no matter where you are. That is what it means to be alive. Remember that you are never *really* alone. We will reach out with our love and always be with you."

The moist smell of damp earth wrapped itself around me, my guardian as I crossed the field at sunset.

Miles from nowhere, and I'm finally free.

༄

I hear you now in sounds that rise and fall
I know you now within my heart
I am you now and I am full

—RUSSELL HUME

Endnotes

1. THE JOURNEY BEGINS

[1] This explanation of protecting one's self from poisonous jellyfish by wearing women's pantyhose or a wet suit or dry suit is not intended as an accurate method of protection. Please go to the appropriate authorities for information on protecting yourself from the sting of poisonous jellyfish. The author will not be responsible for anyone swimming in jellyfish-infested waters, with or without protection.

2. WEIRDOS AND WASHOUTS

[1] During the time I lived in the Daintree area, there were a few different ferry masters and substitute ferry masters. For ease in telling this story I have combined them all together into one person called Clyde. All the ferry masters who operated the Daintree River Ferry were fascinating characters whom I greatly admired. They were interesting to talk with, knowledgeable about the area, patient with the tourists, and often bursting with wild and wacky stories.

[2] I researched the subject of four-wheel driving and winching and had some of Aussie's old-timers help me verify what I remembered. Some of these blokes have used four-by-four vehicles and winches since they were knee-high to grasshoppers. I have described the use of the winch and the four-wheel drive as I best I can remember. Any inaccuracies are on my part, as I have not winched up cliff faces, through bog holes, over logs, or driven through rapidly moving streams since my early days in Australia. Not yet anyway!

3. THE OLD MAN BY THE SEA

[1] I chose to use the word antivenom in this book because it is more widely known. The correct word is antivenin, which is used by the scientific community and is the correct spelling in Webster's Dictionary. According to my Concise Oxford English Dictionary, the word can be spelled antivenin or antivenen. Antivenin is an anti-toxin that protects against snakebite or venom.

4. GOIN' TROPPO

[1] In writing this book I used the word autism for two reasons. Prior to "rainforest life" I had never heard of autism. While living in the rainforest, autism was the word spoken to me by the trees, and the word autism is more widely known than Asperger's. Since writing this book, I have learned that I had Asperger's syndrome (a mild form of autism) or possibly PDD (pervasive developmental disorder), which falls under autism spectrum disorders. Today I am completely free of all symptoms.

5. THINGS EATING THINGS

[1] I used the word God in a couple of places in this book because it was the word that fit best for me. However, many other words could be used equally as well, and have been used in other sections of the book (including Mother Nature, Mother Organism, Universal Order). I invite readers to substitute the word they feel most comfortable with.

7. THERE IS NO SEPARATION

[1] The mention of clay's (mud) healing properties in this book is not proposed as medical advice. Readers must seek professional medical care for all their health-care needs. The author is not a medical professional and therefore will not be responsible for any person using any clay, plants, foods, or seawater mentioned in this book for healing, dietary, or other purposes.

8. CROCODILES, FERAL PIGS, AND PITCH BLACK

[1] Although I have tried to make the snakebite information in the Mad Matt story as accurate as possible, please note that it is not intended to be advice on snakebite treatment or the handling of snakes. Seek a qualified local herpetologist to learn about the snakes and snakebite treatment in your area. The author will not be responsible for the outcome of any person treating a snakebite wound or the outcome of anyone handling any snake anywhere. Snakes are best observed from a distance.

9. DO NOT INTERVENE

[1] The author will not be responsible for anyone who emulates the author's antics and adventures by cutting themselves while whittling wet wood; endangering themselves while climbing wet cliffs; driving through wet rushing creeks, wet muddy moguled fields, and wet leach-infested bog holes; or performing other foolish feats of daring while wet (or otherwise). Approach Mother Nature with respect and common sense or with a good bush guide, and in all cases of injury seek immediate professional medical help.

Robin's Glossary of Strine: (Australian Slang)

THE WORD **STRINE** is a nasally contraction of the word Australian. (From the mouths of my Aussie friends.)

→ **About as useless as tits on a bull**
Has no use at all.

→ **Aggro**
Aggravated.

→ **Arse, Arsehole(s)**
Rear end or ass; a jerk; a mean person; a jackass.

→ **Arvo, T's arvo**
Afternoon or this afternoon. (*Very cool, sharp.*)

→ **Aussie**
Australian person.

→ **'Ave a go, mate**
Have a try. (*Must be said with an Australian accent to reap the full benefit.*)

→ **Barbie**
Barbeque or cookout.

→ **Beaut** (sometimes **Bewdie**)
Beautiful; excited approval; something has gone really well; excellent; very good.

→ **Billy**
A container (a tin) used for boiling water over a campfire.

→ **Bloke**
Australian male.

→ **Bloody**
Universal intensifying adjective: sometimes used more than once in a single sentence [Example: "That bloody bloke (man) is a gasbagging (chattering) bloody galah (pink and gray Australian bird)."]; sometimes used in the middle of a word [Example: Fan-bloody-tastic—it adds extra emphasis or enthusiasm to phrases and words]. (*I abso-bloody-lutely LOVE it!!!*)

→ **Bloody oath**
You really approve of what someone is saying.

→ **Blowies**
Blowflies; very large and noisy flies.

→ **Board shorts**
Long cotton shorts that surfer's wear—usually made from brightly colored cloth.

- **Bonnet**
  Hood of a vehicle.

- **Boofhead**
  Friendly term used to greet someone not too bright [Example: "How's it goin', you ol' boofhead?"]. (*Yup, sounds real friendly to me. Uh huh, sure.*)

- **Brekkie, Breakie**
  Breakfast.

- **Bugger me dead**
  Extremely surprised at something; frustrated. (*This one I won't even touch. Use your imagination.*)

- **Bullbar (sometimes Roo bar)**
  A strong metal bar that attaches to the front of your vehicle to protect you and the vehicle in case you hit a kangaroo. (*Please drive carefully and remember that a bullbar is not an excuse to hit kangaroos.*)

- **Bush**
  Rural Australia; the woods; scrub.

- to **Cark it,** (sometimes **Kark it**)
  To die.

- **Choof off**
  To go; leave [Example: "Well, I best choof off now. I'll see youse later, mate. Ta-Ta."].

- **Cozzie, Cossie**
  Swimsuit.

→ **Crikey, Crikeys**
Exclamation (good or bad) over something; surprise at something [Note: The i in crikey is said like the i in bike; Crike (like bike) y (ee)].

→ **Crook**
Ill; sick; out of sorts or something that's not functioning.

→ **have a Cuppa**
To have a cup of tea.

→ **Dacks, Daks**
Pants, jeans, or shorts. (*Snappy word, huh?*)

→ **Damper**
Unleavened bread cooked in a camp oven or fry pan over a campfire.(*Have a little bread with your grease, mate.*)

→ **Deadset**
Without a doubt—an exclamation that can be used as a question or a statement: Really? It's a fact!

→ **Dog and Bone**
Telephone. (*Australians love to say things that rhyme.*)

→ **Dog's breakfast**
Messy or a mess. (*Okay, it's like this: you wake up after a rough night, look in the mirror, and say, "Bloody strewth! I look like a dog's breakfast." Don't you just love those Aussies?!*)

→ **Donga**
Dwelling. (*Careful here—not to be confused with the word below.*)

→ **Donger**
Penis. (*As one of my Australian friends said when I once asked him the meaning of this word, "Yer dick or tool, mate."*)

→ **Drongo**
Idiot or fool.

→ **Dumbarse**
Dumbass; a stupid person, idea, situation, etc.

→ **Dunny**
Toilet (used to be the word for outhouse). (*Sure beats saying, "the John" or "the restroom," or worse "the toilet." I mean, come on, let's add a little panache here.*)

→ **Eh?**
Didn't catch what someone said; pardon me; something tacked onto the end of a sentence when someone is seeking agreement; an acknowledgment or agreement. (*Just use it whenever you feel like it. No one will notice.*)

→ **Esky**
Insulated ice box or Styrofoam cooler. (*Snappy word for the picnic setting.*)

→ **Exy**
Expensive.

→ **Fair dinkum**
Someone or something that's really genuine [Example: "He's a fair dinkum Aussie,—said about a guy who has lived all his life in Australia.]; also used to question validity [Example: "Fair dinkum, mate? (Are you serious man?)"]. (*For the obvious reasons, most Yanks*

find this a hard one to say. No worries, mate. The Aussies will set your mind at ease; they say it with flourish.)

→ **Fanny**
A woman's private parts. (*I learned very fast when and where to use this word. After I said, "There's a stick poking me in the fanny," and a bunch of Aussie guys started hooting it up, I was more careful.*)

→ **Fart-arse around**
You're not getting on with the job at hand; you're goofing off.

→ **Flat out**
To do something fast.

→ **Galah**
Obnoxious; noisy; often stupid-acting person—taken from the noisy pink and gray parrot, the galah. (*A beautiful bird, one of Australia's most beautiful, unworthy of such a degrading name. Poor birdie.*)

→ 'ave a **Gander**
Have a look.

→ **Gasbagging**
Talking a lot. (*Of course.*)

→ **G'day, Gidday**
A friendly welcome; good day; hello; hi.

→ **Gob**
Mouth.

→ It's/she's a **Goer**
Something that will definitely occur; it works; it's all set.

- **Gold Coast**
  The Gold Coast is a beautiful tourist area located on the eastern seaboard of Australia, about 80 kilometers south of the city of Brisbane.

- **Good onya, mate**
  You're happy with what someone is doing.

- **Happy as a bastard on Father's Day**
  Unhappy or depressed. (*Where do they come up with this stuff? I love it!*)

- **Happy as Larry**
  Very happy. (*In case you haven't met Larry, he's a very happy bloke.*)

- we's **Home and hosed**
  We've made it; it works; a positive outcome.

- **Jack of that (this)**
  Fed up with something; disgusted with something.

- **Joey**
  Baby kangaroo.

- **Knackered**
  Exhausted; done in; puzzled.

- **Knackers**
  Testicles.

- **Larrikin**
  A rowdy, reckless, and mischievous boy or man.

- **Mad as a cut snake**
  Upset; unpredictable; volatile.

→ **Make tracks**
To leave; depart.

→ yer **Mate**
Your buddy or friend.

→ **Mini Moke**
A very tiny automobile—the first one in Australia, the Morris Mini Moke, had thirteen-inch wheels and cost roughly $1,295. (*I rode in one once—had no seat belts—and it was basically a lower metal frame with a canvas "upper" over a metal frame. And we're not talking old army issue jeep here, nothing that rugged—or at least it didn't appear very rugged to me. It was low to the ground—my feet felt like they were two inches above the tarmac—front-wheel drive and very light. I felt a bit like I was riding a skateboard down main street Coolangatta. If we'd been hit by another vehicle, the end result would be similar to a Mack Truck running into a mosquito.*)

→ **Mozzie, Mossie**
Mosquito.

→ to **Muckle**
To latch onto or grasp.

→ **Mud map**
A map drawn on a piece of paper to give someone directions. (*Called a "mud map" because they used to be drawn with a stick or finger in the mud or dirt.*)

→ **Mum**
Mom or mother.

→ to **Nick**
To steal.

→ to **Nick Off**
To scram; go now; get lost.

→ **Oldies**
Parents.

→ **Outback**
Remote inland Australia; (sometimes) anywhere remote or away from the cities.

→ **Oz**
Australia.

→ **Paddock**
Any fenced area, irrespective of size, used for crops or stock; a field.

→ **Petrol**
Short for petroleum; gasoline.

→ **Piss, pissed**
Booze; drunk.

→ **Pommy, Pommie, Pom**
English person—originally believed to be the name given to the convicts taken to Australia from England: P.O.M. (Prisoners of Mother England).

→ to **Pong**
To smell strongly (usually an undesirable smell) [Example: "He ponged somethin' fierce."].

→ **Quick Smart**
In a hurry; do something quickly and immediately; straight away.

- **Ratbag**
  An obnoxious person; a dishonest person; to behave inappropriately. Can be applied to an object as well.

- **Right**
  To be okay [Example: "Youse right there?" American translation: "Are you okay?" (Do you need anything?); Example: "Youse right as rain." American translation: "You're all set." "You're okay."].

- **Right-o, Righty-o, Right-eo**
  Okay or that's right; a question seeking approval.

- **Rob-o**
  The Australians have this delightful way of adding an o to the end of a person's name (Rob-o, Tom-o, Jack-o, Dan-o, Greg-o, etc.) or adding an "o" to the end of certain words like righty-o, right-o, smoke-o, etc.

- **'Roo**
  Kangaroo.

- **Rooted**
  To be really tired (most common use); washed up [Example: "Bill's career is rooted."]; to have sex with someone (root). (*I'd think twice before I said this one.*)

- **Saltie**
  A saltwater crocodile.

- **Scrub**
  Comparable to the word *bush*.

- **Seen better heads in a piss trough**
  Someone is ugly.

→ **Sheila**
A young woman, (usually used by the old-timers)—may have originated from the large number of Irish female immigrants who were called Sheelagh.

→ **She'll be right, she'll be sweet**
Everything will be all right or okay.

→ **Shove off**
To tell someone to go away, in an angry tone; to say that you are about to leave.

→ **Sparrow(s) fart**
The crack of dawn—to wake at sparrow fart is to rise with the birds.(*Has anyone actually ever heard a sparrow fart???*)

→ **Strewth, Struth**
Shock; amazement; verification; frustration (at something or someone). (*Originating from "God's truth," "it's truth," or "'s truth."*)

→ **Stickybeak**
Nosy; someone who can't mind their own business; to take a look at something. (*What a great word; it doesn't get better than that!*)

→ **Stinger**
The poisonous box jellyfish.

→ **Stubbies**
Small bottles (375 milliliters) of beer; a brand of men's shorts.

→ **Suss it out**
Check something out.

→ **Ta-ta**
Good-bye.

→ **They's**
They is. [Example: "They's the best bloody mates a bloke could 'ave."].

→ **Tinnie**
A can of beer; a small aluminum boat. (*Big difference here in meaning, so make sure you get the right tinnie if youse headed into shark-infested waters.*)

→ **Too right**
You bet it is; you bet; term of agreement.

→ **Torch**
A flashlight.

→ **Troppo**
Going crazy or insane—especially used by people in the tropics. (*One goes a bit batty from the isolation, heat, flood rains, insects, mold, more insects, more mold.... Everything takes on a surreal or weird quality, but you don't really care 'cause youse gone troppo.*)

→ **Tucker**
Food. (*Youse done some mighty hard yakka (work) and now you want some bloody good tucker, mate.*)

→ **Underdacks or Underdaks**
Underpants; underwear; briefs.

→ **Vegemite**
A typical Australian food—a dark brown, almost black spread made from yeast. (*You have to grow up on the stuff to really*

appreciate it, or else after many long years of wondering what it's all about, you go slightly wacky and develop a taste for it.)

→ **Wanker**
A male who thinks he's the greatest, but is actually rather stupid. (*Oh yes . . . well, I'll refrain from further comment.*)

→ the **Wet**
The rainy summer season in northern tropical Australia.

→ Castlemaine **XXXX Bitter**
A brand of Queensland beer.

→ a **Yank**
An American.

→ **Youse, Yewse**
You; you is.

Contributing Writer

Russell Hume wrote the poetry at the end of each chapter. Much of his poetry is inspired by the ancient deserts of the southwest, and the words express his wonderment of the area and his love of life. Russ enjoys backpacking into the wild, even camping in winter's cold so he might have the backcountry to himself.

Hume grew up in northern New Mexico. At the age of twelve, when his friends were watching *Gilligan's Island*, Russ was taking notes from the television series *Kung Fu* and sharing them at school as his own inspired notions. In high school and college, while most of his peers were working out relationships in the back seats of cars, Russ was reading Carlos Castaneda's books, writing his own poetic philosophy, and discovering spirit. I don't think I've ever seen Russ when he wasn't carrying his scruffy old army knapsack, which contains a tattered notepad and a stub of chewed pencil.

Russ is an exuberant, motivational, and humorous orator. One of his latest passions is performance poetry, in which he reads his work to musical accompaniment. When not writing and performing, he runs his design business in Santa Fe, New Mexico, where he currently lives with his wife and daughter.

About the Author

ROBIN EASTON WAS TWENTY-FIVE when she left the United States to live with her husband in the remote tropical Daintree Rainforest of Queensland, Australia. This ancient forest transformed Robin's life so completely that she was inspired to write *Naked in Eden*. The Daintree is one of the world's oldest tropical rainforests, home to a vast number of rare and threatened species. Kangaroos, birds, and bandicoots befriended Robin in the rainforest. Her bare feet shared paths with foot-long centipedes, bird-eating spiders, leeches, and ticks. She learned to handle and identify some of the world's deadliest snakes. Her rainforest stories entertain, educate, and inspire.

Robin has since spent much of her adult life in wild and remote areas, including Australia's tropical and subtropical rainforests, Alaska, and Maine's North Woods. She has also traveled to New Zealand, Tasmania, Mexico, and Canada and has lived throughout Europe.

Driven by her passionate love of the wild, Robin has been involved in helping to protect remote areas like the lowland Daintree Rainforest and the Ruahines of New Zealand.

Robin Easton is a writer, inspirational speaker, nature facilitator and educator, performing artist, nature photographer and photo journalist. She has performed and recorded on both the East and West coasts, and appeared in magazines and newspapers throughout the U.S.A. and Canada, and in an award-winning NBC News affiliate piece, Paul Harvey News, KBLA Radio, Huffington Post, The Nature Connection, The Green Hour, KSFR, Inspire Me Today, and others. Robin shares her writing, photography, and music at www.robineaston.com

About the Naked Lady cover painting: several years ago my friend Linda Marie, an art therapist, wanted to test some new projects she was developing before she used them on her clients. I was one of her guinea pigs. She instructed me to paint a picture of the most peaceful time of my life in three minutes. She gave me a tiny brush, a little piece of kitchen sponge, a glass of water, a kid's watercolor set, and a pad of paper, and then she timed me. I was pleasantly surprised at the scene that revealed itself. I had painted my precious unforgettable time in the Australian Rainforest.

www.ingramcontent.com/pod-product-compliance
Lightning Source LLC
Chambersburg PA
CBHW031055080526
44587CB00011B/698